RH
At the
Extinction

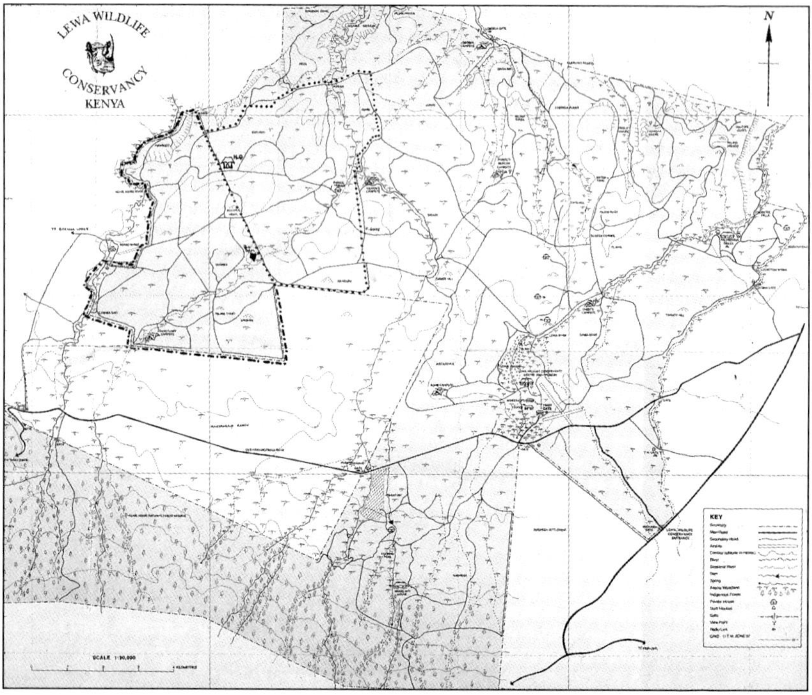

Lewa Wildlife Conservancy
Kenya

RHINO
At the Brink of Extinction

Anna Merz

LONGHORN
Publishing

Longhorn Publishers
PO Box 124, North Riding 2162
Johannesburg, Republic of South Africa

*To darling Ricky
and in memory of my parents
Leonard and Noel Fawell*

*All donations towards the maintenance
of Ngare Sergoi will be gratefully received.*
The Ngare Sergoi Charitable Trust
c/o Bill Hall, La Landelle
Route des Landes, St. Ouen, Jersey
Channel Islands JE3 2AE

First published 1991
HarperCollins *Publishers*
ISBN 0-620-24640-5

2nd Edition 1994
Ex Africa

This Edition 1999

Typesetting by TOPS Desktop Publishing, South Africa
Printed by Colorpress (Pty) Ltd, South Africa

Contents

Acknowledgements

I thank the President and the Wildlife Department of the Government of Kenya for all their support and co-operation and for the emphasis they have laid on the protection of the rhinos in Kenya. I especially thank the directors, past and present, of the Wildlife Department; the co-ordinator of the Rhino Rescue Project, Peter Jenkins; and the veterinarian Dr Dieter Rottcher.

I thank David and Delia Craig and their family for their great generosity in allowing so much of their land to be used for the Ngare Sergoi Sanctuary; for accepting me, a stranger, into their midst; and for their unfailing help and support. I am particularly grateful to Ian Craig for his dedication to the rhinos and elephants on the land and security he affords them. I thank my neighbours, Tony and Rose Dyer, for their assistance and encouragement and I express my especial gratitude to Francis Dyer, who has put not only enthusiasm and hard work but also unfailing good humour into his job as sanctuary manager. I also thank our employees past and present for their enthusiasm and hard work, for their courage and for all they have taught me.

I thank Andy Lodge and the Ngare Sergoi Support Group that he founded for their very generous contributions towards the running cost of the sanctuary. I thank Halvor Astrup and John Street for enabling the extension to be built and the support group, Halvor Astrup and John Cook for financing the purchase of the three white rhino cows (Makora has already made his appreciation obvious). I am grateful to everyone who has contributed to the sanctuary with either financial or moral support in any way, great or small.

I thank Cynthia Salvadori for bringing editorial order to my manuscript and Clement Salvadori and John Cohen for their practical assistance in producing a legible text.

Finally I would like to thank all those photographers who have allowed me to reproduce their photographs free of charge, above all Neil Leifer and Gerry Ellis.

Note on the Third Edition

It is eight years since the first edition of this book appeared. This third edition includes an additional chapter telling about the events in Lewa Downs after 1991. At the same time, because some of the original photographs were lost, we have had to look for others to replace them. Hence this third edition is revised by the inclusion of a new map of Lewa Downs and several new illustrations, by the addition of an entire new chapter written by Anna Merz, and by the deletion of appendices I and III of the original. We hope that the additions will make this edition even more interesting than the previous ones. While Anna Merz now resides in the Waterberg Mountains of South Africa, together with five dogs, she is still actively involved with the work that is going on at Lewa Downs. We hope that this book will help us to appreciate the nature of the rhinoceros and provide some necessary funds to ensure the continued protection needed to safeguard it from the dangers surrounding it.

Dr Kees Rookmaaker

Foreword

I have met many remarkable animal specialists during my life, but none so extraordinary as Anna Merz. What Joy Adamson was to lions, Dian Fossey was to gorillas, and Jane Goodall is to chimpanzees, Anna Merz is to rhinos.

To see Anna calmly taking a walk with an adult rhino, as if it were a pet dog, is unforgettable. The black rhino has always been pictured as a bad-tempered, violent and unintelligent beast, but she has put the lie to all that. She has shown that they are, in reality, remarkably bright and sensitive. Nobody in the world knows these amazing animals as she does and it is marvellous that she has taken the time to record her experiences in this book. Rhinos need all the friends they can get, and she is the best one they ever had.

Although she may be modest about it, she is truly risking her life for her rhinos. Despite armed protection to prevent the poachers from attacking and killing her animals and removing their horns, she is always in danger. But nothing short of a bullet or a spear will stop her. After I had visited her in Africa I came away with a vivid memory of her and her work. To say that she is dedicated is an understatement. Her life, quite simply, is rhinos. And their company and their protection is reward enough.

I long to go back one day, to see her again and to come close once more to her spectacular armoured friends. In the meantime I can relive the atmosphere of my last visit with great enjoyment by reading the pages of this book. I can promise you that, after finishing it, you will never see rhinos in quite the same light again.

Desmond Morris

Oxford 1991

1

The Idea

It would be just, most anything just, to man who speaks of vermin and destroys as never botfly nor bubonic plague.
Loren Eisley

How did I ever come to get involved with rhinos? I think my concern with vanishing species goes back many years. One of my earliest memories is of being taken by my father to the Natural History Museum to see a dodo, that strange and wondrous fowl, and of my father telling me that never, wherever I might go, could I ever see a real living dodo because they were all dead. Man had killed them all. This episode had a lasting impact on me.

Years later I married and went to live in Ghana. There, in front of my own eyes, I saw animal and plant species becoming extinct, and I began to realise how terribly quickly this could happen. Down came the forests. Torrential rains removed the soil. Rivers, which once ran with clear water through the forests all year, became seasonal. In the dry season they dried up and during the rainy season they became mud-filled torrents which carried the precious soil out to sea. With the forests went the creatures that lived in them. As the human population increased, so did large scale commercial hunting for food and the animals began to disappear from the savannah as well as the forest, and to reappear in the markets as 'bush meat'.

In 1958 we were living in a flat near the central Kumasi lorry park at which lorry loads of antelope arrived every morning. Many were carried alive with their legs broken, others arrived already smoked and salted. Meanwhile in the market leopard skins were stacked high, either for sale to the local chiefs or for export along with the country's two main products timber and cocoa. I was shocked but what could I, an ignorant stranger, do?

As the years passed the supply of bush meat in the market dwindled. When we travelled up north we saw no more animals, not even footprints. The land which had once carried large herds of kob, roan antelope and hartebeest was empty. The wild animals had not even been replaced by domestic stock, for the tsetse flies, the scarcity of water and the coarse elephant grass made the area unsuitable for cattle. Greed and a total lack of forethought had killed the herds that, if properly managed, could have been of lasting value to the people both as a sustainable source of 'bush meat' and as a tourist attraction.

Later, when I was working as an Honorary Warden for the Game Department, one of the things I was asked to do was to travel around the country finding areas where wild animals still existed and where it might be possible to protect them. But when I spoke to the village chiefs I always heard the same story: ten or twelve years earlier there had been many animals and plenty of bush meat, but now the animals had 'travelled'. "Where?" I used to ask. The answers varied: across the Volta River, across those hills, into Togo, into Upper Volta. Anywhere but here. However, the true answer was that the wild animals had all been trapped, snared or shot and their 'travels' had been in lorries to the nearest big market towns.

In 1976 my husband and I came to Kenya to retire. At first I was overwhelmed with the amount of 'game' everywhere. We visited the parks and reserves and saw animals in abundance. There were wild animals outside the parks too, even near Nairobi - we ourselves met a rhino on one of our earliest walks on the Ngong Hills 6 km from our house in the Nairobi suburb, Karen. However, it was not long before I realised that all was not well, for I began to recognise signs similar to those I had seen in Ghana. Shops in Nairobi were full of trinkets made from skins, dikdik horns, elephant tusks and lions' teeth; and I visited warehouses stacked with huge piles of zebra and colobus monkey skins. The trade in wildlife products was obviously out of control and this I had seen before.

It was then that I became particularly aware of what was happening to the black rhino. These great beasts were going and going fast. Unlike in West Africa, the animals were not being killed in order to feed an exploding human population. Their huge, pathetic corpses were being left to rot and be eaten by vultures. The rhinos were not dying for lack of habitat, for huge areas of East Africa are arid, covered with dry thorn scrub and of little use to people, but provide all a rhino needs to live and reproduce happily. They were being killed for the most ridiculous reason imaginable - for the two horns the unfortunate beasts carry on their noses.

These horns are the rhinos' undoing, for they were and still are being massacred for them. In the last century there were hundreds of thousands of black rhinos in Africa, south of the Sahara. In Kenya alone there were tens of thousands. Between 1944 and 1946 a man called Hunter was employed by the colonial Game Department to clear the rhinos from 50,000 acres of Kamba tribal country. He killed nearly a thousand of the poor creatures. Despite such slaughter, by the end of the 1960s there were still possibly 20,000 black rhinos left in Kenya, but during the next decade 90 % of these animals were killed.

When we came to Kenya in 1976 I knew nothing about rhinos, but I had fought a losing battle against similar destruction in Ghana for twenty years and felt strongly on the subject. An animal that has survived the vicissitudes of forty million years of evolution should surely not be dispatched by *Homo* (not so) *sapiens* in half a century. I attended a lecture given by Dr Esmond Bradley Martin, the world authority on the trade in rhino horn, who has perhaps done more to try and save the world's rhinos than anyone else. From Dr Martin I learned that most of Kenya's rhino horn was going to North Yemen; that the price was sky-high and rising; and that rhino horn was at least four times more valuable than ivory and, weight for weight, one of the most valuable commodities in the world. Kenya's remaining rhinos were all too obviously very, very endangered.

There are stringent laws against hunting in Kenya, but they are hard to enforce, especially when it comes to animals as valuable as rhinos. There is virtually no security, even in the government parks and reserves poaching is rife. In the northern and eastern parts of Kenya in particular, this poaching is mainly carried out by bandits known by the Somali word *shifta*. Large bands of shifta from Somalia, armed with submachine guns, join up with the local Kenya Somalis to poach on an unprecedented scale. The name 'Somali' has two different connotations, one national and the other ethnic. Unfortunately for the peace of the Horn of Africa, the two do not coincide. A 'Somali' can refer either to an inhabitant of the modern nation of Somalia, whose citizens include a minority of Bantu speaking tribes; or it can refer to an 'ethnic' Somali, a member of any of the closely related Somali speaking tribes whom colonial boundaries divided between Somalia, the Ogaden region of Ethiopia and northeast Kenya. Poaching by Somalis has political overtones. Rhino horn and elephant ivory are their main objectives.

In the Middle East, and in North Yemen in particular, rhino horns are used as status symbol dagger handles - nearly all are made in Sana (North Yemen). In the Yemen ownership of such a dagger is equivalent to that of a black Mercedes car in Ghana. Meanwhile, in the Far East there is a traditional belief that rhino horn can cure a very wide range of diseases and disabilities; and in a few places in India it is used as an aphrodisiac - although in South East Asia, contrary to European popular belief, this is about the only thing it is not used for. In China beautiful cups and bowls were carved out of rhino horn as it was believed they were effective against poison. These incredibly lovely and antique works of art - some of them dating from the Ming dynasty and made before 1644 - are now being ground up to provide powder for a medicine which, if it works at all, can only be by an act of faith. The highest price of all for rhino horn is in Taiwan where it is used as bullion to back the currency. All research on the rises of rhino horn has been conducted by Dr Esmond Bradley Martin on behalf of the W.W.F. and appears in his book "Run Rhino Run" and in numerous articles.

Everyone I spoke to in those early years described rhinos not only as short-sighted but also as bad-tempered, stupid and solitary. I began to be brainwashed on the subject. Surely all those who lived in the land of rhinos must know what they were talking about. However, I still had the conviction that even stupid, bad-tempered, solitary animals should not be driven over the brink of extinction, especially by something as idiotic as a lust for carved horn dagger handles and medicine of dubious efficacy. I have no children, but if I had I would not wish them to grow up in a world where my generation had been responsible for the extinction of so strange and wonderful an animal. Surely somehow, somewhere I could do something to help the black rhinos of Kenya.

Now, several years later, I know a little more about rhinos, enough to view them as fascinating and to see them as beautiful.

There is still much to learn, but I hope I know enough to write this book. I hope too that by telling of my personal experiences, I can make a few more people care sufficiently to arouse public opinion and put pressure on their governments to act on the rhinos' behalf. Even at this late hour, when their populations are a tiny remnant of what they were in the early years of the century, their race towards the final precipice of extinction can be halted if only enough people care.

2

The Beginning

Who is to care - all being permitted, violence, cruelty, lust?
I answer, because I care. Loren Eisely

The creation of Ngare Sergoi

During 1980 and 1981 I was finding life in Nairobi increasingly frustrating. I could see that the same events were about to take place in Kenya that I had spent twenty years helplessly watching in Ghana. It was the same story - the forests were coming down, the wild animals were vanishing and money was all that appeared to matter to most people. In Ghana I had tried so hard working for the Game Department but had achieved so little. However, I was determined to persevere in Kenya and thus came up with the idea of creating a sanctuary specifically to help the black rhino. I had some money, but not enough to both buy land and provide adequate protection for the rhinos on it. Moreover, as a non-Kenyan, I could only own a maximum of ten acres and that hardly helped. I would have to have assistance. So, feeling rather a fool, I began to travel around the country looking for an area suitable for rhinos and a landowner sympathetic towards them. The suggestions I made to various farmers and ranchers were not well received and it soon became apparent that no one was prepared to part with enough land to breed white mice, let alone black rhinos.

After a rather unhappy period in Nairobi during the 1982 attempted coup, we booked ourselves in for a week's holiday at Wilderness Trails, the tented camp belonging to David and Delia Craig on their ranch, Lewa Downs. In 1896 the British established a Protectorate over much of what is now Kenya; English farmers were encouraged to settle and in 1920 it became Kenya Colony. When the colony became independent of Britain in 1963, many of the settlers left. Others such as the Craigs, however, decided to stay on and become Kenyan citizens.

The ranch covers some 45,000 acres of rolling thorn bush plains on the northern slopes of Mt. Kenya; and when not covered in cloud, the mountain dominates the view to the south. Together with Sambo, our much-travelled dog, we drove around the mountain via Nanyuki and arrived, slightly late, for lunch - a picnic at a beautiful spring with the Craigs' son Ian, whom I knew slightly, and his wife Jane. During the following days we walked and rode and went for game drives. Although Lewa Downs was (and is) a working ranch, there were wild animals everywhere, truly wild but not at all shy. One morning Ian took me walking near a herd of elephant, they were not the least disconcerted and this alone spoke volumes.

My mind was alive with ideas and I decided to discuss them with Ian. He turned out to be very enthusiastic but insisted that I talk to his father. I was terrified, for I found David an awe-inspiring person who rather reminded me of my own father. To make matters worse, I had had so many negative responses to my proposals that I felt this was my last chance. On the last morning of our stay, just as we were ready to leave, I broached the subject. I was so nervous that I was almost incapable of coherent speech, but to my astonishment, instead of saying an emphatic "no", David asked me two questions. Would I give references and did I know anything about rhinos? I said "yes" to the first and "no" to the second, and from then on my life changed.

David and Delia invited us back to their home to discuss plans. They were sympathetic from the start. There had been rhinos on Lewa up until ten years earlier but they had disappeared. Not one was killed on the ranch, but as soon as they left its safety they were murdered. Slowly I began to realise that Lewa Downs could become both my home and the place where I might at last, after a lifetime of failures, realise my dream of helping a species that was in danger of extinction.

At that stage many people asked me, "why rhinos"? Did I particularly like them or have a 'thing' about them? The answer was very simple: the rhinos are in Kenya and I was in Kenya, and the rhinos were in terrible trouble. There were only a few hundred left and, to make matters worse, few of those animals were in viable breeding groups. Many were solitary individuals sitting on inaccessible mountains with no chance of meeting a mate. Nor was there the slightest possibility that they could be protected *in situ.*

The Craigs and I discussed the possibility of catching some of these isolated individuals and releasing them into a sanctuary where they could breed and lead normal lives (within the limitations of a fence); and where it would be possible to give them adequate protection against poachers by means of a sophisticated electric fence and a dedicated, well trained and well paid corps of trackers. Although each animal would be individually guarded from a discrete distance, the plan was that they should never be disturbed and their lives never interfered with in any way. It was very fortunate that at this stage of the operation I had little real concept of what my ideas entailed, or I might have been discouraged by the enormity of the task before me. I have always been a dreamer of dreams but am not a very practical person.

In the many discussions with the Craig family that followed, it was agreed that they would allow 5000 acres of their land to be used as a rhino sanctuary. (In 1988 they agreed to give us the use of another 5000 acres and this became known as 'the Extension'.) These acres made up the western end of the ranch through which flowed the river which gave the sanctuary its name, the Ngare Sergoi. The name is a Masai one meaning 'River of Donkeys', or the place where the Masai watered their donkeys - each hillock and rivulet has its Masai traditional name, for the whole area used to be the grazing lands of the Laikipiak Masai before they were dispossessed by the British.

It was also agreed that the Craigs' cattle would continue to graze throughout the sanctuary. We all felt that this was important for two reasons. Firstly, from the political aspect, it was advisable that the land should not be removed from food production. Secondly, it would provide an important and interesting experiment to ascertain if cattle and rhinos could be raised together without detriment to either species. If this could be shown to be the case, it might have important implications for the future of the rhino.

On my side, I was to finance the building of the sanctuary and to guarantee its running expenses. There was a third side to the agreement too, the government - for in Kenya all wild animals are the property of the government under a law made by the co-

Security is a major concern in rhino conservation.
(below: Gerry Ellis)

lonial government in order to control the capture of wild animals to be sold to zoos and circuses and to prevent animals being killed in order that their babies could be hawked on the streets as pets. Peter Jenkins of the Wildlife Department was asked to act as our advisor, and I promised that I would accept all his stipulations. Ian, with his enormous experience of game and cattle protection, would organise the security arrangements.

Once we had made our agreement we went ahead fast. The first thing was to erect a fence as poacher-proof as possible. Peter designed the fence and Elephence Ltd. was given the contract to build it - it was to be 20 km long and 2.5 m high. The posts, of pressure-treated Australian black wattle, 3.2 m high, were to be set 1 m deep in the ground, 12 m apart and strung with seven wires carrying 5,000 volts, interlaced with earth wires and topped by an overhang of barbed wire. The power was to come from energisers run on lorry batteries which were charged by solar panels. The whole fence was to be monitored by an electronic device which would inform us if anything touched it, and also which part (within just over 1 km) had been touched. It was going to be quite some fence.

Construction began in February 1983. To get it started, I had to acquire a tractor and a bulldozer, the former a brand-new bright red Sametract, the latter a second-hand Caterpillar. With these we scraped the lines for the fence and began building roads. Next came a major housing project for our employees. With the exception of our gardener Kiptamoi, a Kipsigis tribesman who came with us from Nairobi, all our staff were hired from the area around Lewa. The drivers, fence gangs, clerical staff and labourers are mainly drawn from the Meru tribe; and our trackers are Ndorobo, traditional hunters and gatherers who live in the forests nearby. The term Ndorobo is a nickname given by the Masai to all the small groups of forest dwellers scattered on the mountains throughout the once-vast Masai grazing lands. The nickname means 'poor people', for the forest dwellers had no cattle, the only thing the Masai consider of any worth. The Ndorobo in the area near Lewa now speak Masai as their home language and call themselves Mukogodo Masai, or simply Masai. As time went on we realised that we were having to employ a good many more people than I had anticipated (over sixty at present) –

luckily we had got some second-hand mini-ports as part of the bulldozer deal.

We established the sanctuary headquarters near the original West Gate, and there we had the office, stores and garage, as well as the holding boma and, later, the manager's house. (A 'boma', from the Persian word for 'garrison' or 'place of safety', has been incorporated into Kiswahili - the lingua franca of East Africa - to mean any sort of enclosure, from a chicken coop to an administrative centre. It is a Swahili word so commonly used in Kenyan English that 'paddock' and 'pen' are virtually never heard.) We also put up a small guard house at the East Gate and for added security located several small camps in strategic locations. For ourselves, Karl and I selected a site on the edge of a gorge which contained a spring-fed pool and swamp which was known as 'the Marula', the Swahili name for the reeds that grow there. A joined pair of charming reed-thatched rondavels, destined to become our guest-house, was built for us to live in while Karl supervised the erection of our 'proper' pre-fab house.

It was rapidly becoming obvious that we were going to spend a great deal more than we had originally estimated; but if Peter said something was necessary for the safety of the rhinos, then it had to be done. We were all determined that if we were going to create a rhino sanctuary, we were going to create a very good one. As the work got off the ground, David pointed out what I was fast beginning to realise, that there was no way I was going to be capable of running the sanctuary on my own. Thus Francis Dyer came into our lives.

Francis is Ian's cousin whose parents own Ngare Ndare, the ranch to the west of Lewa Downs, and are our nearest neighbours. The decision to hire him turned out to be an excellent one. Like me, Francis had no preconceived notions about rhinos and rhino management and was thus able to adapt to what was required very quickly. In a short space of time he also turned himself into an expert house builder, mechanic and fence builder and quickly grasped the complicated workings of the fence's monitoring device, workings which to this day remain a mystery to me. To my great pride he is now regarded as the electric game fence expert in the country. At the same time he started to learn to fly - his father and all the male members of the Craig family were already expert pilots - and Ian and I acquired half shares in a Super-Cub plane, essential for catching rhinos and for keeping a lookout for shifta.

In 1983, while our guest house was being built, Karl and I continued to live in Nairobi. Much of our time was spent driving back and forth, for Lewa Downs is a five-hour journey from the town. At the same time I thought it would be a good idea to find out as much as possible about rhinos before the first one entered the sanctuary. I hoped to learn about all five species, but that was not possible. I had to be content with trying to learn what I could of the African black and white rhinos and the Indian one-horned rhino.

Bill Woodley kindly invited me down to stay with him at Tsavo, a national park, and I learned much from listening to him talk as we drove around and from reading the various papers which he lent me. Of particular interest were those by John Goddard on the Tsavo rhinos. However, Bill was not able to show me a single rhino, although when I had visited the park as a tourist in 1969 I had seen sixteen during our first morning's drive around Kilaguni Lodge. It was depressingly obvious that times had changed.

The rhinos of Chitawan

Having seen work start on the fence early in the month, Karl and I left Kenya in the middle of February for a six-week trip to India and Nepal. For Karl it was to be a holiday, but for me it was to be a working holiday to learn about the rhinos in that area. We landed in Delhi and went first to the Kanha National Park where we experienced the excitement of seeing a tiger, that most magnificent of all the great cats, in its natural setting and from the back of an elephant. We also visited the Taj Mahal and the Kaladea Ghana Bird Sanctuary before flying to Katmandu in Nepal and then on to our major objective, Tiger Tops in the Royal Chitawan National Park. By the time we left Katmandu for Chitawan I had acquired two important letters of introduction and was hopeful that they would enable me to borrow a copy of Andrew Laurie's three-year study on the Indian rhino in Chitawan.

When the plane landed on the dusty grass airstrip there were both elephants and Land Rovers awaiting us. From the steps of the plane we ascended an elephant's back, moved off sedately and were soon splashing across a small river and arriving in the Chitawan Park. The park covers an area of approximately 1000 square kilometres of which about 80% is composed of jagged, knife-edged hills covered with mixed 'sal' forests - deciduous trees with grassy undergrowth. The remaining 20% is the river's alluvial plain, known as the 'terai', and this is the rhinos' main habitat. It is a strange and beautiful area, best seen from the back of an elephant, for the grass grows up to three metres, dwarfing the two metre high elephant grass of West Africa. On the higher ground there are trees, but the rhinos mainly stay in the long grass areas, using the ox-bow lakes left by the meanderings of the river as wallows - for, unlike the African rhinos, the Indian ones spend much of their time in water.

On that first elephant ride we saw our first rhino. With her deeply folded skin, short single horn and very long ears she looked quite different from either of the African rhinos. At first I misjudged her size, as she was dwarfed both by the grass and our elephants, and thought she was smaller than the African rhinos. In fact the Indian female is about the same size as the black rhino and the male is considerably larger, with a massive neck and shoulders. Two days later I was introduced to Dhanbahadur, Tiger Top's head tracker, a small, slender man with a shy smile. His command of English was scanty but his knowledge of the Chitawan was incredible. He was the best tracker I have ever been out with. From then on my days were spent walking with him and to him I owe all I learnt. Tigers were his great love, but he accepted that rhinos were the animals I wished to see and did everything he could to oblige me, including showing me their huge heaps of dung. Unlike the black rhino, the Indian rhino does not scatter his dung but piles it up to serve as sign posts. These heaps convey information - by scent and perhaps by other means - not only as to which animals have passed by, but also information about their reproductive state. We spent the first few days in the forest, but despite Dhanbahadur's best efforts we only had a few good rhino sightings. I realised that if I really wanted to see rhinos we would have to leave the safety of the forest and concentrate on the ox-bow lakes and long grass areas which are their preferred habitat; and if I wanted to see them behaving naturally, we would have to go in on foot.

The thought was rather unnerving as visibility in the long grass was poor and hazards were plenty, for in addition to rhinos and tigers some very large marsh crocodiles inhabited the area. However, by this time my trust in Dhanbahadur was complete and he in return knew my limitations regarding running and tree climbing. At this stage Karl had had enough of rhinos and removed himself to look at the Annapurna range. Therefore I spent most days out in the 'terai' with Dhanbahadur, the Tiger Tops organisation providing us with endless picnic lunches and sometimes starting us off on one of the elephants. Dhanbahadur was so skilled that we managed to see six to eight rhinos daily. I began to recognise them as individuals and also began to make some sense of their vocalisations. Every night I studied Andrew Laurie's paper.

We often saw one particular cow and her calf. At noon one day we were sitting in a perfect position, on top of a high bank on a promontory running out into an ox-bow lake. Below us the mother rhino lay at ease, eyes closed but ears constantly on the move. Her calf lay behind her, almost afloat, sometimes putting his head under the water and blowing strings of bubbles, sometimes paddling around his mother. It was all very peaceful, until we heard a noise. A heavy 'pad, pad, pad' behind us, coming nearer and nearer. I turned my head slowly. Behind us stood a tigress - huge, beautiful and awe-inspiring. I do not know exactly how close she was, but I could see the pattern of her whiskers. Her head was held high and her eyes were watchful - I think she was as surprised as I was. I stood up slowly, but Dhanbahadur, who could have leapt up any of the small trees nearby with ease, but realised I could not, acted with speed. Grabbing my hand, he jumped down the bank and into the lake. I was taken by surprise and landed in the water almost on top of him with a tremendous splash and right behind the rhino, who immediately took off with her calf in the direction she was facing.

Expecting at any moment to be grabbed by a crocodile, Dhanbahadur and I swam swiftly across the lake and scrambled up the opposite bank. At the top we stopped and looked at each other. For a few moments there was no sound, then all hell broke loose. Tigress and rhino, both in retreat, must have had a head-on collision. We saw nothing, but the noise was tremendous.

We ate our somewhat damp and muddy lunch and gave things time to calm down. Dhanbahadur then suggested we look for rhinos in a different direction and moved off down a narrow tunnel through the grass. Suddenly he whispered, "run" and I ran. Two rhinos crashed past and all I saw was wildly waving grass. I then sat shivering with fright until Dhanbahadur found me, but, strangely enough, I think that day's adventures cured my fear of the 'terai'.

Before I left Tiger Tops, I wanted to have a really good sighting of a big male rhino. Dhanbahadur found one for me, but unfortunately there was no nice convenient bank from which to view him. So he went on a little and then returned, indicating that I should wriggle on my belly in the same direction. Following instructions I wriggled, and when told to, lifted my head. There he was, a huge male, all of 3 m away. At this moment, Dhanbahadur nearly made me laugh by whispering, "very dangerous animal, if he get up, you run." Quite how he thought I should achieve that when lying on my tummy in the mud and facing the wrong direction I do not know.

On an elephant ride early one morning towards the end of my stay, we found a very calm female rhino with a large, half-grown calf gazing quietly at the elephants. She urinated copiously and then when she had finished, to my intense surprise, all the elephant handlers urged their beasts forward, shouting at the rhinos which departed at speed. The handlers then slithered off their charges and made a mad scramble for the rhino's puddle, shoving handfuls of urine-saturated mud into plastic bags produced from their pockets. Astounded, I asked Dhanbahadur what was going on. "Very strong medicine, very valuable", he replied. This seemed to bear out Dr Martin's report that in the east all parts of the rhino are of value, not just the horn. When the sad time to leave came, I really felt that, thanks to Dhanbahadur, Dr Laurie and the generous cooperation of the Tiger Tops management, I had learned a great deal. I had spent many hours watching rhinos feeding on the long grass. I had seen how they pushed the grass and saplings down by walking over them so that they could feed on the juicy tips. I had looked on while females suckled their calves and had watched them wallowing and sleeping. I had sometimes seen eight or nine rhinos in a fairly small area but had noted that, except for cows and calves, they were never really together. If one rhino was in a wallow and another arrived, either the newcomer or the occupant left at once. So I presumed that in any given area they all knew one another and had established a pecking order. I had also learned that the Indian rhino, unlike the African species, has two very large lower incisors which are deadly fighting weapons. According to Dr Laurie, Mr Dhungel (the Warden) and Dhanbahadur, fighting is common and adult breeding males will attack sub-adult males, often with fatal results. Even if the losers are not killed outright, they often die of infection from the wounds they receive. Certainly all the males I saw had scars on their necks and shoulders and when I asked Dhanbahadur the cause, he always replied, "from fights". I wondered if fighting would prove to be a problem with black rhinos when confined to a 5000 acre sanctuary.

Catching rhinos in Natal

Our holiday over, we returned to Kenya and as soon as possible drove up to Lewa Downs to see how work was progressing. While I went around the fence, Karl inspected our guest house. Everything was going well. We could now contemplate the next step.

I had been wondering more and more about catching rhinos. It was quite obvious that to kill a rhino is very easy and requires little skill, but to capture an animal of that size without injuring it in any way is a rather different matter. I had heard and read about the all too many animals that had died in the course of capture and translocation. Everyone seemed to accept that losses were usually inevitable. Knowing nothing whatsoever about the matter, I was nevertheless determined that any animal the government gave us permission to catch and translocate would survive and without injury. While I had been in the Chitawan there had been much talk of translocating some rhinos from the park to two new parks set up in an area where rhinos had recently become extinct. In the course of these conversations it was frequently mentioned that the group who regularly moved rhinos with only a 1% loss rate was the Capture Unit of the Natal Park Board and I was determined to meet these experts. So in November I packed my bag and went.

When I arrived at Pietermaritzburg, alone and having had a very bumpy flight, it was cold, dark and pouring with rain and there were no taxis - the whole idea seemed a bit crazy. However, the next morning the sun was shining and as I presented myself at the Natal Parks Board headquarters and found everyone kind and helpful, I was sure that I had done the right thing in coming. After a morning of discussions I hired a car and went north up the coast to Matubatuba where Peter Hitchins took me to his farm. Peter is one of the world's leading experts in all aspects of black rhino behaviour and management and we talked until late that night, then started again in the morning. He then sent me on for practical experience to Rodney Henwood at Hluhluwe.

Rodney is the chief capture officer for the Natal Parks Board and a most impressive character. He has caught between 800 and 900 rhinos and has only lost five in the process. He took me down to the rhino bomas at Umfolozi and I spent the rest of the morning there, paddling around in the mud and looking at rhinos (both black and white) and at bomas and crates, while juggling with spectacles in the rain and trying to note down all I was told. The most important thing I learned was that the animals are always held in the bomas for at least two weeks before being dispatched to their destinations. During this period, travelling crates are attached to the bomas and the rhinos are fed in the crates so that they get quite used to going in and out of them. This procedure makes the rhinos much easier to handle and much less stressed by their journeys.

That afternoon I watched while four white rhinos were darted in their bomas and then pushed into crates. These were winched up on to a recovery vehicle which was then driven alongside a huge transport vehicle into which the rhinos were off-loaded, each in its separate compartment. The whole complicated operation was conducted with speed and efficiency by Rodney, his assistant and a very well trained staff. I was most impressed.

These rhinos were destined to go to the huge de Beers game ranch near Kimberly, nearly 1500 km away and I persuaded Rodney to let me accompany him. We left in a variety of vehicles just before dawn and arrived after midnight, but the journey was not at all tedious for I learned so much talking to Rodney *en route*. We slept in the vehicles until it was light enough to find the ramp that had been specially built for this operation. The back of the huge transport lorry was then let down and the first rhino prodded off. It did not seem at all distressed by the long journey, but came out perfectly calmly and slowly wandered away. When it was out of sight, the second one was unloaded and so on until all four were gone. There were no dramas at all and the advantages of having the rhinos boma trained were made very clear.

We then drove a further couple of hundred kilometres with the ranch manager to catch another four rhinos that were to be moved to the de Beers ranch. These rhinos were not waiting in bomas, we had to locate them in a huge ranch, but luckily the area was flat and fairly open. Rodney, two of his men and I stood in the back of an open Toyota. I was holding on with one hand and clutching five colour-tagged darts ready to hand to Rodney upon request in the other. We found one rhino very soon, a splendid, huge, mature bull. With Rodney roaring instructions to the driver, we took off after him at 60 kph cross country with an apparent disregard for holes, stones, bushes and other minor obstructions - the rhino was going flat out and so were we. I hung on for dear life with my one free hand. It was an exciting chase. As we drew level with the vast grey rump, Rodney balanced himself in an incredible fashion, held the rifle with both hands and neatly shot the dart into the galloping animal. We then veered off and continued to follow him at a slightly less violent speed. After ten minutes the rhino started to circle and high step, beginning to look rather drunk. It was both comic and sad to see such a magnificent animal behave in such a ludicrous fashion. At the right moment, Rodney jumped out with a rope and looped a noose around one hind leg, fastened it to a tree and had the animal down, all with the most impressive ease and speed. I was allowed to come and help push the rhino up from his side to his brisket, and then Rodney set to work on him swiftly. He removed the dart, treated small sores, administered an antibiotic, treated the animal's eyes (for the drug used dries up the mucous membranes and damage can result if care is not taken) and prepared the recovery drug; all the time telling me exactly what he was doing and why. Meanwhile, I was jotting it all down, despite being without my spectacles and having a slightly shaking hand. The recovery vehicle, which had been summoned by radio, was then manoeuvred into position and a crate off-loaded in front of the rhino. His head was lifted on to the crate's ramp and ropes were arranged around his body. When Rodney was satisfied that all was ready, he injected the recovery drug into a vein in an ear, then moved to the back end and prodded the rhino under the tail with an electric cattle prod. The animal was up and on his feet in that crate before either he or I was aware of what was happening. The whole operation was carried out with the minimum noise and fuss and the maximum speed and efficiency, and I understood how Rodney had earned his reputation. The next five hours were spent searching for the other three rhinos which had vanished. As the area was flat and sparsely bushed, you would not have thought that they could have done the disappearing act as well as they did. The sun was blazing hot and there was a searing dry wind. I got very burnt and had a thirst the like of which I had never had before, but we had to find those rhinos, otherwise they were doomed - for the owner of that ranch was anti-rhino and wanted them moved off his property. Eventually, at three o'clock, we discovered them in a group under a tree. They all took off together, the calf in front, followed by the cow and the male behind, just in the order Rodney had predicted. Once again he did his balancing act and after about six exciting minutes placed three darts in three galloping rumps.

The calf was the first to falter and one man jumped down with a rope to secure it while we carried on. The cow was the next to high-step and Peter jumped off with a rope to secure her. We continued after the big bull. The disappearance of his family had maddened him. Half his mind was on getting away, half was on knocking hell out of us. He turned, charged and was suddenly more or less on top of us, a two ton, enraged animal. Just when I thought our last moment had arrived, Rodney roared at him and he stopped within touching distance, jamming on his brakes so violently that we were engulfed by a cloud of dust. Several times the rhino made as if to charge again, each time Rodney roared. At last the drug started to take effect and Rodney jumped down with rope in hand, took off after him and got the noose on a leg and the end around a tree. The rhino turned and charged him, but Rodney stood his ground and then at the last moment jumped aside and, pulling the rope with full force, brought the beast down. This time I was allowed to help treat the three rhinos and load them, but it took time because the recovery vehicle had to come for each animal separately and ferry it to the waiting transport lorry. It was just getting dark when I scrambled up into the passenger seat of the transporter for the 250 km drive back to the ranch.

Luckily the moon was up when we reached the unloading area. The rhinos were still under the influence of the drug and were difficult to unload, particularly the cow who had the firm idea that she was going to stay *in situ* and murder everyone who tried to prod her out. The speed with which she could swipe with her horn, not to mention the power behind the swipe, was most unnerving. However, eventually all three were unloaded and we departed for a quick supper and gallons to drink. After we had eaten and it was well past midnight, we went down and unloaded the old bull we had caught first.

Rodney was up at dawn the next morning, anxious to check the welfare of the rhinos. We did not actually see any of them but spotted plenty of tracks and Rodney was satisfied that all was well. So after breakfast we started the long drive back, spending one night *en route* at the farm of some very charming friends of Rodney's who run a small game ranch; and I was taken to see the four white rhinos which are amongst the major attractions there.

We were back in Umfolozi the next evening and I spent most of the next three days down at the bomas learning how to feed and care for the rhinos. I was also taken up in the helicopter used by the Capture Unit and given a practical demonstration of how a rhino could be driven over a considerable distance, five to six kilometres, so that it could be darted near a track or place from which it could be retrieved without great difficulty. It was a slightly unnerving but fascinating experience as the helicopter swung round trees and gently forced an increasingly irate rhino to go exactly where the pilot wanted it.

The Natal parks, like all the parks in South Africa, are fenced and therefore the animals within them have to be carefully managed. It is intensive management of the sort I had not seen practised anywhere else in Africa and I found the whole system very interesting. The parks cover their expenses both from tourist revenue and from selling animals to other parks and reserves and to private game ranches (of which there are many). The numbers of animals that have to be disposed off is calculated according to the rate at which the species breeds and the carrying capacity of the park, which, of course, is highly dependent on rainfall. Since space is restricted, priority is given to the endangered species, of which the black rhino is the most important. Therefore other browsers such as kudu and impala have their numbers regulated to ensure adequate browse for the rhino. On my last evening in Umfolozi I was taken for a drive in an area of the park that is normally closed to visitors and there I saw six black rhino, four adults together and a female with a sub-adult calf a short distance away - living proof that if they know each other and if there is adequate food and cover, the black rhino, usually described as a 'solitary beast', will live in amicable proximity.

From Umfolozi I drove to the Kruger National Park. Black rhino had been translocated there from Natal, and I had an interesting three days finding out how they had been released and how they had adapted to all area that struck me as very different from their homeland. In Kruger it was really hot and the whole park appeared drought-stricken - and my host there, Anthony Hall Martin, told me that a lot of the animals would have to be culled (a polite word for killed) if the rains failed again.

Pilanesberg Park

The final course on my educational tour was given in Pilanesberg National Park in Bophuthatswana. Pilanesberg is only a small park (600 km square) but a beautiful one, situated in all old volcanic area. I arrived in the middle of a violent dust storm after an eight hour drive and was duly installed in a staff caravan which I shared with a large supply of mosquitoes, cockroaches, two rats and a pregnant skink. I had several skirmishes with the rats which set up house in my handbag and devoured much of it, including all my biros. One night they even joined me in bed which resulted in my becoming entangled in the mosquito net and whacking my own foot while they escaped having had a lot of fun.

Pilanesberg was of particular interest to me because thirty rhinos from Natal had been translocated there, and because Chris Freeman from Natal worked there. He had been Rodney's predecessor in the N.P.B. Capture Unit and I hoped I could learn much from him - and I did. Like Rodney, Chris was tough, extremely interesting and willing to share his knowledge with me. He took endless trouble to work out lists of equipment and to tell me how to prepare for various emergencies and he gave me all the papers relevant to the release of the black rhinos from Natal. I spent much time walking and looking for those rhinos but they favoured the densely wooded valley bottoms and, as I had neither my dog Sambo nor a good tracker with me, my courage rather failed me in that thick scrub. I tried to see them by climbing the mountains and peering down from aloft, but this did not work for they were too well hidden. However, I had some lovely walks and scrambles and saw a lot of white rhinos as well as many other beasts and birds.

I had hoped I might be in on a rhino capture, but the only capture on the park programme just then was that of two ostriches due to be sold to a game park. As I knew that there were ostriches on Lewa and felt it important to learn about all the animals in the sanctuary, I accepted the invitation to go along. The operation began after dark when Chris and I and three others set off in an open truck. The group of ostriches we were after was quite a large flock on an area of open plain near a lake. They had been located just before dark and sure enough there they still were. When Chris switched the searchlight on them they immediately became very confused and ran off with us in hot pursuit. As we drew close, a net gun - a weapon invented in New Zealand for the capture of red deer - was fired at the chosen fowl. The gun went off with such a bang that I nearly jumped out of my skin and the poor bird went down with an awful thud.

I already had my instructions, I was responsible for the care of the bird's head and neck. It had been impressed upon me that the results of a kink in the neck were very serious for an ostrich, as it can cause strangulation. So I sat on the ground with the whole length of neck carefully held between my legs and its head in my lap. I had not realised what incredible eyelashes these birds have, nor how appealing their large dark eyes and the absurd clumps of spiky feathers on their heads are. In due course the bird was trussed up to Chris' satisfaction and lifted into the back of the truck. I sat on the floor with my back to the tail board and the neck once more between my legs, but this time the head was under my shirt to protect the eyes from the dust. We then set off in full cry after the next bird, but I was so enveloped in a cloud of dust and so shaken about, that I saw nothing of the chase which finished abruptly when the net was fired.

This second bird was also installed with its neck between my legs and head under my shirt. By this stage I was beginning to wonder what livestock was deserting the birds for fresh pastures, as I got increasingly itchy. However, I had to stay put as, with two birds safely in hand, we set off on the 60 km journey to their new home. Chris was apparently hungry, for he drove in a hurry while I bounced up and down in my cloud of dust and saw nothing at all. But suddenly we came to an abrupt halt - Chris had seen a rhino in the road - and I flew up into the air, still clutching my two heads, and no doubt would have sailed straight out of the truck decapitating both birds in the process had not my two companions, who were sitting on the birds, grabbed my legs in full flight. I was very sore for days after.

One evening Peter, one of the park staff, took me to a dam where he had sometimes seen black rhino, but instead of black ones we found a large white one, very obviously stuck. A big bull hovered nearby, going to her from time to time and sniffing her. Each time she struggled more frantically. Convinced that she was unable to extricate herself, Peter went to fetch Chris while I stayed to watch. By the time they returned with a lorry full of bales of hay, it was well after dark. The male was still in the vicinity and a leopard had begun calling from the far side of the wallow. We unloaded the hay bales, hoping that the rhino could trample them into the mud and get herself out, but three hours later she was still stuck. Obviously something other than hay was in order. However, as Chris saw no way of extricating her until he could get hold of the workshop keys, we left her there and returned home. I felt very sorry for that rhino that night.

Chris fetched me early next morning with rescue tackle and helpers already loaded on to his truck. We found the rhino still stuck and very much alive. I was deployed to try to distract her front end while Chris attempted to get a net around her back end. So as he floundered around in the slippery mud in over a metre of water behind her, I waved sticks at her nose and tried to keep out of range of her wicked horn. She, poor thing, was furious and must have thought we were torturing her for fun.

At one point she did a complete backward somersault and began to head out to sea blowing bubbles. This could have been a disaster, for due to the peculiarities of their anatomy - their short necks and the nuchal hump on their shoulders - white rhino cannot swim or rather cannot hold their heads and noses above water. Somehow Chris looped a noose around her nose and we all heaved and got her turned round so that her nostrils at least were above water again. Then he managed to get the net back around her rump. One man operated a winch anchored to a tree, to which a rope coming from one side of the net was attached. On the other side of the net a rope lead to eight men on a block and tackle rig. While I held another winch attached to her nose rope. I had never used a hand winch before and only had a hazy idea of how to work it, moreover, this was rather a temperamental one that had to be frequently readjusted. As I had not got my specs, I could hardly see what I was doing when I did figure out how to do it - and to complicate the situation yet further there was a branch just over my head that got in my way whatever I did.

Chris was directing operations from the rhino's rear, up to his neck in mud and water - but the lady herself had no intention of helping her cursing and sweating would-be helpers and continually thwarted our efforts. However, after about four hours, she suddenly popped out on to the bank, on to her feet and ready for murder. Turning quickly to deal with Chris, she got entangled with both net and nose rope and went down with an awesome crash. The others rather wisely departed at speed. For one awful moment I thought she was going to slide down the bank back into the dam, but Chris moved with alacrity and cut her out of the net. Again she was on her feet and out for murder - and still firmly attached to me and my winch. But somehow, as she charged, Chris got the rope around a tree and himself half up it; and somehow - when I thought I had only three seconds left to live - he pulled her round and off balance and, as her head came around, leaned down and cut the noose from her nose. He then roared at her and, tail tightly curled, she headed swiftly for the bush.

The whole operation had been very well managed, as indeed is the whole park. Pilanesberg National Park was created because of the personal interest of the president of Bophuthatswana and it was created not just to idealistically conserve wildlife, but to be of economic benefit to the little country. It is proving its worth to the citizens in several ways. Firstly, the park makes money from tourism; it has both a tented camp and a very small luxury lodge. Secondly, it makes money directly from the animals, both alive and dead. Since the park is so small it has to be very carefully managed and the numbers of animals strictly controlled. Some of the surplus animals, like the ostriches I handled, are captured and sold to other parks and reserves. Others are shot, but they too bring in money. Trophy hunting is allowed under strict regulations in one part of the park. The hunter pays through the nose for the privilege and gets to keep the trophy head or skin, while the meat is sold cheaply to the local people from the abattoir that has been built just outside.

This abattoir also handles the animals that are 'cropped'. In a small fenced area, especially an area such as Pilanesberg which is subject to drought, the number of surplus animals must be reduced. Such calculated killing is far better than letting the numbers rise uncontrollably with the result that the overpopulated area is devastated, and the animals die anyway of starvation. The culling keeps the park population in check, provides inexpensive meat to the people around it, so that they do not resent the land being taken away from farming or ranching, and brings in additional funds as well.

As a result of these multiple-use management practices, Pilanesberg is a very viable little park. Although some of the practices are not at present applicable to Kenya, where sport hunting is strictly banned and 'game' meat is not marketable, the park is run in a way which I think many other countries could well emulate. I certainly came away from there having learned a good deal about the potential of well-run small parks, as well as how to extricate rhinos from dams.

3

Catching Rhinos

I know what only man has known this far, that there existed time before we came. Loren Eisely

We spent Christmas of 1983 in Nairobi but as soon as the holidays were over we started packing. On 11 January, 1984 we moved to Ngare Sergoi. The move itself was chaotic and so were our first six months there. We lived in the attractive thatched rondavels which have since become our guest house while Karl struggled to build our permanent home. It really was a struggle, for the whole operation was fraught with language difficulties, transport complications and lack of skilled labour. Most of our belongings remained in packing cases. Wind and dust were our constant companions. Tempers were frayed and our little collie Remus bit our labourers at fairly regular intervals.

Meanwhile, as Karl wrestled with the house, Francis and I embarked on the job of learning how to run a rhino sanctuary; but first we had to get some rhinos. We had put word out that we were offering a reward for information as to the whereabouts of any rhinos in the area north of Lewa. This vast, arid area of acacia scrubland, broken by jagged mountain ranges and rocky hills, is the homeland of pastoral peoples; the Samburu, close kin to the Masai, just to the north of us, and beyond them others such as the Rendille and Boran and to the east some of the Somali tribes which have moved in more recently.

Traditionally these people lived in peaceful proximity to the wild animals, generally only hunting the predators that threatened their herds of camels and cattle, sheep and goats. But times had changed and poaching had become so rampant in the area that hardly any rhinos were left. However, we knew - hoped - that there must still be a few and so set up a network of informants to find out where. Then whenever information came in, we could check on it ourselves with our own people.

The first, futile search

One such report was from a mountain to the northeast of Lewa and just east of Shaba, the reserve made famous by Joy Adamson's work with leopard. I set out to investigate early one morning in the Suzuki, taking Thomas, one of our trackers, with me. By noon we had reached the Uaso Nyiro river in the Shaba Reserve. This was as far as we could go by car, we would have to wade across. As there was going to be a full moon that night, we were able to dawdle a little, waiting until the worst of the heat was over to continue. So while I surveyed the river with a certain amount of trepidation, thinking all too vividly about crocodiles, Thomas made 'Samburu tea'. Cold water, tea leaves, sugar and powdered milk are stirred together in a saucepan and boiled wildly until well stewed – it is a most excellent drink and very sustaining.

Thus fortified we crossed the river, happily without incident, and fairly soon came across rhino tracks heading north towards the mountain. We followed the tracks and soon found some droppings. In those days I was not sure of the difference between rhino and elephant droppings so, after Thomas had searched around in his nether garments to retrieve my spectacles which I had given him to carry, we both knelt beside the exciting bits of dung and discussed the implications in a variety of languages. We must have looked rather comic, for I sported a strange hat of tattered white straw which drooped forlornly and Thomas was adorned with a red checked tablecloth over his shorts and carried a spear in one hand and a yellow plastic water container in the other. Whenever he concluded from my colour that I was becoming seriously overheated, he would stop and pour a cupful of water over my hat and down my shirt - a very good way of keeping off the boil.

We set off again, but shortly lost the tracks in rocky ground. However, we decided to continue in the same direction over the arid plain towards the mountain. The going got steeper and rougher and very thorny. Before long my trousers were in tatters and my legs bleeding. Thomas, born and bred in such country, did not get impaled with anywhere near the regularity that I did.

Anna Merz (Neil Leifer)

As we struggled to reach the saddle in this confusion of thorn and rock, Thomas suddenly pointed. I looked upwards to see a giraffe above us moving effortlessly with its long and elegant legs across terrain which required more climbing and scrambling than walking. As we watched, the giraffe stopped for a short moment and stood above us, burnished red-gold against the black rocks and the deep blue of the cloudless sky, a beautiful sight. We continued onwards and upwards, constantly surrounded by klipspringers – tiny antelopes, 55 cm at the shoulder, which bounced about from rock to rock on upright hoof-tips as if to mock our human clumsiness – until we finally reached the northern peak just before sunset. The view more than repaid the climb, but of our rhino there was not a sign. So resignedly we scrambled down and walked back across the plain in the brilliant moonlight. Listening to the lions roaring nearby, I was glad that Thomas had brought his spear. Back at the riverbank, while I washed in the river, Thomas cooked a meal of maize flour, cabbage and corned beef and we washed it all down with gallons of stewed tea. We then wrapped our blankets around us and lay down by the fire which Thomas kept going all night. During the night, elephants passed by so closely that we could hear the rumblings of their bellies; and from time to time, when other strange noises came too close, Thomas would get up and hurl a branch in their general direction.

At four o'clock in the morning we reheated the remains of the tea and re-crossed the river and the plain in the moonlight. I kept close to Thomas and his spear as the lions did not sound very far away. We reached the southern side of the mountain at dawn and followed a dry river bed up over a series of rock falls. In several places I wished for a rope and once or twice Thomas had to help me, so I was more than a little surprised to see elephant droppings. How on earth they managed to climb up those rock falls I could not imagine - and what a sight it would be to see them doing it. Later I was to learn that rhino too can negotiate slopes that would defeat any horse or mule, even those bred in Afghanistan on which we had trekked in the Hindu Kush.

The southern part of the mountain was a vast tangle of serrated peaks, boulders and thorn bushes. Elephant and kudu tracks abounded, but of rhino there was again no trace. We returned via a dry torrent bed, so steep that even the elephants had avoided it, a family of baboons watching our progress with interest. Then we drove back to Lewa, tired and sadly rhinoless.

The arrival of Godot

The Wildlife Department and a very competent veterinarian, Dr Paul Sayers, had captured a male rhino in the Kitengela, the conservation area that is adjacent to Nairobi National Park. He had had to be captured because he persisted in leaving the park boundaries and straying into an area where he was in danger of being killed. Since then he had been kept in a holding boma near Athi, just inside the park. On 10 March we received a message saying that he was to be sent up to us, and, although the Wildlife Department knew our fence was not yet completed, that he had to come to us the following night as that was the only time that Dr Sayers was free to accompany him. I was to leave at once for Nairobi.

Twenty minutes later I was *en route* in my Suzuki and that evening I met Paul. He had organised the medical side - the drugs for tranquillising and so on - but not the documentation. Nor had I. Paul also told me that I would have to organise a digging operation as there was no ramp at the holding boma and even without a crate the animal weighed nearly two tons. It was Saturday night and I had no labour and not even a pick-axe with me. I managed to get hold of Peter Jenkins of the Wildlife Department early the next morning and told him my tale of woe. He was remarkably polite for one woken before seven on a Sunday morning, but his advice was to go home and wait until other people organised things. However, that would have meant moving the rhino without Paul and I felt that we had to move him with his help that very night. Peter finally agreed and I spent the morning on the phone, receiving instructions.

At five o'clock that evening we all assembled at Athi. Francis came with a lorry and two drivers; Paul had the medical equipment to deal with all the emergencies that might - but happily did not - arise; and Peter had performed miracles and arrived with two friends who had vehicles with winches, plus a borrowed ramp.

Meanwhile, the object of all this fuss, a big bull rhino, was standing in his crate letting out anxious little squeaks - absurdly small noises from such a large animal. Eventually, after considerable trouble with winches and cables, the crate was loaded, with the wretched animal facing backwards, and securely roped down. We then left the poor rhino to calm down while we went back into town for a much-needed meal.

At ten o'clock that evening we returned and an hour later we were on the road. An armed escort vehicle drove ahead (one of the Wildlife Department men had told me how one rhino in transit had been ambushed and killed); then came the lorry with the rhino (and me, standing by his crate); and my Suzuki, containing Francis and Paul, brought up the rear. It was a slow procession. Every ten minutes I climbed up the crate to peer anxiously down

The rhinos are usually kept in a holding boma before and after being moved. This makes them easier to handle and less stressed by their journeys.

at the rhino and every two hours we stopped to enable Paul to inspect his charge. Each vehicle that passed us or followed us excited my overwrought imagination and scenarios of holdups and rhino-nappings exercised my mind. The rhino occasionally let out a worried squeak. I think he and I were equally anxious, but I was a lot colder.

As I talked to him and he squeaked back at me, it occurred to me that he was not behaving in the manner I had expected from a brainless animal; and for the first time it crossed my mind that perhaps these animals were somewhat maligned and not as stupid as everyone had assured me they were. Perhaps living with them and learning about them would be interesting after all, and not the let down I was expecting after my work with chimps in

Ghana. The thought warmed my heart if not my body as we drove slowly through the night heading north around Mt. Kenya. As we passed by the tiny township of Naro Moru it was still pitch dark, I was frozen and both rhino and I were unhappy, but as we reached Nanyuki, some 30 km further on, a spectacular dawn made me feel better. Although the unfortunate rhino could not appreciate it, caged as he was in his very solid crate.

At nine o'clock in the morning we drove through the sanctuary gates and down to the holding boma. It was a very proud moment. The arrival of this animal gave reality to my dream of helping rhinos. Here he was, a large, unhappy and very unpredictable fact, and not just one of what Karl used to describe as my 'wild ideas'. The Wildlife Department had named the rhino Ngotho, but I re-named him Godot, having waited for him, our first rhino, for so long.

The capture of Shaba

Now we had one rhino, we simply had to get another. Although Thomas and I had failed to find the rhino on the steep, ridged mountain north of Shaba, we knew that there was one up on a mountain just east of Shaba and had put guards there in an attempt to protect it. We decided to move in force to the mountain on 23 February. I began the day by losing the tips of two fingers to the teeth of my pony who inadvertently bit me when I was giving her worm tablets, and had to make a mad dash to the little Nanyuki hospital, then another mad dash to our departure point. The lorry and the tractor and trailer had left the day before. The Wildlife Department helicopter, with Ted Goss (head of the Capture Unit), Dieter Rottcher (the vet) and our little plane were to join us on Saturday. Sunday was 'D-Day'.

We left in a convoy of four vehicles, one containing a large and very angry lion, a confirmed cattle thief trapped by Ian the previous night, accompanied by a Wildlife Department vehicle to get him through the Isiolo checkpoint. It was very hot by the time we got to the lowlands, and we had to stop periodically to water the tarpaulin covering the lion's crate. However, we eventually arrived in the Shaba Reserve and immediately sought a place by the river to release one hot and very angry lion. Ian managed this operation with great skill, pulling the trap door up by means of a rope which he had slung over a branch and then attached to the back of his vehicle. We onlookers retreated to our own vehicles and rolled up the windows. Ian moved his car forward, the trap door went up, and the lion bounded out giving a roar of rage and departed at speed in the direction of the river, looking magnificent. Game abounds in the reserve so we hoped for the best for him. Having disposed of our feline travelling companion, we then looked for a campsite for ourselves closer to the mountain. We found a beautiful spring, but it turned out to be well populated with leeches and the mosquitoes that night were bad.

We spent the following day planning our attempted line of action. Late in the afternoon Ian, his friend Bob and six other men were driven to the far side of the mountains where they would climb to the top and try to pick up fresh tracks at dawn. Unfortunately I was not allowed to go with them, a decision which did not please me; but I realised that with my injured, bandaged hand I would have caused undue delay while attempting to scramble up the steep slopes.

On Sunday we in the base camp made tea before dawn and then William (Ian's brother and a brilliant pilot) and I drove to the little plane. At first light we were in the air. I had only flown in a small plane once before, but did not have time to be frightened as I was too occupied trying to spot the rhino. We made radio contact with Ian and the others but they had found no tracks, so we landed the plane for half an hour and then flew up again. This time Ian and his men had found tracks. Moreover, both he on the ground and William from the air had had very brief glimpses of the animal. They had sighted it near a dense tangle of boulders and bush where the mountain came down to the plain in a series of steep rock falls - difficult country for a klipspringer and surely impossible for a rhino. Little did we know then of the abilities of rhinos.

Ted and Dieter then joined the search in the helicopter and for the next two and half hours we flew in strips at tree top level over that precipitous mountain. I peered down and scanned the ground, the wind nearly taking my eyes out, but there was no time to feel either sick or afraid. We then went on to search the vast plain, but there was still no sign of the rhino. By this time Ian and his companions had also descended. They had got news from a Samburu herdsman that 'our' rhino had been off the mountain for at least two hours. It had come down at speed through terrain we had all considered impossible and had given us the slip nicely. The helicopter had already landed. William tried coming down on a rough road, but after three attempts concluded there were too many trees as well as an anxious elephant in the way. He finally landed on the little airstrip and we all returned to the camp to decide on our next line of action, while Jane, Ian's wife, fed us.

After brunch we drove to the small manyatta where our old Samburu informer lived. (A manyatta is the name given to the small collection of huts surrounded by a thorn bush fence where the nomadic people of Kenya live, some are permanent settlements, but most are not. At night all the cattle, sheep and goats are kept within the stockade). On his advice, William, I and six men walked for two hours in a large semicircle around the patch of very thick bush at the base of the mountain where our rhino had allegedly descended, but there were no signs of tracks. We met again at the manyatta for more talks. Ian and I were both determined that having driven the animal off the safety of its mountain home, we should at least try to follow it up. So William departed in a truck to get his plane, while Ted and Dieter stood by with the helicopter. Meanwhile Ian, Bob and I and our three best men went back to that patch of tangled bush.

Slowly and silently we crept into the tangle, until we came suddenly upon an area full of fresh rhino spoor and rank with its scent. Ian whispered that I should be ready to leap up a tree and I nodded assent, knowing full well, however, my limitations in that respect even with two fully-fingered hands. Then a black patch of bush moved. There was a furious snort. A hand grabbed me and knocked me down behind a tree so that I missed the ensuing action when the fleeing rhino charged right between Ian and Bob, narrowly missing them both. Luckily Ted and Dieter were hovering in the helicopter overhead, for Dieter took aim and placed his dart perfectly in the rump of the galloping rhino. Rhino and helicopter then departed at speed.

Ian told two of our men to run back to the vehicles and follow us. Bob and Kinyanjui, the head of Lewa Downs' security force, ran after the noise of the helicopter, with me panting in the rear, going as fast as I could with heart pounding, head bursting and fear in my heart for that rhino. I trotted about 4 km, guided by the circling plane, and arrived just as Ian and Ted took off in the helicopter. Dieter was bent over the prostrate form of our huge quarry as it lay in the full sun. It was a female.

I could not believe our luck, but there was no time to gloat. While Dieter gave her the necessary injections, Kinyanjui and I covered her with branches, hung our dampened shirts over her and applied ointment to her eyes. The helicopter soon returned with more water, but without Ian who had gone to retrieve the tractor which was of course kilometres away, with no road in the vicinity. The rest of us did not have the strength to turn the great beast on to her brisket, but at least I was able to get her nose out of the dust and raised across my legs while water was poured over us both. Dieter stood by with watch in hand to monitor her breathing, and I sat with her great heavy head on my legs and prayed the tractor would come soon.

In due course - although it seemed ages - the tractor and all our people arrived. The sledge was off-loaded from the trailer and the rhino, trussed up with padded ropes, was hauled on to grass-stuffed sacks and tied securely down. We pulled the rhino-laden sledge up on to the trailer and then we were off. Dieter and I sat by her head in a cloud of dust, me still without my shirt which was covering one of her eyes. A Game Department escort vehicle, with rifles at the ready, followed close behind. On the way, we passed a lovely herd of elephant and a cheetah on her kill with two tiny cubs, but had no time to stop and admire such scenes.

It took about two hours to reach the little holding boma that had been constructed for the occasion and another forty minutes to off-load the rhino. I was stiff from the journey and also worried, for she had been on her side far too long. Eventually she lay unroped in the little pen, accompanied by Dieter who gently injected the recovery drug into a vein in her ear and then climbed out. Still she lay prostrate. We re-entered the pen and sprinkled water over her. Slowly and unsteadily she lurched to her feet and stood there looking angry, bewildered and magnificent. In the gathering dark we left her to recover with an armed guard mounted over her. Then shortly before midnight, Ted, Dieter and I drove back and gave her water - to have given her a drink earlier would have been dangerous to her health. She seemed fine and we left her in peace. Later, when she was crate trained, the rhino we had christened 'Shaba' was brought safely to Lewa.

Alas, I missed that journey as I was in hospital having my hand re-broken and reset.

Releasing the first rhinos and the arrival of Morani

On 18 April Peter Jenkins pronounced the sanctuary facilities 'adequate', although we still had neither radios nor a monitoring system on the fence. His approval meant that we could now release our rhinos from the confines of the holding boma into the wide open spaces of the sanctuary. We decided to release Godot that very evening.

I perched on top of the log wall while Ian, Francis and two of our men pulled out the heavy poles that constituted the gate. Patiently, and with very obvious curiosity, the great beast waited until the gap was wide enough, then calmly walked through the opening. For about half an hour he sniffed around the precincts with interest and then quietly walked off into the dusk.

No sooner had we given Godot his freedom than another rhino arrived. This was Morani. He was a very calm rhino, for after his mother had been poached in Amboseli Park, he had been hand-raised for six months. The trouble was he was too amiable and had taken to hanging around the lodge and unwittingly terrifying tourists. So it was decided to remove him before he caused a crisis and we were asked to take him. He arrived in due course and settled down happily in the holding boma. Shaba posed a far greater problem in the holding boma than either Godot or Morani. She was a wild, wild rhino.

Since we had caught her ourselves she was, and still is, my pride and joy, but she did not reciprocate my feelings. Every day I visited her at regular intervals, always bringing her lucerne (alfalfa) or horse nuts or some choice bit of browse. However, as soon as she saw me she would charge me with ears flattened and her nose wrinkled, making a fearful roaring noise. She would pull up just as her nose touched the wall. Each post was stout and strong and set deep into concrete and I knew that no rhino was strong enough to break through, but it was all I could do to keep still and continue to talk to her gently. We did not want to keep her in the holding boma too long, but I feared that if I could not calm her down before we released her she would smash herself, the fence, the vehicles and whatever else she might encounter. Eventually I began to despair of ever calming the frantic animal down and ran out of conversation, until I had the brilliant idea of reading to her.

I climbed on to the platform above her head and out of her reach and started to read aloud. I continued this programme, reading for several hours each day or as long as my voice held out and it worked. One wonderful day Shaba walked up to me and accepted the usual proffered food from my hand. Within a week we felt she was ready to be released. Like Godot she stood expectantly at the gate and quietly walked out as soon as it was open.

Then the trouble began - but not the trouble we had expected, instead she simply would not go away. She walked all around the holding boma, eating grass and sniffing everywhere with much interest and we had the greatest difficulty in eventually creeping over to our cars in the gathering dark. I returned early the next morning with lucerne for Morani and to my astonishment Shaba was back in her pen and squeaked for food when she saw me. We had to coax her out with lucerne and close the gate behind her. Still she hung around and later that morning took violent exception to the tractor that arrived with a trailer-load of browse for Morani. To the great consternation of the driver she tried to tip the tractor over, but was fortunately unsuccessful in this enterprise and eventually moved off. Morani was released later that same day and three days later they were spotted together in the valley just below the holding boma, where Morani was seen to make three attempts to mate Shaba.

Unloading Rongai and Amboni

On 25 April we were expecting the arrival of two rhinos that had been captured by the Wildlife Department a few weeks earlier, but they failed to turn up and we could not think what had happened to them. At eight thirty that evening I was in the bath when our Land Rover arrived and the driver told me that two lorries with two rhinos, plus escort vehicles, had arrived at the West Gate. I rushed over to find a scene of vast activity at the holding boma. About forty game scouts were trying to unload a large male rhino in the glare of various headlights. I stood by the lorry and watched the proceedings. Slowly, and with infinite caution, the rhino started to emerge from his crate. He was about halfway out when suddenly everyone in sight leapt on to the nearest available object and I was pulled up a rather unstable ladder by an unexpected helper.

I turned round to see what all the commotion was about and could just make out the tip of a horn and a prehensile upper lip around the corner of the holding boma. Slowly the whole huge head of Morani appeared. His ears were pricked and his expression was one of intense curiosity. The moment was awkward in the extreme, but also very funny. As soon as I was sure that the head did belong to Morani, I told everyone what a calm and friendly rhino he was. Many of the game scouts knew him and were soon laughing as much as I was. Meanwhile, Morani was totally fascinated but also somewhat blinded by the headlights. First he tripped over some logs and lost his balance in a most undignified way. Then he reversed somewhat violently into a Land Rover. To relieve his feelings and add to the general confusion he went on to give a fine dust-digging display with his horn. Finally, in a playful manner and without malice, he tried to tip over the lorry, crate, rhino and all. Eventually he backed off, allowing us to proceed with unpacking our new rhinos while he surveyed matters from a more reasonable distance. Luckily, neither of the new rhinos - Rongai and Amboni - seemed unduly perturbed by Morani's activities, and quite ignored his presence as we got first one and then the other into their pens.

The capture of Womba

The next arrivals came from parks and a private sanctuary and are described individually in another chapter; but the next rhino we captured ourselves came from the Mathews Range, the mountains visible to our north. As recently as the early 1970s the Mathews supported a large population of elephant and rhino. Then the shifta moved in and very heavy poaching followed. The animals were nearly wiped out in that disastrous decade, but we heard rumours that there were between one and four rhinos left in the mountains behind Wamba, the very small town at the southeast edge of the range.

If there were any surviving rhinos there it would be impossible to protect them - they would certainly end up being poached. So the Wildlife Department's Rhino Management Committee decided that all attempt should be made to catch them and move them to the safety of our sanctuary. First we had to build a holding boma at Wamba and, although only temporary, it had to be very strong. The problems of transport also added to the difficulties and the cost, but eventually it was finished and we set off to look for a rhino to put in it.

On Wednesday 22 January Ian, Jane and Bob moved to Wamba with several of our trackers. A couple of days later I followed with Errada, our best tracker. We wedged ourselves into the back of William's Toyota for a very dusty and bumpy three-hour drive to the camp that Ian and the others had set up in a beautiful valley leading into the mountains, about 3 km from Wamba. Then Ted Goss arrived in his helicopter with Dieter the vet and the team was complete.

The rhino was no rumour, Ian and Bob had glimpsed it that day, high up in the range to our north, moving with a herd of buffalo. The mountains looked wonderful from a distance. The higher northern peaks were clad in beautiful cedar forest, but the southern part of the range, where we were, was nothing but impenetrable thorn tangle nearly three metres high. At best you had to stoop and as often as not you had to creep through the thickets on all fours.

Early on Friday morning we all moved off, just as it was beginning to rain - something it rarely does in those parts, and certainly not in January. Ian, Bob and the Game Department scouts went to the north where the rhino had been seen on Thursday. Errada, myself and two scouts were to climb to a pinnacle on the southern range where we could watch the opposite slope for the rhino. Ted and Dieter stayed in camp to be near the helicopter. We were all linked by radio. It took us three hours to reach our pinnacle - well-scratched and soaking wet - and the rest of the day passed equally slowly. It was very cold up there and to add to our discomfort it continued to rain on and off, but we dared not take shelter for fear of missing the rhino. Ian got one glimpse of it high in the forest, but that was all. So at about four o'clock he called the search off.

Back at the camp, Jane had hot tea and masses of food ready for us to devour before retiring to our tents. My tent, which weighs all of one kilo, is tiny. I can kneel in it and lie down in it, but there just is not room to deal with sodden clothes - it was an

Anna and two of her trackers observing rhinos (Gerry Ellis)

uncomfortable night. Just before dawn I unearthed a dry shirt but had to get back into soaking shorts and shoes. Fortunately it had stopped raining, but our world was still pretty wet. This, however, made the tracking easier. At first light we picked up fresh tracks, for the rhino had watered that night in the main valley, less than a kilometre from our camp. However, the tracks were somewhat confusing as the animal had wandered around feeding.

By midday we had followed the tracks up over the watershed to the east and were perched on a variety of vantage points watching Bob and our tracker Shambaini searching in the dense bush-filled bowl below us. Shambaini was obviously at a total loss, so Ian decided Errada should help and he and I scrambled down. I followed Errada in fascination, watching him cast about in the thick scrub until his trained eye caught the sign of the rhino's passing. Then we crept slowly forward with Bob and his radio bringing up the rear; the bush becoming increasingly impenetrable and visibility almost nil as we moved downhill.

Errada then stopped suddenly on top of a little gully and just beneath us there was a crash and a snort that brought my heart up into my throat. A superb rhino erupted from the thicket just below us and with head and tail held high crashed down the gully. From his vantage point above us, Ian saw it almost at the same moment as Bob radioed contact. Minutes later Ted and Dieter took off in the chopper. They had no difficulty in locating the rhino but as the terrain was difficult and miles from the holding boma, and as the turbulent air was throwing the chopper about, they decided that to try to dart the rhino would be taking too great a risk. They radioed us their decision, and the four of us had a long and hot walk back to camp. When we arrived we found Tim, a helicopter pilot, and his client with a second chopper - a welcome addition to our party.

The next day, Sunday, had to be our last day as Dieter had to be in Nairobi that night. A lot of money had been invested in the enterprise and we could not bear to have it fail. The Wildlife Department scouts, however, refused to cooperate. They said they did not work on Sundays, and anyway the mountain was too 'hard'. The rest of us drank tea in the dark and finalised our plans.

Even before it was light, Errada and I set off to check the valley up to the watershed for tracks; and soon after we left, and as soon as it was light enough, both helicopters flew over to drop a team to inspect the watershed itself. Ian and his men were dropped where we had left the rhino the previous afternoon and Errada and I reached the watershed as they were still searching below. Much time was wasted casting around, until we realised that the hurricane caused by one chopper had obliterated the tracks where the rhino had recrossed the watershed and gone along the southern flank of the valley. But eventually the tracks were traced and Ian and five men followed them, while Errada and I went along the southern crest to see if the rhino had gone over any of the saddles. It was obvious from the tracks that the animal was disturbed and moving fast along the side of the slope towards Wamba, so eventually Ian radioed to say that we should come straight down from our ridge, cross the valley, climb up the other side and try to observe from there.

Following these instructions was not easy. We started with a most appalling descent. The slope was very steep, the scrub almost impassible and visibility nil, but when we got about a quarter of the way down we came upon very fresh tracks. I called up Ted in the helicopter and also Ian; but Ian was convinced that we were mistaken, that he was on the freshest track and that the rhino had merely doubled back. Meanwhile, Ted and Tim were both hovering overhead, when suddenly Ted called down that he could see the rhino and that it was virtually beside us - and, moreover, was I aware that we were on top of a sheer rock wall?

It was an interesting situation. Errada and I looked at one another, expecting that at any moment one or other chopper would drive an enraged and terrified two tons of rhino on top of us; and there we were with nothing to climb and nowhere to go. However, five minutes later, to our enormous relief, Ted called to say that the rhino had crossed the saddle and was heading fast towards the plain - exactly where we wanted it to go.

Ian and the others were already in hot pursuit, Errada and I were most definitely not. I could not clamber back up the way we had come down, and I was not at all sure that we could get down either. We would have to try sideways. We edged our way along the top of the rock wall and then slowly crept down. Near the bottom I heard Ted radioing to Ian that Dieter had darted the rhino, and there I was, on the wrong side of the ridge and unable to help. We eventually reached the valley and I started running towards the camp until Jane came on the radio to say that we should go to the first clearing we came across and wait for Tim who was on his way to pick us up. Two minutes later Tim hovered over us in his chopper and Bob leaned out to haul us both in.

Within moments we were dropped neatly beside Dieter and the recumbent rhino which he had already treated. He had also cleaned a horrible deep spear wound in its neck, but despite the severe wound, the rhino, a superb male with a big horn, was in excellent condition.

About twenty minutes later the Capture Unit lorry arrived. The sledge was unloaded and with everyone helping - including the Wildlife Department scouts - the two dead-weight tons of precious rhino were rolled on to the sledge and strapped down. The sledge was then winched up on to the lorry, and Dieter and I scrambled up. The journey was very rough, for there was no track at all and it took about forty minutes to bump our way to the boma. After we arrived there was a very nasty moment when the sledge nearly capsized as it was being slid down from the lorry, but we eventually got it safely off and then manhandled the huge beast from the sledge and into the boma.

Dieter went in with the rhino and as soon as the gate was closed injected the recovery drug into the ear vein and scrambled out. I watched in terror. Would the rhino be alright? First he had been overheated by the prolonged chase and then drugged and subjected to a long journey in the lorry. However, when Dieter threw buckets of water over him, the poor animal lurched dizzily to his feet. All was well.

Three days later his travelling crate arrived from Nairobi so the Capture Unit could begin crate training him; and on 14 February he was delivered to our holding boma. We named our new arrival Womba, to remind us of where we had found him. We were also very glad we had found him and found him alive, for in the course of our expedition around the mountains we had come across the corpses of three dead rhinos - all with their horns chopped of and their faces horribly mutilated.

The capture of Sabatchi

To the east of the Mathews where we had collected Womba is the huge flat-topped massif of Ololokwe, alias Sabatchi. Soon after we came to live in the sanctuary, Ian told me that there were rumours of rhinos there and that he and a friend were going to look. I was invited to join them.

We parked the Toyota at the bottom of the northeast flank of Ololokwe and scrambled up a very steep, rocky goat track through dry, thorny scrub. The going was hot, dusty and rough. Ian kindly carried my rucksack and he and Mark waited patiently for me at intervals. Compared with them I was very slow, but eventually even I made it to the top. The difference in scenery up there was incredible. Lush and lovely cedar forests covered the plateau and there were huge rocky outcrops, springs and small streams.

We soon found what we were looking for - rhino tracks and droppings. We also came across some Samburu grazing their cattle. The Samburu do not hunt rhinos or any other 'game', and consequently we saw the tracks of many wild animals up there buffalo, bush buck, duikers and others. However, for the time being we abandoned the search and made camp for the night. The next morning saw us searching around again, but although we found more rhino tracks we did not catch as much as a glimpse of even one rhino. We headed back to the Toyota, Ian and Mark, both incredibly fit, charging straight down the mountain. I followed slowly behind with one of Ian's trackers who periodically helped me to my feet when I fell. Back at the car Mark handed me a drink and kindly remarked that I had done "very well for an old lady". The two looked at me with astonishment when I roared with laughter; was it Robbie Burns who talked about seeing ourselves as others see us?

After this expedition there was much discussion with the Wildlife Department about what should be done to protect the rhino on Ololokwe. To attempt to catch them up there would be too dangerous, for after being darted a rhino might very well run over one of the many sheer cliffs. To protect the rhinos *in situ* was the obvious answer; they formed a small but viable population, the mountain top was a glorious place for them, and the Samburu posed no threat to their safety. Once this decision was made, protracted discussions took place between the Wildlife Department and the Frankfurt Zoological Society, which was considering funding a rhino sanctuary on Ololokwe. We were prepared to help with the organisation of the guard team, to keep in radio contact and even to put an airstrip in on the top of the mountain where our Super Cub could land in an emergency; but I could not afford to finance the protection project.

Early in 1985, while there was still talk but no action, the shifta moved in and we heard rumours that no rhinos had survived. However, the Wildlife Department asked us to check, and we sent trackers. At that time they found no trace of any rhino, but later we heard that a single rhino's tracks had been seen to the west of Ololokwe. It appeared that the rhino had come down from the mountain and that it was now the sole survivor of the little group. We determined to attempt to catch it.

In early April William drove me to where Ian and Dieter were already camped and searching for the rhino. It was a beautiful area midway between Ololokwe and the Mathews and recent good rains had made it green and lush. We camped near a small dam under a full moon and were off in the moonlight before dawn the next morning. Charlie Wheeler, Ian's farm manager, got a glimpse of the rhino and called up Ted Goss in the helicopter. Ted took Dieter aboard, located the rhino and Dieter successfully darted it. I happened to be in the wrong place and missed all the action, although the noise of the helicopter showed us which way to head. By the time I arrived, the rhino was already down and the lorry had been sent for.

It was an immature female in poor condition, which we all thought surprising considering how lush the vegetation was. The lorry took a long time to arrive as it had to hack its way through this thick bush, and it was a very rough trip out again. After her uncomfortable journey, we unloaded the rhino as gently as we could into the temporary holding boma that the Wildlife Department had constructed for her. Dieter gave her the recovery drug and we poured buckets of water over her until she struggled to her feet. The next day we departed, leaving the Wildlife Department's Capture Unit people to get her crate-trained and ready to transport to the sanctuary.

The capture of Kikwar

Early in January 1990 we heard rumours of a rhino in the northeastern part of the Mathews range. Since poaching in the area was still rampant, it was imperative that we investigate as soon as possible. By dawn of Monday 15 January we were on the road. This time I was accompanied by two of our trackers who know the Mathews area well, and also by Andy Lodge, the coordinator of the Ngare Sergoi Support Group, and his colleague Bill Pittenger who were both visiting the sanctuary. (Andy was working for the Columbus Zoo in Ohio when he first visited the sanctuary in 1985. After he returned to the USA he began raising funds to help us, and to that end founded the support group. In 1989 he left his job to devote himself to full time fund-raising.)

Shortly after noon we reached the village from whence the rumours had originated and began making inquiries. The villagers told us that until the shifta had arrived the previous year, there had been three rhinos; two had been killed but yes, it was true, one remained. They took us to a nearby salt lick and showed us tracks and a dropping, but such evidence was too old to be adequate to set the somewhat complicated wheels of rhino capture in motion. We had to have absolutely fresh proof of a rhino's existence.

We drove several kilometres nearer the mountains and then, leaving Andy and Bill to guard the Suzuki, the trackers and I tramped off. Around four in the afternoon we were walking up a narrow, dry riverbed, and there in its sandy floor found what we were looking for - tracks that had been made some time since the previous evening. That was all we needed. We hurried back to the car and as the dusk began to fall I drove as rapidly as I could (which was not fast at all, due to the condition of the road) to within radio range of our sanctuary network. It was dark when we reached the hill where I was able to call the East Gate and report the good news that we had found definite signs of the rumoured rhino being alive. We then made a fire and brewed up tea and I lay down for the night confident that Ian would have the logistics of the capture organised in the minimum time.

However, even I was astonished when we reached home mid-morning on Tuesday and Ian told me that we would be moving north on Friday - and so we did, quite a caravan of us. There was not only Ian, Jane, myself, Andy, Bill, William with the Super Cub, Dieter with his veterinary equipment and Ian and William's cousin Tim Ward Booth with a helicopter; but also a driver and many men with the Capture Unit rhino transport crate and lorry, Colin and Rocky Francombe from another rhino sanctuary, and Jo Ordonez, an American who had come to visit our sanctuary. That evening we all assembled in a valley to the northeast of the Mathews. A wide, sandy riverbed walled on each bank by thick bush was our caravanserai, and a trickle of clear water ran at our doorstep. The valley was enclosed on three sides by the jagged peaks of the mountains, and this whole setting gave us a wonderful sense of remoteness.

As Saturday dawned Ian, Colin, Jo and I and six trackers set out to search for spoor. An hour later it began to rain, not much but enough to obliterate any fresh tracks. We split into three parties, each with a radio and two trackers. All day, hour after hour, we walked and searched, the apparent hopelessness of our search ameliorated by the beauty of the country. The short rains had been more copious and gone on longer than usual, and the normally arid scrub had flourished into dense green leaf. Flowers were blooming everywhere, some tiny and delicate, others hugely conspicuous. The air was scented and butterflies of all sizes and colours flitted from blossom to blossom.

For walking, however, the country was not as beautiful as it looked. Most of the now rampant vegetation had thorns. The spiked and hooked acacia bushes were relatively easy to negotiate, but the meadows were sheer hell. In amongst the deceptively inviting waist-high grass and flowers were hidden tens of thousands of sharp spiked burrs, so many that my lower regions were quite covered with prickles. I felt like a hedgehog who has had his skin put on inside out. Even worse were the cutting vines that lurked in the grass and lacerated our legs so badly that each step became a pain. As my legs became bloodier I tried to think of flowers and butterflies and rhinos, but as the hours passed such positive thinking became increasingly difficult.

At three o'clock Ian called the search off for the day. Tired and dispirited we all returned to camp from our several directions to be welcomed by Jane who has a genius for camp organisation and, in particular, cooking. Although my legs looked revolting and felt worse, Jane's excellent meal so revived me that I went out again with a tracker to check another couple of kilometres up the main riverbed. We found tracks of lion, hyena, buffalo and elephant - but none of rhino. However, when we returned to camp by moonlight we were greeted by Ian with the news that fresh rhino spoor had been discovered by a local herdsman. That boded well for the morrow and I lay down in the sand under my mosquito net feeling quite optimistic. My spirits, however, were soon dampened, for I was woken at five o'clock in the morning by heavy rain. As the Suzuki was beside me I grabbed my sleeping bag and jumped in, to be joined minutes later by a damp Dieter.

By seven o'clock the rain had stopped but our chances of finding fresh tracks were washed out. I and two trackers searched one area for four hours, and then returned to camp to snatch a quick lunch before Tim and the helicopter whisked Ian, myself and the trackers farther up the valley. Ian and one man went in one direction, I and my tracker in another. It rained again, then the sun came out, and then it rained again - and so it continued for most of the afternoon. We got alternately soaked and steamed and my legs started to look like messy raw steaks. None of us saw any sign of rhino, but we all had our various adventures.

On our way back to camp in the late afternoon, my tracker and I had a close encounter with a very startled elephant. I jumped into a thorn bush as the elephant waved his ears and trumpeted at us, but luckily he thought better of charging and left us to go on our way in peace. Meanwhile, while we were all slogging on foot,

William was scouring the area from the air with the Super Cub – until its one engine failed. He then managed to make an emergency landing in the riverbed and escaped unscathed, but the little plane would not fly again until repaired.

That night it poured with rain again and we were all most uncomfortable. I started to feel really ill and by morning was worse. While Ian and the trackers searched the landscape, I lay in the riverbed all day feeling and being miserably sick. Jane dosed me from time to time with a rehydration drink, but aside from her thoughtfulness the less said about that Monday the better.

To our grateful surprise that night was fine, and at dawn even I felt reasonably well. William drove me, Jo and two trackers in the Suzuki and dropped us as high as he could go in a small riverbed. Within ten minutes we had found fresh tracks at the point where the rhino had crossed the gully and headed east. We called Ian by radio, gave him our position and then set off after them. The rhino had clearly been moving steadily, not pausing to feed. As always, I was lost in admiration for our trackers' skills. Where I saw nothing of significance on the ground, for them it was covered with signs. Slowly and doggedly we worked our way east through the thick bush for two and a half hours. Then suddenly one of the trackers turned, grabbed me and we jumped simultaneously as the long-sought rhino erupted out of the bush ahead of us and fled.

We immediately radioed 'contact' to Tim in the helicopter and to Ian. A few moments later Ian arrived and as we stood talking he suddenly said, "get up that tree", luckily pointing to one within my limited climbing capacity. Seconds later, three elephants appeared, clearly alarmed by the activities of the helicopter, but fortunately so nervous that when we shouted at them they rushed off. In the meantime, Tim was doing a brilliant bit of helicopter herding. In half an hour he managed to drive the rhino towards the main riverbed which was accessible to the Capture Unit lorry, and Dieter beside him darted it.

Half an hour of fast walking downhill brought us to the scene of action. There lay a beautiful male rhino, estimated by Dieter to be seven or eight years old, fat and in perfect condition. However, loading conditions were less than perfect, for the area in which the young rhino had fallen was one of thick bush. We cleared the bush as best we could and then off-loaded the crate and ma-

Once the rhino is darted and down, its respiration and temperature are carefully monitored.

noeuvred it into position in front of the comatose, blindfolded rhino. One end of a rope was bound round his nose and threaded through a hole in the far end of the crate, while we all held on to the other end, silent and tensed ready to pull with all our might at a word from Dieter. Next came the critical moment. Dieter injected the recovery drug into a vein in the rhino's ear and when the animal staggered up, reached behind and gave him a poke with an electric cattle prod, at the same instant shouting "pull". We all pulled - and the rhino was safely in the crate with the door closed behind him in a matter of seconds.

The next step was to winch four tons of rhino and crate on to the lorry. This would have been easy, except for the fact that the winch had broken when the lorry had got stuck in the riverbed. So we struggled for hours to get the crate aboard using a block and tackle and all available man power; and, as the rhino had to be loaded back end first, he spent a wretched time being tipped nose downward. It was unnerving and exhausting, but eventually at half past two that afternoon, less than five hours after he had been darted, the rhino was on his way to our sanctuary. The Cap-

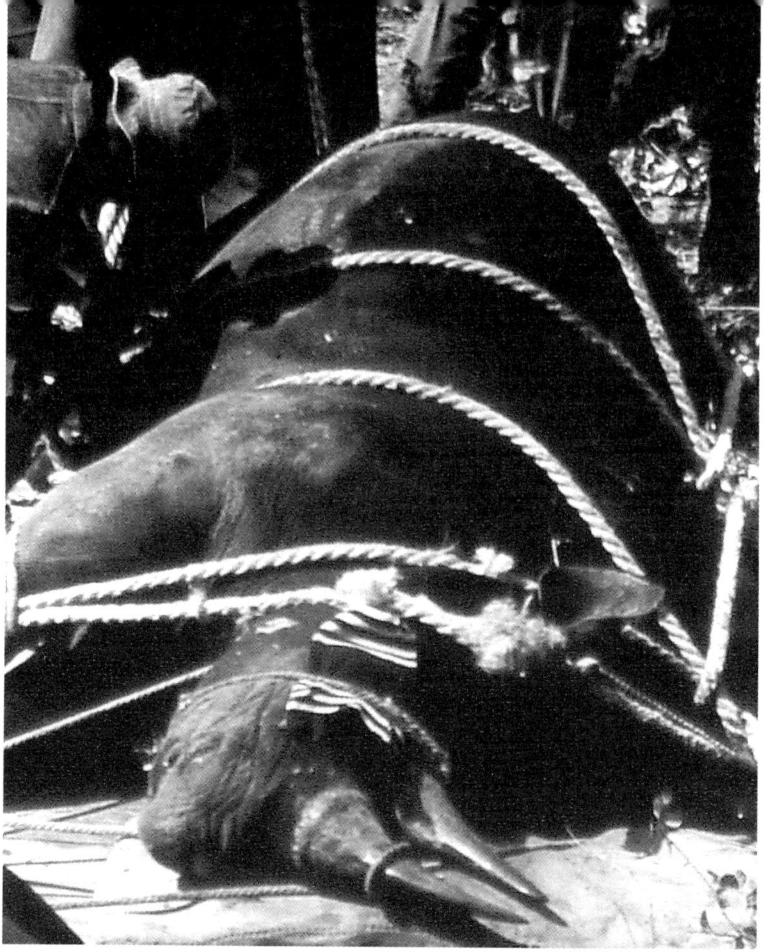

Moving a darted rhino requires much manpower.

ture Unit named him Kikwar after the hill near where we had found him.

Our excitements, however, were not over. We still had to deal with the downed Super Cub. William had radioed to Nairobi for an engineer and Tim had collected him, as well as extra fuel, from the airstrip at Wamba early the morning of the capture. By the time we got back to our camp the Super Cub had been mended and William made a splendid take-off from the riverbed. But seconds later the engine failed again and he crashed into the trees. Tim, who was hovering above, immediately flew over and to our vast relief radioed back that he could see William standing on his feet and waving his arms to indicate he was unhurt. To our amazement even the plane was not badly damaged and we arranged for the Capture Unit lorry to return to carry it to Nairobi for repairs. However, on the main road near Ololokwe a wheel came off the lorry, the driver lost control and the vehicle turned turtle down a bank. So, sadly, our little red plane which had made more than 50 rhino translocations possible was a total write-off after all.

Later that overly eventful afternoon Tim flew me home over the Mathews in the helicopter, enabling me to see an area of great beauty which I could never have seen any other way. We also saw some magnificent elephants, but unfortunately not all of them were alive. Throughout the landscape were shattered the giant bones of the victims of the shifta and I was more relieved than ever that we had managed to rescue at least one more rhino from a similar fate. Late that night the lorry arrived and Kikwar was securely installed in our holding boma; and a week later he was released into the sanctuary.

4

Rhinos as Individuals

Animals are beginning to look better than my own kind.
Loren Eisley

The object of creating the Ngare Sergoi Sanctuary was simply to try to keep some rhinos safe so that they could breed. It was, and is, an exercise in security and management, not a scientific experiment. Not only is the entire fence patrolled daily, but the rhinos are also under constant surveillance by more than a dozen Ndorobo trackers, the elite of our 60 - 70 employees. They work singly or in teams, equipped with field glasses and radios - a few have rifles. Each person or team is assigned to an area (we rotate them regularly) and responsible for keeping track of whatever rhinos are there. Early on we decided that my role - other than paying the bills - would be to monitor the rhinos daily. For this purpose I have my own tracker, who comes to the house each morning after breakfast, with whom I go 'rhinoing'. From the first day I carried a notebook, a habit I had started in Ghana, and noted down which rhino was where, what it was doing and whether it was in company or alone. As my observations increased, so did my fascination with these creatures and I very soon became aware that the African rhino is neither dull nor stupid.

If you take the trouble to get to know them, most animals turn out to be individuals; and the more intelligent the species, the more this rule applies. All the rhinos in this sanctuary certainly have very marked personalities which have emerged after years of observation. I hardly think that they are unique; it is merely that by living amongst them and caring about them, we have been privileged to get to know them well.

Mwingo, a female black rhino

Godot

Godot was the very first rhino to enter our sanctuary. He behaved very quietly and calmly in the boma where he was held for over a month until the fence was completed, and I think this was because he was intelligent enough to realise that he could not escape from it. He had been captured, boma-ed and translocated several times before and therefore tolerated those who came to feed him and endured my near constant presence. He came when I called and accepted food from my hand but he had been hunted and wounded and therefore still mistrusted people.

Godot was not a very big rhino in terms of height, but he was massive and compact, with the powerful arched neck and shoulder development of a stallion. He always looked alert, with his ears pricked and his head held high. When he trotted he raised his tail up in the air - an action almost like that of a hackney horse and surprisingly graceful for so massive a creature. Yet his was a presence to be reckoned with, for power and determination emanated from him. Whether he had the typical character of a dominant male or whether, as I suspect, he was something of a Napoleon amongst rhinos, I still do not know. All of us feared him and with good reason. Apart from Makora and Morani, he was the only rhino in the sanctuary who would not high-tail away in fear if he got the slightest whiff of human scent. If he was far enough away he would run off, but if you were too near he would try to remain hidden until he thought you were within charging range. He had practically all of us up trees at one time or another.

Once, soon after his release, he came out of a bush at me. I turned to run, tripped and fell, but instead of flattening me he snorted in disgust and turned and trotted off tail in the air. I could not but wonder whether it was because he remembered the scent that for five weeks regularly came with horse nuts and lucerne and gentle talk. My trackers did not laugh at this idea, they have always affirmed that rhinos have much intelligence; Errada in particular has said this to me time and time again.

Like our white rhino Makora and unlike all the other rhinos, Godot travelled the length and breadth of the sanctuary endlessly, patrolling the area by day and night and keeping us all on our toes. He did have his favourite 'houses' in which to lie up by day and utilised particular suitably shaped rocks for masturbating and then rubbing his chin on. However, seeing him parked under a tree at one end of the sanctuary in the morning was no guarantee that I would not collide with him on my afternoon walk with Samia (the orphaned rhino calf I was hand-raising) and the dogs several kilometres away. It became the job of Errada and later Orogai to keep very close tabs on Godot and to keep me informed of his whereabouts. On one occasion Orogai saw me and Samia on a direct collision course with Godot and had to run right across the valley - no small distance - to give me warning, arriving just in the nick of time to escort us home giving Godot a very wide berth.

Although Godot was often seen alone he was an intensely social animal and my notes show that he was seen almost daily with one or other of the rhinos, males as well as females. Even if he was not actually seen with the others during the day, his tracks would show that he had been socialising at night.

In January 1988 the 1987-88 drought was at its very worst. Every day revealed more deaths. Those animals that were still alive were very hungry. The rhinos were getting a small ration of lucerne, but to feed the other animals was impossible. Foolishly, I did try to feed the beautiful greater kudu that lived in the Marula below my house. They knew me well and were not afraid, and I put some lucerne out for them near the house. Within a few days Godot discovered this. At first by night, and then also by day, he would arrive at the house at any hour. I would hear a snort and there he would be, standing but a few metres from my garden fence.

Samia, the baby rhino, was terrified of him and whenever she heard or smelt him she would rush to the fence yelling madly for me. I would have to lead her into her stable and stockade where she spent the nights, because without a rhino mother to protect her I was very afraid that Godot would smash her against the fence. At frequent intervals a team of carpenters and labourers had to come over from Headquarters to reinforce the stockade; what kept Samia in with ease would not keep Godot out. In his annoyance and frustration at not being given lucerne and at not being able to get into the garden or at Samia, he flattened half the thorn trees growing outside the compound.

Even trying to have someone with a radio on Godot's tracks all day did not always work. He would manage to give his tracker the slip, then turn up unexpectedly and cause a crisis. With Godot glaring at them from just a few metres off, people who came to the house to visit me either could not leave their cars to come in, or could not get into their cars to depart. I was reluctant to go anywhere myself in case in my absence Godot attacked Samia. I would have to lock her up, and it was not good for her to be locked up so much when she was meant to be free. To add to the complications Karl had a stroke and, despite the vigilance of his nurse and the rest of us, was remarkably adept at going for walks outside the garden at unexpected moments. It was not possible to drive Godot off; had we shouted at any of our other wild rhinos, or even just let them get our scent, they would run away. Not Godot.

I was convinced that total disaster was not far off, either for Karl, for our household staff or for Samia. Eventually news of my predicament filtered down to Nairobi and Dieter flew up to see what was happening. Flattened trees and possessive scrapes all around the house confirmed only too clearly what was going on. Dieter asked me if I wanted Godot translocated and sadly I had to say, "yes". I was somewhat consoled when he explained that genetically it would be a good idea anyway, for Godot had already sired four calves and a fifth was probably on the way since he had recently served Stumpy. In small sanctuaries it is important to avoid inter-breeding, so Dieter suggested that Godot should go to Oljogi on a swap.

On 2 April Godot mated Stumpy for the second time and the next day Dieter arrived, with scant warning, to capture him. Godot was on the plain above the North Valley, near Stumpy and Shaba and when Dieter darted him he ran down to the valley and into a very rough area. He fell badly and was only breathing three times to the minute, so Dieter injected him with a small part of the recovery drug. Godot recovered enough to get up and run further into the valley and had to be re-darted. This time he went down in the most impossible place in a small gully. However, we managed to get the tractor and trailer right down to him, but he then struggled up to a sitting position, hooked his horn under the trailer and nearly had it over. Eventually we roped him up and hauled him out on the sledge and then up on to the tractor. My heart was in my throat a few times as the tractor negotiated the steep hairpin bends on the road up from the North Valley, but everything held and we got him safely to the holding boma.

The next morning when I went to feed him he seemed well - hungry and aggressive. On 15 April I started crate-training him and, as I expected, he gave no trouble at all but walked calmly into the crate as soon as he realised the lucerne was there. On 22 April a Wildlife Department lorry came to collect him. He walked straight into the crate and stood quietly while the back was closed and the crate pulled out and loaded on to the lorry. It was only when he was loaded that I learned that Godot's destination was not Oljogi but the newly completed rhino sanctuary in the Meru National Park. This did not make me at all happy - there was almost no security in Meru Park at that time and the shifta were having a field day with the elephants there. But there was nothing I could do about it; although I have always regarded wild animals as belonging to themselves, officially Godot was government property.

My distress was well-founded. Seven months later a gang of shifta massacred the small herd of tame white rhino in Meru Park, an event which received world-wide publicity. What was not publicised, however, was that the black rhinos too were killed. No details were ever disclosed, the rhinos just 'disappeared' and repeated searches in Meru both on the ground and by helicopter have revealed no living rhinos. I feel very bad about this and partly to blame for Godot's death. My only consolation is that he has left one son and three daughters behind.

Morani

Our third rhino arrived from the Nairobi Animal Orphanage on 17 April, 1984. He was an eight-year old male whose mother had been poached in Amboseli Park when he was between six and eight months old. He was taken to the orphanage attached to the Nairobi National Park and fed by hand; and his keepers called him Morani, the Masai term for 'young warrior'. He was later taken back and released in Amboseli, but there suffered constant attacks from the resident dominant male who terrified him to such an extent that he took to hiding in the bar of one of the tourist lodges. That obviously would not do, and Morani was sent back to the orphanage and from there to our sanctuary.

Morani was a total contrast to Godot. Dr David Western, an eminent zoologist working in Amboseli, once told me that he thought Morani might have been castrated during one of the battles. His testicles certainly bore the scars of a very nasty wound possibly made by a horn. Be that as it may, a more sweet-natured and gentle animal I have seldom known, although on occasion he could be very erratic. Morani and Shaba were in the holding boma together, in adjacent pens, and from the start Morani obviously conceived a great affection for Shaba. We released them within a day of one another, and ever since their release they more or less stayed together. If Shaba left Morani he would be seen wandering around looking rather disconsolate. He largely ignored the other rhinos, except for Makora whom he disliked very much, which was foolish considering the difference in size.

Morani was always at ease with people, and would usually come when I called him. He was a great asset for tourists, not only because he was gentle but because he was easy to find. He kept to a relatively small area to the south of my house, and had a habit of lying up in old cattle bomas in the full sun, when other rhinos would be less visible, resting in the shade of trees. Why Morani did this I do not know, but perhaps, as he came from Amboseli which is at a much lower altitude, he felt cold here.

He was not as heavily built as the other adult rhinos. He was thin when he came here, even before the 1984 drought started, and during it he got thinner despite being fed lucerne as it progressed. However, he always had fewer sores and was less troubled by flies than the others, perhaps as a result of his lying up on high open ground. Another strange habit of his was eating the plant stramonium, the seeds of which are poisonous to many animals and its leaves generally shunned by all, but he ate it with apparent relish and it appeared to have no ill effects on him. He also loved cattle, and they could wander all around him. I have even seen calves licking between his back legs while he took no notice at all. However, for some reason he did not like donkeys (we keep a few for carrying food and water to the camps) and we would sometimes see him chasing them along the road at a brisk trot.

Otherwise Morani got along perfectly well with all the wild animals, except on one occasion when he acted totally out of character and killed a female eland. Unfortunately I was in Nairobi at the time and missed this strange drama, but it was recounted to me in detail on my return. It seems that Morani was lying up quite near to Shaba when an eland, getting wind of one of the trackers, ran towards the bushes where she was lying hidden. Morani came hurtling out from his bush and charged and killed the eland in a very determined fashion, horning her for some time after she was dead. Perhaps Morani thought Shaba was being attacked, or perhaps he was suffering from the allegedly hallucinatory effects of eating stramonium. We shall never know and in any event, he never did anything like that again.

Like the other males, Godot and Makora, Morani had one particular rock which he used for masturbating. He would rub his penis on it for up to ten minutes, breathing heavily all the while, and when he ejaculated he would give several little happy-sounding squeaks, squeaks that I only ever heard him make.

As Morani was so gentle, I often used to follow him. If he realised I was perched on a rock or a branch near him, he would come over and make what I later learnt was the greeting breathing and because of his amiability he was an excellent photographic subject. On one occasion in May 1986, Ian particularly wanted to get a photograph of him with the Super Cub in the background, but first we had to wake him up. Ian repeatedly flew the plane over him at tree-top level, but Morani was so unconcerned that he refused to get up and co-operate. I had to go back to the house and get lucerne with which to bribe him; and only then did he condescend to rise to his feet and be photographed with the plane.

In July 1986 a female, Solia, started moving into the area that until then had been the exclusive preserve of Shaba and Morani. Errada our tracker, so wise in the ways of the bush, warned me that this would cause trouble with Godot. I could not understand why Godot, who had already mated with Shaba and had never before objected to Morani, should take exception to Morani being near Solia when he was allowed to be with Shaba. Errada said he did not know why, but he was sure it would be so and he was right.

During the night of 23 August Morani and Godot had a fight. I think it was a very one-sided battle, and Morani was badly walloped on his backside. Three days later he was quite obviously in trouble; he was very stiff and the tracker whose job it was to keep him under observation reported that he could not urinate. Strangely, that day he left his normal area and walked right over to Headquarters, which he had only ever visited twice before and then only because he had followed Makora there to do battle with him. I realised then that something would have to be done to save his life. We already had Amboni in the holding boma but we moved him out of two sections and prepared them for Morani. I went to him with an armful of lucerne and called. He must have known that he was in serious trouble and needed help, because he followed me right down and into the pen and then let me wash and disinfect his wounds. I must have hurt him, but apart from a few little grunts he stood quietly and made no attempt whatsoever to hurt me. On each of the next two days I bribed him into the crush and Francis injected him with an antibiotic while I washed the wounds and then sprayed them with Terramyacin. Morani was always incredibly good and gentle throughout.

By the middle of September all the swellings had gone down and Morani was looking fit again. Godot had been coming round on most nights to check up on the situation and we all realised that there was no way in which we could release Morani without his being beaten up again. He was no match for Godot in either character or physical strength so we would have to make other arrangements. Thus on 24 September I sadly took up an armload of lucerne, bribed Morani into a travelling crate and watched while the Wildlife Department's men loaded him on to a lorry to return him to the Nairobi orphanage. I was very depressed to see him go, for I was really fond of him and he had taught me so much.

Womba

Womba was a big, young male rhino whose mother, we were told, had been poached when he was a calf. I have already described in detail how we caught him near the town of Wamba in the Mathews Range. He was in lovely condition, except for an unhealed spear wound on the side of his neck behind his left ear and from Womba's behaviour we all believed that the wound had seriously affected his hearing.

Once caught, the young rhino was kept in the holding boma we had built near Wamba town - and then, when he was crate-trained, the Wildlife Department brought him to our holding boma. He arrived on 14 February, 1985 and settled down easily. He would come and eat lucerne out of my hand but at the same time would indulge in a series of roars and squeals, making it clear that he loathed people and was only suffering my presence under duress. I did not blame him, considering his history and the fact that he was the only rhino left in an area that twenty years earlier had probably had hundreds.

We released Womba after just one week. On his first night out he burnt his nose on the fence and then met up with Stumpy near the boma. On the following night he scorched his nose again. In the morning he was found still loitering near the boma and in the company of Solia and a big bull buffalo. Thereafter he remained within the immediate vicinity of the holding boma, limiting himself to a range of only a few acres.

At midday on 16 March, Godot approached Womba and there was much huffing and puffing but no action. Three nights later Godot returned and the two had a fight that was audible to all around our Headquarters camp. The morning revealed Womba with a little blood on his face but no serious damage, for which we were all very thankful. Godot then seemed to lose interest and Womba spent at least one night, 23 March, with Stumpy and her calf. Then Godot reappeared at the holding boma and on 2 April and once more on 11 April, the two fought very noisily - but again neither combatant appeared to be in any way damaged. The 25 April was a pitch dark night and I was sleeping on the roof of my Land Rover, which was parked by the holding boma, watching over the new rhino, Sabatchi. Godot encountered Womba outside. It was a terrifying night. I sat in my sleeping bag clutching my little collie Remus while the earth shook with the thunder of those two huge creatures as they galloped up and down the road, one roaring like a lion and the other trumpeting like an elephant, I knew not which was which. They separated before dawn and when we saw them later that morning, Godot by then kilometres away, remarkably both seemed to be intact.

We released Sabatchi on 29 April and she too stayed close to the holding boma, although she ranged a little farther afield than Womba. The two newcomers seemed to be friends, but Godot was not. From then on further nightly battles took place all around the holding boma and the browse in that area became badly knocked about. By the end of June, although the two bulls had not really hurt each other, Womba had lost a lot of condition and yet he still would not move.

This situation, with both the vegetation and Womba's condition deteriorating, continued on to mid-November when Peter Jenkins came to visit us. He suggested that we cut off the supply of water to the pool near the boma to force Womba to move away. This we did, but initially Womba still would not move. First he tried, but failed, to dig up a waterpipe; a few days after that he tried, but failed, to get water from Francis' house. Finally he gave up and moved and went to drink at the waterhole on the Top Plain - but he got his own back on me by digging up the waterpipe attached to my house.

For the next two weeks Womba moved all over the sanctuary. His condition started to improve and we were very hopeful that all would be well. Until on the night of 10 December, on the steep hillside above Morani Camp, the big fight took place, judging from the tracks, the battle raged up and down the hillside and it looked as though at one point Womba had had a bad fall down one steep portion of the slope. The following morning we found Godot a long way off and Womba standing in the river just above Morani Camp, looking very sore and covered with a vast number of what appeared to be fairly superficial cuts. By midday he was sleeping away from the river, but the flies surrounded him in a thick cloud. During the night he moved to the Simba Lugga and the next morning Errada and I watched him trying to lie down, but he seemed unable to and the flies were on him thicker than ever. The next day he was lying further up Simba Lugga, under a dry waterfall. With Errada's help I crept close to him and he smelt really bad. I was fairly certain that he could no longer move and his breathing was very erratic. The tractor could not possibly reach him nor was it possible to contact Dieter. Late that evening Womba died.

Early the next morning Francis and some of our people carried out a post mortem, while I sat on a rock taking notes. The visible cuts on his body gave no indication whatsoever of the extent of the damage beneath. The whole of the upper part of his left front leg, shoulder and ribs were bruised and the lungs damaged. The spleen had two splits in it and two ribs were broken near where they joined the breast plate. There was also a deep gash by his testicles, his penis was very swollen and his bladder was very full.

Bill Woodley, whose experience in such things is vast, told us later that if a rhino dies as a direct result of a fight, it is usually from wounds inflicted by the opponent's horns which tear deep holes and gashes. But apart from the wound near the testicles, this had not happened to Womba. So either Godot battered him with the side of his horn, or his injuries occurred when he fell.

In hindsight perhaps we should not have chased Womba away from the holding boma, but I think the end would have still come in time. Had another sanctuary been ready to receive him, we could have moved him, but there was no suitable secure place available. After the death of Womba, I worried increasingly about our other three male rhinos: Morani, Amboni and the still very young Kelele.

Sabatchi

On 22 April the Capture Unit drove the young female rhino we had caught near Mt. Sabatchi (Ololokwe) to the sanctuary and we unloaded her into the holding boma. She settled down quietly and did not seem unduly perturbed, even by the uproar created by Godot and Womba, and after a week we released her. She walked out of the gate calmly, and started grazing at once. We called her, like many of our rhinos, from her place of origin, Sabatchi.

From the start, Sabatchi was a very gentle little rhino and neither afraid of people nor vehicles. She periodically met up with Womba and seemed to get on well with him, but she was much afraid of Godot. She took to sleeping most days in the immediate vicinity of Headquarters, quite often either on the veranda outside the office, which made life rather complicated for us, or in the workshop with rather similar results. Once she walked right through Francis' house. From the start she was thin and she never really recovered condition. My own belief was that she had been deeply stressed by the death of her mother and the rest of the Ololokwe group; that she never really got over the strain imposed upon her while she was still very young, and that she was therefore very susceptible to infection.

At the end of October, after consulting with Dieter, we started supplementing her diet with lucerne. She ate it happily but it did not seem to help. Just before Christmas she moved, to my surprise, from Headquarters all the way over to my house. I locked up Samia, still a baby, as I did not want to take any chances. Sabatchi had a good roll in a heap of ashes and slept outside the staff kitchen, which rather complicated their cooking operations, and that evening returned to Headquarters. A few nights later she drank at the water hole on the Central Plain and was clouted by another rhino, although there was a difference of opinion between the trackers as to which one had clouted her. The following morning she was back at Headquarters. This time she had what appeared to be a very minor wound on her hindquarters and a discharge of yellow mucus from her nose. By the next day the discharge was worse and smelt rotten. We collected samples of it and also of her urine, but since it was the Christmas holiday period we could not get hold of either Dieter or any other vet.

Sabatchi's condition deteriorated rapidly over the next few days. She moved stiffly and was obviously weak and listless. I did not know whether she was sick because she had been walloped or walloped because she was sick, but I strongly suspected the latter. At last, early on the morning of 7 January, we received a message that Dieter was on his way. I went over to Headquarters only to find that Sabatchi had gone down just outside the holding boma. With much help we managed to get her propped up on her brisket and wedged into that position with sacks hastily stuffed with freshly cut grass. Dieter arrived at noon and gave her antibiotics, iron, vitamins and cortisone, but to no avail. She died after he had left, at half past three that afternoon.

I called Dieter on the radio. He was just about to leave Lewa, but Ian agreed to fly him over to the Ngare Ndare airstrip, appreciably closer to Headquarters. Meanwhile, Dieter told Francis and me what portions of Sabatchi's anatomy we should bring to the plane for him to take down to Nairobi for a post mortem examination. We started cutting. In the middle of this gory, horrible job, my first husband and his second wife arrived for their holiday with us. I had so wanted to have everything looking lovely to receive them; instead I had prepared nothing, was covered with blood and stank into the bargain.

In due course the results came back from Nairobi. Sabatchi had died of a streptococcic infection of the lungs and the bronchial tubes. She had presumably had the infection for months, and probably prior to her capture. It was very sad to have made all that effort for nothing, especially as she was such a sweet and gentle little rhino - and the office seemed sadly vacant without her recumbent form on the veranda.

Shaba and Jupiter

Of all the rhinos Shaba has been my favourite (except of course for Samia), perhaps because she was the first rhino we caught ourselves, and perhaps also because she was, in the early stages, such a trouble. Without doubt she is a survivor; a rhino with a lot of intelligence, individuality and guts. She is small, with very small neat feet, but at the same time compact and powerfully built, with a strong curved neck and beautiful shoulders. She broke the tips of both her horns while in the holding boma at Shaba and one tip was given to me by Ted Goss. Having lived twenty years in Ghana I am well acquainted with 'juju' charms and I regard the horn tip as my personal 'juju' and wear it on a string around my neck for luck, but, for obvious reasons, only while in the sanctuary.

Shaba is more active than the other rhinos, possibly because she is younger. She moves widely all over the sanctuary, but her favourite area seems to be near the house and because of this I seem to have spent considerably more time watching her than any of the other rhinos. She is still a perpetual source of pleasure and fascination to me.

Soon after she was released, Shaba moved over to the area south of our house and there joined up with Morani. They became inseparable companions for a few months. Thereafter she started moving all over the sanctuary and was nearly always with some other rhino, and sometimes with several together. She made the rounds of the males, Godot and Amboni, but invariably went back to Morani. Her behaviour on occasions looked remarkably flirtatious, and she certainly played the field, frequently in full view of the house.

Two particular incidents I remember well. Once when she was having a nap in the grass she was startled by the unexpected appearance of a giraffe. She jumped up and floated off doing a beautiful passage, that lovely elevated trot that horses perform in advanced dressage. The second incident occurred when she was feeding about half a kilometre from Godot and a helicopter flew over low. Godot took no notice, for he had never had any reason to fear helicopters, but Shaba quite obviously remembered the trauma of being chased and darted from one. She panicked and galloped across a small gully straight to Godot and stood facing him nose to nose as if for reassurance. He apparently did reassure her, for after a few moments she quite visibly calmed down and soon they moved apart and started feeding again.

Shaba gave birth to a calf on 28 May, 1986 and we named him Jupiter after HMS Jupiter - the captain and crew of which had recently made a generous donation to the sanctuary. He started developing a very distinct personality at an early age and he is obviously Godot's son, every bit as determined and forceful a character as both his parents. In temperament he is totally different from the first two calves born in the sanctuary, Bahati and Samia, who were sired by other males. Jupiter was extremely independent and adventurous and we noticed that by the age of six months he was eating more browse than either Samia or Bahati had eaten at that age. (Samia in particular ate predominantly grass until she was well over six months old.) While watching him, I was often thankful that fate had landed me with Samia and not him to rear.

Once Shaba was sleeping and Jupiter, then only a few weeks old, wanted her to get up. He walked around her, prodding her with his nose and minute bump of a horn, but his mother took no notice at all. Eventually an idea came to him. He managed to get both his front feet up on her face and putting his little nose into her ear, blew into it with the full force of his lungs. This really worked! Shaba came to her feet shaking her head in a bemused fashion. It was all Errada and I could do to keep from laughing out loud. On another occasion Jupiter and his mother were walking across the hillside opposite the house, heading for the Marula. Rongai and Kelele were heading in the same direction but some distance behind them. Somehow Jupiter did not appreciate this and began to scrabble to and fro between the two females, neither of whom took much notice of his mad gallopings. Quite what he hoped to achieve I do not know, but it was most amusing to watch. Eventually all four rhinos moved out of sight and into the valley.

Rongai, Amboni, Kelele and Julali

In the days when Karl and I used to walk in the beautiful country to the north of the Aberdares Country Club, on the plateau between Mt. Kenya and the Aberdares Range, we often saw rhino tracks, and on occasions we even heard the animals themselves. Then in 1983 the poachers moved in and the rhinos were being killed off fast. However, three remained on a ranch that had perfect habitat for them but did not have the infrastructure to afford them adequate protection against modern style poaching. In the middle of April 1984 the Wildlife Department captured these three and held them at its nearby Mweiga headquarters. From there they were sent to our sanctuary.

On 29 April the first two arrived, a large mature female called Rongai and a young male, who could have been her son, called Amboni - both named by the Wildlife Department. These were the two rhinos that Morani 'helped' to unload. We released them from the holding boma on 6 May. Rongai wandered off looking very calm and relaxed, but Amboni seemed nervous and in no hurry to leave the boma, although he did finally depart during the night. When I drove over the next morning he was out on the Top Plain and he came after the Suzuki at a fair gallop until he got entangled in a herd of giraffe which distracted him from his pursuit. A couple of days later Karl and I were enjoying the sunset from Morani Point when some low-flying army-jets screamed by. The noise gave Karl and me a bit of a shock but Amboni a far worse one. He suddenly materialised beside us, shot across the road and thundered down into the valley below. By 23 May Amboni had joined up with Rongai and thereafter they were almost always to be seen together.

Kelele arrived from Mweiga the day after we had released the rest of his family. He was christened Kelele, the Swahili for 'noise', because he made so much of it. He was a very immature male and after we released him he rushed around the sanctuary calling continually, and generally behaving as if he was most upset. He was estimated to be five years old, but clearly did not like being on his own. However, as soon as he met up with Rongai and Amboni he calmed down and then became inseparable, we were all convinced that they were mother and sons. Godot also spent a good deal of time in their company.

Rongai wandered less than any of the other rhinos. She established her home range in the main valley north of our house, and would go as far south as the East Gate Road. She was up on Fumbi a lot, and also used the Simba Lugga and, to a lesser extent, the Middle Valley; she never went into the North Valley or the West Plain, nor into Morani's area. She was also frequently in the Marula and on the slope opposite our house.

Towards the end of January 1986, Rongai was looking and acting as if she might be pregnant. She also tried to drive Kelele off several times, but was never very successful. She gave birth to her calf on 29 January. That morning Kelele was with her, but by noon he had left and joined Godot up on Fumbi. The next day, both came down to visit Rongai but she chased them away. On 2 February the calf was dead. The following day Rongai was seen with Amboni and Kelele, while Godot remained up on Fumbi. Thenceforth Rongai and Kelele were again inseparable until the end of August when Rongai chased Kelele off again. Thereafter he was mainly on his own, although he met up fairly regularly with other rhinos, including Rongai until she calved again in mid February 1988.

This calf was born on 16 February, at the height of the 1987-88 drought and we called it Julali, the Swahili for 'drought'. The situation was most worrying. We provided Rongai with a daily ration of lucerne but nevertheless she lost weight rapidly. Julali, however, did well, for Rongai was evidently an excellent and experienced mother despite her earlier trouble. She refused to let Kelele or any other rhino near her, and occupied herself solely with her little calf. The rains finally arrived in April and thereafter Rongai put on condition rapidly. By early April the calf was eating grass and by May she had started browsing on Solanum plants. She was very playful and used to like to bounce around her recumbent mother and play with her feet. At this stage Julali was as clumsy as a young puppy and would frequently take headers over Rongai's outstretched legs.

Kelele suffered badly from the drought and when he could no longer expect protection from Rongai he became much more cautious in his behaviour and was obviously fearful of Godot. Even after Godot was removed in April 1988, Kelele continued to stay close to Rongai's home area, although he also took to following Stumpy and Juno and their calves up to the plains and into the North Valley. Only now at the age of approximately ten years old is Kelele really starting to fill out and to behave with increasing confidence.

Amboni was estimated to be about eight years old when he came to us. He was a nice young male, not very powerfully built, with heavily fringed ears which made him very easy to identify. Although he mainly stayed with Rongai and Kelele, he was also often with Godot. They would sleep side by side and walk and feed near each other. Very often all four rhinos were seen together. By the end of 1985 Amboni was in magnificent condition. I would often see him, surprised by something or having got wind of us, moving off with that wonderfully proud elevated trot, ears pricked and huge neck arched. At that time he was also regularly seen with various females besides Rongai - Shaba, Juno, Solia and Stumpy - and he was on very friendly terms with them all.

Early in 1986 Amboni's behaviour started to change. More and more often he was only to be seen in a very restricted area near the north fence up on Fumbi. He would lie there all day, often meeting with Juno, who also favoured that area, but no longer with any of the others. At night he would go down to the river to drink but would always return to Fumbi before dawn. Godot was sometimes seen with or near him and we saw no signs of aggression, but it seemed that Godot had made it clear to Amboni that if he moved away from that area there would be trouble. Meanwhile, Amboni was becoming less alert and his magnificent neck less impressive.

At the beginning of July I did not see him for several days, until I spotted him on 6 July. I could just make out his ears as he lay in his usual place, concealed by a thorn tree with low-hanging branches and by the long grass that grew in its shade. He had always had a habit of lying parallel to an overhanging branch so that its shadow and the line of his back merged, so except for his constantly flicking ears, his camouflage was perfect - I do not know whether this was instinct, coincidence or intelligence. I was about to leave, when Samuel the tracker shocked me by saying that he thought Amboni was sick. I then decided to break one of our firm rules and to disturb him intentionally so that he got up. I asked Samuel to give Amboni his scent and in the meantime Orogai helped me up a nearby tree. Amboni came to his feet and I was horrified to see how terribly thin he had become, in addition he was quite obviously very weak.

I called Ian and Francis on the radio and we discussed the situation. That evening Ian came over to see Amboni, and we all agreed that we should ask Dieter to come up and look at him as soon as possible. Although the rhinos in the sanctuary are treated as wild animals and are generally not interfered with in any way, the poaching outside has been so appalling that each of our rhinos is very precious. If there is anything we can do to prevent it, we will not let them die.

Dieter said he would be up early on 8 July. I knew that it would be quite possible to dart Amboni where he was, but that there would be no way we could get the tractor and trailer in to move him to the holding boma. The roads in and out of the main valley were too steep and rough. So I spent many hours on 7 July looking at Amboni and wishing there were some way I could communicate with him and get him to understand that, for his own sake, he should move to the other side of the main valley where we could get the tractor to him. But I knew in my more rational self that such communication was impossible. That night I lay awake and worried about Amboni and what we could do to help him.

Early next morning our trackers went to locate Amboni. I was feeding my horse when I heard over the radio that he had been found lying under a tree on the Top Plain, just a few yards from the road. Rhinos are very much creatures of habit and usually lie up in their chosen areas, under their favourite trees - but Amboni was now lying in a place which he had never used before. When Dieter prepared to dart him, the rhino got up and faced him, standing quietly head on. We knew that if, when darted, Amboni ran in the direction he was facing, he could very well get to the bottom of Simba Lugga before the knockout drug took effect. From there we would not be able to load him.

As Dieter's shot rang out and the dart whammed into Amboni's neck, I willed him not to move; and to my astonishment, he stood completely still until the drug took effect. Then he slowly went down. I do not believe in miracles but I find it difficult to offer any logical reason for Amboni's behaviour, first in getting himself to such an accessible site and secondly for staying there. But it did happen, and we were thus able to save his life.

We loaded Amboni without difficulty and took him to the holding boma. Dieter made tests and took a number of blood samples, and injected him with an assortment of drugs including one for 'tryps' in case the poor beast had that, although it seemed unlikely. ('Tryps', or sleeping sickness, is the disease transmitted by the tsetse fly, and caused by the single-celled parasite, trypanasome.) Finally he injected him with the recovery drug and Amboni soon staggered to his feet, looking - and no doubt, feeling - terrible. In due course the results of the tests came through and showed that he had a partial kidney collapse and also an infestation of worms; the latter probably caused by his staying in a very small area for a long time, for we had had a spell of unusually damp and misty weather and he had had no need to move out to water.

While he was in the holding boma his condition initially deteriorated, and his head became very swollen due to his kidney trouble. We put glucose in his water to encourage him to drink. I fed him lucerne and horse nuts, and twice a day the tractor went many kilometres to collect riverine browse which was kindly made available from Ngare Ndare, the farm belonging to Francis' parents. Dieter had prescribed Imovec to get rid of the worms and when this failed to work, six packets of Equisole did the trick, and out came the most incredible number of worms. We had to shift Amboni from one pen to another to keep him clean.

At that time we also had Morani in the holding boma, so both we and the tractor crew were more than occupied in looking after the two. During the nights Godot rampaged around outside, no doubt informing the two gentlemen within of what he intended to do when he could get at them - and this posed a serious question, what were we to do? There was no sense in patching up the two ailing males and then releasing them under Godot's angry nose.

Luckily real progress had by this time been made in the construction that was turning Nakuru National Park into a rhino sanctuary. The holding bomas were already completed and it was decided that Amboni should be the first rhino to be translocated there, a decision that made us all very happy. At the beginning of October Joshua, one of our men, and I started to crate-train him. It was very easy and he went into his crate perfectly calmly from the first. After a few days Joshua would climb on to the top of the crate and bang around making huge noises, while below him I fed Amboni lucerne and assured the poor rhino that there was nothing to worry about.

On 18 October the Game Department lorry came to collect him. He stood calmly in his crate during the whole noisy business of loading and departure. His journey to his new home was made without incident, and he was the first rhino to be released in the newly created sanctuary at Nakuru National Park.

The Solio rhinos

Solio, a 15,000 acre game reserve in a huge cattle ranch near Naro Moru, has had the most fantastic success in breeding both black and white rhinos, and must be about the only place in the world suffering from overpopulation. To relieve the pressure and help us stock our sanctuary, the Wildlife Department bought us three black rhino cows.

Juno

In February 1980 a female rhino had been captured in the Nyeri Forest and taken to Solio. Four and a half years later, on 5 August, 1984, she was brought to Ngare Sergoi, the first Solio rhino to be moved to our sanctuary. She behaved calmly in the lorry that delivered her and as we knew she was used to electric fences, we released her the evening of her arrival. On her first day in the sanctuary she chased our fence gang once and touched the fence twice, but after that she settled down easily. I named her Juno after the goddess of fertility, for she was believed to be in calf when she was chosen to come to us. Indeed she was, and gave birth six weeks later but sadly the calf died after only three days.

Once Juno was over that crisis she became very sociable and was often to be seen with other rhinos, especially Stumpy, Solia and Godot. She has always behaved as if she is a reasonably elderly animal, and has a very quiet and gentle temperament. We are all inclined to confuse her with Rongai, for they have very similar horns, extremely high withers and sagging backs. This I suspect may be partly a matter of age, for elderly female rhinos generally have sagging backbones, whereas the younger females have straight backs like the males. Juno is possibly a bit larger than Rongai, indeed I believe she is our largest rhino, despite the fact that she has very small feet (only 25 cm in diameter). She is so much bigger than Shaba, that when seen together Shaba could be taken for her half-grown calf. She is also quite a lot bigger than Godot, being much longer in the body, although less compact and powerful looking.

As Juno prefers being up on the open plains rather than down in the valleys, she is usually fairly easy to observe and is seen almost every day. She is a very destructive feeder, chewing on one bush until she has totally demolished it. She has a real passion for wild asparagus and also has no inhibitions about using her horn to break off branches and break down small trees. Invariably if we come to a tree that has been flattened, Juno is the culprit. The only other rhino that could compete with her in this destructive respect was Amboni. Godot also flattened trees but he did this when he was annoyed rather than hungry.

Stumpy and Bahati

The second rhino we received from Solio had originally been captured in the Kibwezi area and was named Stumpy. She was caught on the same day as Juno but came to us five days later, having had a really bad time being captured. After being darted she had fallen down a bank and was thought to have broken a bone in her foot, she was certainly very lame on arrival. Then in the process of being unloaded she somehow got trapped by the hips between two iron bars. Her horn had been loosened and she had also injured an eye, as well as being very thin and generally poorly looking.

If rhinos had pecking orders (of which I have seen no sign), Stumpy would be at the bottom. She is small and not at all well put together. She and Shaba are about the same size but look totally different, whereas Shaba is compact and powerful, Stumpy is long-bodied and ungainly. Because of her condition we held her in the boma for two days, but although she calmed down she would not eat. So Ian thought it best to release her, which we did in the evening. Almost at once she met up with her ex-ranchmate, Juno, which made poor Stumpy look even worse; lame, with bones sticking out everywhere, her skin hanging in folds and covered in huge sores caused by a filarial parasite. My heart bled for the poor beast.

During her early days in the sanctuary Stumpy mainly stayed in the North Valley, watering at night either at the pool near the holding boma or else going down to the main river and then returning. She spent much of the time with her old ranchmates Juno and Solia. By the end of 1984 Stumpy was still very thin, which was not surprising considering the drought, but we were all fairly certain that she was pregnant. Luckily by this time the bone in her foot seemed to have mended itself and she was at least sound again, but otherwise she was still in poor condition. I was not at all optimistic about her chances of producing a healthy calf and of being able to feed it, but to our amazement she calved successfully seven months after her arrival, in March 1985. She looked after her calf extremely well and we called him Bahati, the Swahili for 'luck', but alas, while nursing her calf poor Stumpy got thinner and thinner, although Bahati continued to do well and evidently did not suffer from lack of any nutriment. We have no idea who Bahati's sire was, but his temperament was very like that of his mother, calm and quiet. He was not the least like Jupiter, Shaba's son by Godot, who, although fourteen months younger, started chasing Bahati around at an early age whenever their mothers met.

The first rains came soon after Stumpy calved. I was relieved for her sake but worried that the calf would suffer from the cold. However, he was perfectly alright. By June Bahati had a tiny horn and looked in beautiful shape. By the end of his first year, he was fit and fat but Stumpy still looked very thin. She also had two very bad filarial sores, one on either side of her body, just behind the girth, and in August we noticed that she had somehow broken off about three quarters of her front horn. It has since regrown but lacks the graceful curve of the original. Stumpy took to spending much of her time with Solia, and Bahati would go freely between the two females, sometimes even following Solia if they moved apart. Poor Stumpy looked worse than ever in Solia's company, for she is a good deal smaller and has none of Solia's good looks, her only claim to beauty being the very long and silky hairs that fringe her ears.

Like all young animals, baby rhinos are playful. Although I strongly suspect that they are most playful by night, we have seen them do some very entertaining things during the day. Once, when Bahati was nineteen months old and he and Stumpy were sleeping under an acacia on the Top Plain, the old bull giraffe known as Masikio came wandering up to feed on that particular bush. Stumpy flicked her ears and lifted her head but otherwise took no notice, but Bahati got up and very cautiously stalked the giraffe around the bush, hesitated and then put his little head down and charged at one leg. Masikio casually lifted the offending leg in time and continued to feed. The little rhino turned round and charged again. Once more the leg was raised in time. After a few more charges the giraffe walked over to Stumpy and looked down at her and when she raised her head he moved slowly off. Bahati snorted and bounced round his parent for all the world as if he were asking her to applaud his prowess at giraffe removal.

All rhinos I have seen are nervous by temperament and Stumpy and Bahati are no exceptions. One day I watched them approaching a salt lick and stayed very quiet, hoping to get a good photograph. A solitary cow was lying beside the salt, and for some reason the sight of this apparently perfectly ordinary bovine female so unnerved both the rhinos that it was nearly half an hour before they plucked up courage to approach the salt.

When we opened the Extension in October 1988 it did not surprise me that the wide-ranging Makora was the first rhino of all to explore it. What did surprise me was that, in early December, the usually very nervous and conservative Stumpy was the first black rhino to go into it. From then on she and Bahati spent much of their time there, and became a good deal more difficult to observe.

Stumpy has at last put on a lot of condition and, for the first time since she arrived, looks really fit. After Solia's calf reached its first birthday, she resumed her friendship with Stumpy, and both mothers and calves were often together in a companionable foursome. We were for a while hopeful that Stumpy was carrying Godot's calf, but she did not in the end calve. However, she was seen to be mated by the new male Osupat on 14 August, 1990.

Bahati began to turn into a fine sub-adult male. However, in July 1990, while I was in Europe, he apparently tried to prevent Kelele mating Stumpy. This resulted in a fight in the course of which Bahati sustained internal injuries and sadly he died on 30 July. The postmortem conducted by Dieter revealed peritonitis, cystitis and acute septicaemia.

Solia and Zaria

Solia was the third female black rhino we got from Solio Ranch. She is a huge and magnificent animal, a real beauty. She and Juno are about the same size, perhaps Solia is fractionally smaller, and she is obviously younger. She has the most incredible horn, very long and curved, which ends in a rapier point.

Solia arrived from Solio Ranch a couple of months after Juno and Stumpy, on 1 October. We released her early one morning a week later and she very soon joined up with her ex-ranchmates, and also spent a good deal of time with Godot. Like Juno and Stumpy, Solia prefers being on high ground and is not often in the valleys, but unlike them she is very nervous and highly strung. Consequently, she is much more difficult to observe because she keeps herself very well hidden and seldom uses the same bushes to conceal herself, whereas most rhinos in the sanctuary have regular 'houses'. When alarmed she moves like Shaba, with a high springy trot, head and tail held up. Once she was tracking Stumpy by following her scent, nose to ground, and came very close to the Suzuki before she realised it was there. I sat in it hardly daring to breath, let alone fiddle with my camera. When she did see us, she wheeled around with a terrific snort of alarm and set off at a fast trot looking wonderful. Unfortunately I was too slow with my camera to get any pictures.

On another occasion, when I was out with Errada early one morning, Solia inadvertently came very close to us as we sat beneath a tree. The wind was blowing our scent away from her so we were able to sit still and watch her feeding and moving slowly towards us. She was very alert, her large, sensitive ears constantly moving, and in between taking mouthfuls of grass she would stop to snuff the air. Suddenly a small brown bird flew towards us. It was a greater honey guide and he came to call us to a bees' nest that he had found. For a second Solia stood tense and motionless and then, with a snort of fear, swung around and was gone.

I was surprised that a rhino should respond to a honey guide's call, for the call is not one of alarm but a 'come on'. The greater honey guide is a little brown bird with a passion for beeswax and larvae, but he can rarely get at the combs by himself. So he flies close to humans and, with a very persistent call, will try to lead them to a bees nest in the hopes that they, with their passion for honey will open the nest and allow him to share in the spoils. It is said that the honey guide will also try in the same way to lead the honey badger (or 'ratel') to a bees nest for the same reason. I have also been told that if you refuse to share the spoils with the bird, he will then try to lead you on to a snake or a crocodile. I have heard this both in East and West Africa, and whether true or not it is obviously a widespread belief.

The bird which the rhino does regularly use as an early warning device is the red-billed oxpecker. These brownish birds of the starling family walk around on the animals while they are feeding or sleeping. The oxpecker is looking for insects and renders the host a great service in removing ticks, although it can also cause trouble by pecking at the filarial sores which the surprisingly thin-skinned creatures often have. The oxpecker is extremely alert, and when it sees anything strange it will give an alarm call to which the rhino responds.

Solia was pregnant when she arrived, and she calved on 15 February and then promptly walked off from her baby in a very decisive manner. Errada managed to get me close enough to look at Solia's teats. They were tiny and showed no sign whatsoever of having milk. So Solia was acting wisely, as most animals do in similar circumstances, for by abandoning a newborn baby, a milkless mother cuts short its agony and also brings herself back into season so that she can try again. However, this calf was destined to live, for we rescued it and I will tell Samia's story in another chapter. Suffice it to say here that if ever Solia should meet Samia, they will have no conception of their relationship to one another.

Three years later, on 9 March, 1988, at the height of another drought, Solia, having been well served by Godot, calved again. Remembering what had happened before, I was terrified she would abandon her baby, but this time she proved to be a perfect mother and had plenty of milk.

The following February mother and calf moved into the Extension and shortly afterwards Lesile, one of our trackers, had a very close encounter with them - so close, he was able to sex the calf. Orogai and I had been in radio contact with him and were walking towards him on the broad, black cotton-soil plain. As we walked we lost radio contact, but continued on. We walked very cautiously, for the area is a 'difficult' one, thick with waist-high grass and whistling thorn trees that are too stunted to climb but which are highly obstructive of the view. Suddenly Lesile appeared looking somewhat dishevelled. There followed such an excited spate of conversation that I could not make out a thing that was said. Eventually, when they calmed down, I discovered to my horror that Lesile had virtually walked into Solia who was sleeping and almost invisible. She had leapt up, knocked him down and gone off at full gallop with his field glasses over her horn and also with his radio and his belt.

We proceeded to the scene of action and found that Lesile had been less than three metres from Solia when she got up. We found the radio and the belt fairly soon, but had to track Solia for at least twenty metres before we found the field glasses which had presumably got stuck on her nose. Lesile then proudly informed me that, as the calf had jumped over his prostrate form, he had been able to see for sure that it was a female. I pointed out rather weakly that I would prefer its sex to have remained a mystery than that it should have been discovered in such a manner. However, since we did now know its sex, I named the calf Zaria, a name similar to that of her mother and also recalling the name of a Nigerian town where I had once lived. Recently, from the top of a nearby hill, I had a wonderful view of Solia trotting full speed across that same plain towards me - Zaria was having to go at a pretty good canter to keep up. I have no idea what had disturbed them, but they looked marvellous.

Mwingo

Mwingo, which means 'cloudy', was another black rhino female from Solio Ranch. She had originally been translocated to the Lake

Nakuru Park rhino sanctuary and, although no-one knows quite what happened to her there, she was evidently twice attacked by another rhino and badly damaged. On each occasion she was recaptured and put into a holding boma where she was patched up, but after the second time both Dieter and Peter Jenkins agreed that she should not be released back into that sanctuary again. So well after dark one night, in the middle of February 1989, a convoy of Wildlife Department vehicles brought her to us.

We had built a ramp near the Ngare Ndare Dam, having decided to release her directly into the Extension. The area had received good rain, so the food was excellent there and no other rhinos were as yet using that part of the sanctuary - we thought it would be a perfect place in which she could settle down. When the crate door was opened, Mwingo stuck her head out and started eating the nearest thorn bush. It was not until she had completely demolished it that she bothered to get right out of the crate. Still she hardly moved and we saw the next morning that she had slept at the base of the ramp.

For the first few weeks Mwingo hardly moved from the immediate vicinity of the ramp. She was very tame, presumably from having been handled so much at Nakuru. Supposedly about six years old, she was certainly appreciably bigger than Samia who was then four; and despite her beatings in Nakuru, she appeared to be in good condition. She has very distinctive ears, for they are heavily fringed and notches have been cut out of them.

Recently, Mwingo has started to move a little further afield, but she always returns to the dam to drink. Stumpy and her calf Bahati are the only other black rhinos to have visited that area and we found the tracks of all three very close together. The tracks indicated that they had sometimes been lying up near one another but we never observed them together. Latterly Mwingo has become much more alert and nervous and is now inclined to rush off if she catches our scent. We hope very much that she will settle down well and, after her previous traumas, have no more troubles.

Osupat

Osupat, a superb mature breeding bull, was translocated here from Solio Ranch on 24 June, 1990. As he was used to fences, we released him directly into the Extension. He is a very big and powerfully built rhino, bigger than Godot, and possesses a totally different character from that of his predecessor. He does not like people and has chased a few cars, but with other rhinos his behaviour is infinitely more gentle. On 4 August I saw him with Kelele who was behaving aggressively towards him. Watching from a nearby hill top, I was filled with horror and feared he would massacre the smaller and younger rhino. But after a few skirmishes, which were obscured by clouds of dust, and some noise, Kelele thought better of it and departed uninjured. There has been no known aggression between them since.

On 14 August he mated Stumpy and was very gentle with her - I watched them for three hours. On 13 October he was seen by a tracker to mate Shaba and apparently showed no signs of aggression towards Jupiter. On 3 November I watched him mate Juno and when her calf Juniper charged him, he merely lay down and waited until she had calmed down.

The white rhinos

Makora

Makora was born on 16 June, 1973 in the Meru National Park. His mother had been imported from Natal in 1966 to be one of the founder members of the small herd of white rhinos which the park was so proud of. Makora is now the sole survivor of those animals, for all the Meru rhinos were mowed down with submachine gun bullets on the night of 29 October, 1988.

In 1983 a zoo-bred rhino from America was brought to Kenya to act in a film. When the filming was finished he could not be returned to the USA due to quarantine regulations, so it was eventually decided that he should go to Meru Park to infuse the little herd there with fresh blood. At the time Makora was the resident breeding bull there and he did not take kindly to the arrival of the film star. The Wildlife Department therefore decided to move Makora and asked if we would have him. We agreed gladly.

At two o'clock in the morning on 1 May, 1984 I was woken by a tap on my bedroom door. Fearing some crisis had befallen the rhinos in the holding boma, I rushed out to find Mark Jenkins standing there. He said to come quickly - and to bring a pick-axe and shovel. As I looked slightly appalled at this request which brought visions of graves to mind, he rapidly explained that the white rhino bull had been dispatched from Meru but had been stuck on the road for two days in a broken-down Wildlife Department lorry. Ian had taken the Lewa lorry to go and rescue him, and, as by this time the poor animal was frantic, Dieter had rushed up from Nairobi to sedate it. The rhino was now, presumably, on its way to us in the Lewa lorry, but he could not be unloaded at the holding boma since it was full of black rhinos. The pick-axe and shovel were to build a ramp so that we could unload Makora straight into the sanctuary and the rest of the night passed in frantic activity doing just that. The lorry soon arrived with a very dopey rhino, so dopey that at first he refused to emerge but by dawn he was out grazing, and seemingly none the worse for his ordeal.

Due to his upbringing at Meru, where the white rhinos were kept in a boma at night and herded out to graze during the day, Makora is totally unafraid of people. This has made him a great deal easier to observe at close quarters than most of the blacks, and from the start it was obvious that Makora was a gentle, intelligent and intensely curious creature.

Since he had been raised in a national park, where domestic animals are not permitted, he had never met cattle before he came to the sanctuary. At first he did not think much of them and would move judiciously off when they, already quite used to rhinos, approached him. Now he takes no notice of them. He is more intrigued by my horses - who did not react quite so calmly to his attentions, but they eventually became fairly used to him, especially during the drought when he used to come and eat horse manure. One night he broke into the horse boma and in the morning I found my little mare Topsy looking somewhat shaken but none the worse for her encounter - although I suspect she had lost part of her supper. When my Suzuki was parked near the horses, Makora would often have a good go at opening the rear door if he smelt lucerne inside.

The donkeys we use for transporting food and water to some of the camps are looked after by a wonderful old man who wears a startling red hat of a most unusual design. It looks as if he has wrapped red velvet around an old, handleless saucepan. Makora has no objection to this strange hat, but he does not like the donkeys and from time to time has caused the old man considerable difficulties. One morning the donkeys came trotting down the hill towards my house with Makora trotting behind them, he had brought them all over from Headquarters to visit me. At that stage Samia was still very small and nervous and I was always nervous on her behalf, so the arrival of the cavalcade caused quite an upset to everyone - except Makora. It was one of the very few occasions on which he lived up to his name, Makora being a commonly used Kikuyu word for 'rascal'.

From the start Makora mingled easily with the wild animals such as the zebra and eland, although he sometimes chased the zebra in play. He would roll his tail up into a tight curl, roll his eyes and trot after them, but they were never unduly concerned. From time to time Makora meets a black rhino but normally they take no notice of each other at all and rarely interact. Once I saw him walk towards a tree under which Stumpy was lying with her calf. When he got very close Stumpy rushed out at him, huffing and puffing her indignation at the intrusion. With a very hurt look on his face, Makora hurriedly backed off.

The black male, Morani, however, did not like Makora at all and periodically went for him - which was foolish in the extreme as Makora was so much larger. One Sunday afternoon I was washing my hair when a messenger arrived to tell me to come quickly as Morani and Makora were having a fight at Headquarters. With a towel around my head, I rushed over in the Suzuki to find that the two embattled rhinos had already been separated by Francis' little Jack Russell terrier, Kepe! On another occasion when Morani attacked him, Makora got sufficiently annoyed to knock him over flat on his back. One of the drivers arrived in the other Suzuki at the crucial moment and drove Makora off, so no damage was done.

Makora is a great walker, more so than any of the black rhinos, and trundles along at a steady 8 km per hour. On many nights he seems to cover the entire sanctuary, for in the morning we find his huge footprints on all the roads. This was a worry on full moon nights when the shifta are most active, so a driver was always detailed to follow him if he was near the fence line at dusk. Knowing me and my car well as a provider of lucerne in times of drought, Makora would usually come if I called him. Sometimes, in periods of real shifta crisis, if Makora was near the fence I would go and try to bribe him away to a safer area. Usually he would follow the Suzuki, trotting hopefully behind with ears pricked and nose revelling in the lovely scent of lucerne.

Once when shifta were known to be very close by, I was told that Makora was near the fence up on Fumbi - so I thought it prudent to try to move him to a less vulnerable position. I had a rather eminent visitor with me and, having loaded lucerne into the back of the Suzuki, began to tempt Makora away from the fence. As I was driving down a very steep and rough track calling to Makora, I kept leaning out to look back to see if he was following the car. Somehow I managed to lean so far out that I lost my balance and fell out, all except for my hands which were still clutching the steering wheel. Fate was on my side, however, and instead of having a serious accident we merely stopped with a bit of a bump against a small tree. My poor guest, however, was more than a little shaken and later, over lunch, inquired whether I made a practice of such circus tricks.

Much of our sanctuary is black cotton-soil, and when it rains our roads become impossibly slippery. One day after it had rained and I was driving along very slowly and carefully, I glanced in my rearview mirror and saw Makora coming down the road after me full gallop. There was nothing very much I could do about it, so I just slithered on slowly. As he caught up with me he veered off the road on to the grass and came tearing past, mud flying in all directions, and as he passed he gave a series of terrific bucks. His mouth was open and I could see the whites of his eyes. If he had not got a wicked grin on his face, it certainly looked very like it. Amused though I was, I admit that my knees were a bit wobbly as he tore off into the distance.

When we opened the Extension in October 1988, it did not surprise us that Makora was the first to take advantage of having this huge new area at his disposal. Each morning his tracks showed the distance he had covered during the night, presumably in the endless search for others of his own species.

Makora had certain rocks and tree trunks on which he could at least relieve his physical frustration. He would walk over them until he was in position and rub himself gently to and fro with a pleased expression on his face; but, as far as we saw, he never continued on to ejaculate as Morani regularly did. He also quite frequently used his huge penis as a fly-whisk-come-scratcher, pushing it between his front legs and moving it vigorously back and forth and sideways. Although he and the other white rhinos are as bothered by flies as the blacks, the white rhino does not seem to get the same fly-born filarial infection; so it seems to be specific to the black rhino.

It was always a matter of amazement to me that a huge breeding bull in the prime of life and accustomed to having a harem should remain so sweet-tempered when he must have felt his loneliness acutely. We all determined to do what we could to get him a mate and in the event, he got three.

Makora's three brides

Late in 1988 we were told that we could have three white rhino cows from Solio Ranch. Unlike the black rhinos, the white ones there are the personal property of the owner and we would have to buy them. Unfortunately my finances were not up to it, but it was much too good an offer to turn down. Fortunately two very generous people came forward with the money for two of the rhinos and the Ngare Sergoi Support Group of Columbus, Ohio, run by Andy Lodge, managed to raise the money for the third. Since the three had all been born and bred in the Solio sanctuary and were accustomed to an electric fence, we decided not to keep them in the holding boma but to release them directly into the sanctuary. We then built a ramp in the Extension, having decided that it would be the best place for the new arrivals.

In the late afternoon of 7 December, the first of our new rhinos arrived in a large crate on a very large lorry. She was a lovely, fat little rhino and Dieter estimated her to be seven years old. Our trackers named her Gororika, from the Masai word 'nkorika', an area of bushy trees on Solio. When she arrived she was still suffering slightly from the effects of the capture drug and her journey and was in no hurry to get out of her crate. As we wanted to unload her while it was still light, we had to speed her on her way with a poke from an electric cattle prod. For the next two days she behaved rather wildly and we detailed a tracker to keep tabs on her, but her first encounter with a herd of cows so terrified her that she had the poor man up a tree.

I had to spend the whole day of 8 December in Nairobi, and arrived back just in time to see our second white rhino cow being unloaded at the same spot and moving off calmly as night began to fall. Four days later she joined up with her ex-ranchmate and the two rhinos became inseparable. Our trackers called her Marembo, a Masai term for 'beautiful girl'. As she is estimated to be between nine and ten years old she cannot possibly be Gororika's mother, but she behaves in a remarkably protective fashion towards the younger rhino and always leads the way. It might be that the two are sisters, but we do not know for sure.

The last of the three rhinos arrived on 11 December. As a reminder of her provenance, the trackers called her Sungari, after a hill on Solio which had been occupied by a clan of Laikipiak Masai of that name. She was slightly smaller than Marembo and estimated to be eight or nine years old. As a result of rough driving she had knocked her front horn badly against the crate, we could see it bleeding around the base and it looked distinctly loose. However, she emerged quietly enough and walked off into her new home. Three days later she joined up with the other two white rhino cows from Solio.

On that same day she lost her horn and to my great surprise our trackers found it in the wilderness of long grass and tangled thorn bushes. I knew they had very keen eyes, but had not realised just how keen. It had not broken off but had become detached from the saucer-like hollow from which a rhino's horn grows. We were able to view Sungari clearly enough to see that, although her nose looked a bit bloody, she did not appear to be unduly distressed.

All three newcomers were very nervous at first and bolted off at the sound of a car or the slightest whiff of human scent. Marembo always led and the others followed with their tails tightly curled into knots (unlike the black rhino which, when alarmed, holds its tail straight up in the air like a warthog). Makora in the meantime was having a rather perplexing time. He was to be seen marching around the Extension with his nose to the ground, ears flicking continually and tail in a tight and agitated curl. He was a picture of determination, but the determination was rather misplaced as he usually seemed to be tracking his brides in the wrong direction.

On the morning of 14 December I and my trackers were watching the three females lying in a grove of large yellow fever trees near a spring, when Makora at last caught up with them. Perched on a convenient rock I watched in excitement. The three females got up and presented a united front. Makora moved slowly towards them, ears pricked and tail tightly curled, making the same contact breathing noises I had heard the black rhinos, and in particular Samia, make. Sungari moved a little ahead of the other two and with her ears laid back and nostrils crinkled, snorted at him - she looked exceedingly wicked. Marembo also laid her ears back and snorted. Gororika, being younger, stood with her ears pricked forward and looked very interested. Makora slowly walked in front of all three, then moved a little way off and sprayed urine on a bush. Then he lay down. The three cows moved away a short distance and then also lay down - and that was the great meeting.

At the end of December, Sungari left the other two females and moved into the Mzinga area of the old sanctuary. She stayed there for nearly two months on her own and then rejoined the other two. Whether she went off on her own because she was troubled by having no front horn or for some other reason, I do not know. At any rate, by the end of February her new horn was showing as a quite substantial bump on the end of her nose.

On 1 October, 1989 Marembo gave birth to a male calf which our trackers called N'juku and on 19 March, 1990 Sungari also gave birth to a male, Lari. Both females were totally solitary until their calves were about six months old. Gororika has now also given birth, on 2 February, 1991, but as yet the calf's sex is unknown.

The white rhino females are usually very sedentary in behaviour and - when not with very young calves - seem to be more herd animals than the black rhino females. Makora is with them part of the time, but is still often on his own and still walks vast distances. Since the arrival of the cows, I have not seen him masturbate or use his penis as a fly whisk and scratcher, but this may be because he is spending most of his time in the Extension and so I see less of him. However, he has discovered some new distractions. He managed to demolish the Dyers' telephone line, which has since had to be re-sited outside the sanctuary. He also recently learned how to open the bonnet of my Suzuki which is held down by two spring-loaded hooks. He came upon the car which I had left parked while I had gone out walking. On my way back I noticed him standing by it and as I watched he used his horn to unhook the second hook and lift the bonnet.

When I shouted at him to leave my poor car alone, he dropped the bonnet with a clang and stepped back looking very shamefaced. Luckily he had not had time to dismantle the engine. Another game he has started to play is ball, rolling large boulders into the road. This is somewhat annoying if I am driving alone, as I have to roll them out of the way unaided. Judging from the expression on his face as he once watched me doing this, he clearly regarded my exertions as an extra bonus to his activities.

5

Feeding Behaviour

We need no followers - ours is the right. Loren Eisley

As we acquired our rhinos, we began learning about them and one of the most important things to study was their feeding patterns, for we had to avoid overstocking the sanctuary out of ignorance. According to the books, the white rhino is a grazer and the black rhino a browser. In fact it was their different eating apparatus rather than their colour that gave them their names. The white rhino is so called, not because it is white, but because its mouth is wide. When the Dutch-speaking people first encountered this beast in South Africa, they called it the 'weit' rhino, meaning 'wide'. However, the English thought it meant white, and so they called this great grey beast the 'white' rhino and, although similarly coloured, the smaller species the 'black' rhino. Like elephants, both are usually tinted by the dust or mud in which they have been rolling. So that although the animal's colour says nothing about its species, it does give an interesting clue as to where it has been, as the soils in the different parts of the sanctuary are wholly different colours, ranging from bright red to black and pale grey.

The significant distinguishing feature between the two species is, as the Dutch-speaking people had correctly noted, the shape of the mouth. The white rhino has a broad, square upper lip, whereas the black rhino has a narrow prehensile one which looks like the beginnings of an elephant's trunk. Neither species has any teeth in the front of its mouth, but both have good grinders in the rear.

Up until the very recent past, the black rhino was distributed all over Africa south of the Sahara, with the exception of the heavily forested areas of Central Africa and the rain forests of West Africa. In the far distant past it was also found in northern Africa and what is now the Sahara. The rhino could live almost anywhere, from the deserts of Namibia to the montane forests of the Aberdares.

In 1983 I was invited by Bill Woodley to stay with him in Tsavo and to look around at the type of country which had probably once had the highest population density of rhinos anywhere on the continent. This was the thick thornbush scrub of the Yatta Plateau. It was there that John Goddard did his study on the feeding habits of the black rhino, and Bill loaned me a copy of his report.

That it did not help me much was my own fault. I am not a botanist and did not know whether the same plants existed there as do here. The average annual rainfall is about the same in both places, but Lewa, at 1650 metres, is much higher. It is area of open grass plains with scattered thorn bushes and deep valleys with thicket type scrubland and patches of riverine forest. Rhinos had lived on Lewa before, but in the early days I was very concerned as to whether or not individuals coming from wetter and higher, or lower and drier areas would adapt to the climate and vegetation there. If they did adapt, how many animals could the vegetation support? These are questions that still have to be asked, but the answers may take several decades to come.

Dr Hugh Lamprey, the head of the World Wildlife Fund in Kenya, took aerial photographs of the whole area. Under his guidance Gilly Furnivall did a study of the vegetation in the sanctuary beginning in October 1985 and continuing for five months, thus seeing the vegetation both during the short rains and the subsequent dry period. Her report has been of immense value to us. All our observations, however, are complicated by the fact that the rhino is more nocturnal than diurnal, especially in hot and dry weather - which is what we have most of the time here. Most of the rhinos' feeding and socialising takes place at night when it is impossible for us to observe them.

To determine a rhino's feeding patterns, Gilly and her tracker would trace the route that one particular rhino, the young male called Amboni, had taken the previous night, noting the vegetation that he had browsed along the way. She listed 38 species of trees and shrubs eaten by him alone. Although there are other browsing animals in the sanctuary - giraffe, greater kudu, eland, impala and gerenuk - as well as many grazers - buffalo, zebra, red hartebeest, oryx and Grants gazelle - it is quite easy to discern if a

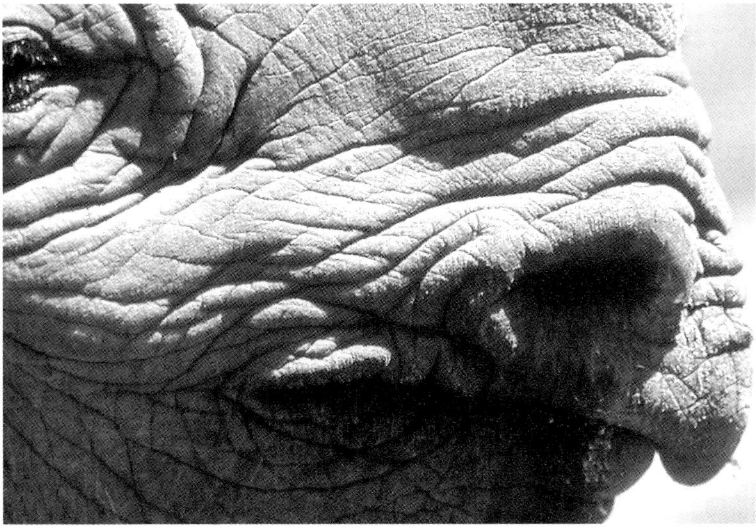

The black rhino's prehensile lip distinguishes it from the white rhino (Gerry Ellis)

particular bush has been eaten by a rhino or by something else. The way a black rhino bites off a twig or a branch is quite distinctive.

I myself have seen Samia browsing fifteen species of trees and shrubs and thirty species of herbs, plus a considerable number of others which I have not been able to identify. She also eats the 'marula' (the local species of papyrus) as well as sedges and grasses. Her preference for 'soft' browse reflects, I think, both her immaturity and her unnatural upbringing. The wide range of food plants is very significant, and I believe that the poor condition, and consequently the poor reproductive rate, of some zoo-kept black rhinos may well be due to their having a much narrower range of fodder.

Droppings also indicate what an animal has been eating. In the wild I used to be confused by the droppings of elephant and rhino, but in the sanctuary the problem does not exist, for we have no elephants here. In any case, the difference was soon pointed out to me. When a rhino stops to defecate, it almost always 'scrapes' its droppings, sending them flying with energetic kicks of its back feet. An elephant never does this, but leaves neat little piles as he goes along. Furthermore, the twigs in rhino droppings are always cut into short, sharply defined pieces, each about a quarter the length of the average matchstick. The pieces are usually not much bigger in diameter than a matchstick, but during drought periods, when the animals are hard pressed for food, I have seen bits of wood the thickness of my little finger in the droppings. In contrast, elephants extrude long twisted bits of fibrous material.

When each of our rhinos first arrived and was kept in the holding boma, we fed them on browse that we cut outside the fence; but we ensured that it was the same as what they would be able to find for themselves when released within the sanctuary. We also supplemented the captives' diet with dry lucerne and horse cubes. Each time we released a black rhino, we noticed that one of the first things it did was to start grazing. This made us look again at the assumption that black rhinos are only browsers and our subsequent observations have shown that grass may constitute between 30% and 40% of their diet. But unlike the white rhino, which prefers short grass spiced with a few herbs but never trees or bushes, the black rhino chooses long grass. This is probably because its prehensile upper lip makes it easier for the animal to eat long grass. Watching Samia, I came to realise the extent to which the lower lip is also used as a scoop. One would seldom be close enough to a rhino in the wild to be able to observe this.

We have tried to compile detailed records of what the rhinos eat without disturbing them. So I have spent many hours watching rhinos feeding, but usually from a distance which renders it impossible to see exactly what they are eating. I often have to write down simply whether they are grazing or browsing or, if I cannot discern if they are grazing grass or eating herbs, 'feeding ground level'. If I can see the plant and identify it, I write it down with the Latin name if I know it; and if not, with the Ndorobo name which eventually enables me to find its Latin name. Since much of their browse is off thorn bushes and trees, my notes are filled with "*Acacia* sp.?"

After the rains, when the sanctuary is full of green grass and herbs and browse, the rhinos are very selective feeders, and each rhino's individuality shows clearly. For instance, Shaba seldom takes more than two or three mouthfuls from the same plant or place, but always moves slowly on, taking in an enormous variety of plants as she goes. Juno is just the opposite, she is a terribly destructive feeder, eating a great deal from one bush or plant before moving on to the next. She often quite demolishes the plant on which she is feeding in the process, something that Shaba never does. Is Juno's unwitting destructiveness due to her having been raised in a wetter, lusher area where she did not have to be so careful to conserve her food supply? Or is it just a matter of individual behaviour? I do not know.

During the dry seasons the rhinos have much less choice, and when there is a drought and no green grass or leaves at all, the unfortunate animals have to survive as best they can on dry twigs and dead-looking sere grass. But survive they do, and a great deal better than many of the other animals in the sanctuary. It is in periods of drought that one of the ways in which its horn is invaluable to its owner becomes apparent. The front horn is used both to hook down branches that would otherwise be out of reach; and also to dig up roots, bulbs and tubers, including the onion-like bulbs of the 'Pyjama' lilies which are considered to be slightly poisonous.

In this area of erratic rainfall, drought is our main enemy apart from poachers. Kenya has two rainy seasons each year, the 'long rains' from mid-March until June and the 'short rains' from mid-October until December, but the amount of rain varies tremendously from one area to another and from one year to the next. On Lewa the average annual rainfall is supposed to be about 50 cm. But 'average' means that we may have appreciably over that for several years and then virtually none during the next year or two. Much of Africa is prone to such violent extremes in rainfall, unlike the more consistent rainfall patterns of the temperate zones.

Some animals are much better adapted to drought than others, for a multitude of different physiological reasons. When we have been stricken by droughts here, as we were in 1984 and 1987, we have seen buffalo, eland, kudu and impala all dying, while the giraffe and the Grants gazelle did not appear to be affected at all. We noticed that in some species the sex of the animal seemed related to its ability to survive harsh conditions. The buffalo bulls, although becoming very thin, almost all pulled through, as did the barren cows; but if a buffalo cow was in calf, or had a calf at heel, both were doomed. This held true for other species as well. During those hard times I dreaded to see any animals born, for usually both mother and child died, often suddenly. The most strangely affected were the common zebra. They never seemed to lose weight or condition, but would simply lie down and die without warning. We even lost a few Grevy's, that bigger-eared, more narrowly striped version of zebra, that is always said to be more capable of surviving drought than the common Burchell's.

In these circumstances it is also the 'little' troubles that kill. As the nutrient quality of the food deteriorates, afflictions that the animal could otherwise surmount without difficulty come to the fore. Some die from blood lost to ticks, from infestations of worms, or from some small wound or ailment. Ideally it is the fitter, tougher animals which began the drought with more resources that survive, but psychology as well as physiology plays its part. Eland are animals with very migratory tendencies and they are very stressed when restricted by a fence. The loss of eland inside the sanctuary was much greater than the loss rate outside, although the food outside was no better. The warthogs, too, suffered greatly, rather to my surprise, and many died; but to my equal surprise, the bush-pigs did not even seem to be affected. They were as fat at the end of the 1987-88 drought as they had been at the beginning. I strongly suspected at the time that one reason for this was that they were much more omnivorous than the warthogs, and that insects and carrion carried them through. Since then, Francis has raised an orphaned bush-pig and he found that it has developed definite hunting and killing tactics, shaking things in its mouth like a terrier and joyfully consuming meat if it gets a chance.

Plants, too, have interesting ways of surviving drought conditions. From research done in South Africa it has been discovered that, in times of drought crisis, certain plants are able to protect themselves from being over-browsed by the secretion of tannin. The really incredible discovery was that the over-browsed plant not only increases its tannin level in its own leaves and twigs, but that, in some astonishing way, its stress is communicated to its neighbours which then also react by increasing their levels of tannin - even though they may not have been eaten at all. It appears that kudu are particularly susceptible to poisoning by tannin, and this may be the reason why so many of our beautiful kudu died in the 1987 drought.

Rhinos do not seem to be unduly affected by tannin, and in

When browsing, rhinos use their prehensile upper lips to help pluck the leaves (Gerry Ellis)

general appear to be more drought-resistant than many of the other herbivores. Like horses and zebra, the rhinos are Perissodactyla - odd-toed ungulates - and digest their food by means of bacterial fermentation in the hind gut. In many respects over the past forty million years or so, the odd-toed ungulates seem to have lost out to the even-toed ones, particularly to the ruminants. However, in serious drought conditions those ruminants which are not specifically adapted to desert conditions appear to suffer more than the rhinos, possibly because the rhinos are able to utilise an astonishingly wide range of plants without poisoning themselves.

In the 1984 drought Juno had lost a calf just after birth; Rongai had aborted hers and Solia deserted hers at birth, for she had no milk with which to feed it. However, we were not sure if these disasters were due to the drought or to the stress caused by translocation (all three rhinos had been moved while in calf), either by the move itself or the drugs used to effect it. No one knew the answer, and in all probability it was a combination of both drought and translocation stress.

However, in 1987 there was no doubt that the drought was causing the rhinos to suffer, they were all becoming noticeably thin. Both Stumpy and Shaba were nursing calves and both mothers, Stumpy in particular, looked terrible, although both the calves, Bahati and Jupiter, looked well. Three of the other cows - Rongai, Juno and Solia - had been mated and were believed to be pregnant. As all three had had crises in the 1984 drought, we feared for them now. Dieter explained that if the intestinal bacteria had at least a small amount of protein-rich fodder to keep them going, the animals would be better able to cope with the huge quantities of dried grass and even drier-looking twigs that they were having to eat. So we decided to try to supplement their diet with small amounts of lucerne delivered daily to each animal.

This was a great deal easier said than done. It was a time-consuming job and not without danger. That we succeeded most days was due almost entirely to the skill, courage and persistence of our tracker Orogai. He and I would set forth with about three sacks of lucerne in the back of my Suzuki. Having heard from the other trackers where the various rhinos were, Orogai would take an armful of lucerne from the sack and creep as close as he could to the recumbent animal, placing the lucerne where he thought the creature would find it when he or she moved off. It was of vital importance not to disturb the rhinos, either by making the slightest noise or by letting them get the smallest whiff of human scent. If the rhino were alarmed it might charge, but even more likely it would go rushing off so that the whole exercise would have been wasted. My heart was in my throat many times as Orogai crept quite ridiculously close to a sleeping rhino. He would never let me help him and he never got chased. He was so adept that I figured he had at least a 90% success rate, for nine times out of ten the lucerne was eaten by the rhino for which it had been intended.

Feeding the white rhino, Makora, was quite a different matter. Being a bigger animal he had a slightly larger ration of lucerne than the black rhinos, and he loved every mouthful of it. He knew very well that I and my little yellow Suzuki were the bearers of good things for him. He also knew that Topsy, my horse, got lucerne and he took to waiting at the stable for me. This did not help when I wanted to go off for a ride, as my poor mare was more than a little disconcerted when the very large bull rhino came trotting after us, huffing and puffing his hopes of a handout. I refused to feed him anywhere near the horse and he quite quickly grasped the idea that a certain tree had been chosen by me as his dining room. I would feed him there regularly every morning. He would almost invariably be waiting for me with his ears pricked and a hopeful expression on his face; and he would give me a greeting huff very similar to the one with which Samia honours me. If I found Makora hanging about the stable, I would call to him and he would trot behind the car until we reached his dining tree.

On one unforgettable occasion I had gone early to feed both Topsy and Makora, as I was in a hurry to drive into Nanyuki and get to the bank as soon as it opened. There was no sign of Makora, but many cattle were hanging around looking hungry, so I took his breakfast back with me. On my return from Nanyuki I was horrified to see a huge backside going along the road ahead of me, obviously intent on visiting the house. I would have had no objection to a rhino guest, except that I happened to have one already, the orphan Samia. I did not know what would happen if the two rhinos met and I was not prepared to risk finding out, for Samia was only a tenth of Makora's size and I could all too easily visualise her being flattened.

Makora and I reached the house together. Luckily there was no sign of Samia, so I hustled the sack of lucerne into the Suzuki, calling at him to follow me. Having seen the lucerne, he was somewhat frantic and took off after me at full gallop, ears pricked and huffing his concern lest his very late breakfast should disappear. Looking into the rearview mirror I noticed something galloping behind him. It was Buffalo, my black hairy hound, who had somehow got out of the garden and was going *ventre à terre* behind Makora. When I reached the tree I slammed on the brakes, opened the back door and put the lucerne down in front of the rhino's breathless nose. The panting dog jumped into the car and I drove hurriedly off before embarrassing questions were asked by the party of tourists who had arrived on the scene unexpectedly and were looking somewhat astonished.

When I grew up in Cornwall, it seemed to me that all animals with which I had dealings behaved in an orthodox fashion and ate the things expected of them. Going to Ghana was rather like walking through Alice's looking glass. No creature behaved in an expected way. When my husband told me that he had a stallion which periodically relieved the monotony of his diet by catching and eating a chicken, I did not believe a word of it - until I saw it happen. Likewise, when my guinea pigs disappeared and my gardener told me the duikers, or 'bush deer', were eating them, I considered him a liar, full of succulent guinea pig himself. Until I caught a duiker in the act, with the guinea pig caught, consumed and swallowed virtually whole, the hind legs still kicking as the front end disappeared. Thereafter I kept my eyes and ears open and my mind prepared for all sorts of surprises.

Even so, I was not quite prepared for the surprise that Samia gave me during the 1987 drought. By this time I was used to the fact that, despite individual food preferences, the rhinos ate almost anything that grew in the sanctuary. Their menus included poisonous plants, such as stramonium, and things which appeared totally unpalatable, such as very dead-looking wood. In 1987, Samia was in her third year and very playful and explorative. Her little horn was growing and she delighted in finding that she had on the end of her nose a very useful tool for manipulating objects. She loved hooking it into things and using it to turn them over and particularly liked moving logs and fallen branches around. I used to take her out for hours during the afternoons and evenings. I would find a nice place for her to explore and sit myself down with a book while she played and fed and rummaged around.

One evening I noticed that she was turning over all the dead wood she could find and I imagined that she was either licking salts, minerals or sawdust from beneath it. It was not until she seemed distressed, shaking her head and rubbing her nose, that I climbed off my log to investigate. She came to me for help and I saw that she had a fighter termite stuck on her nostril. I took it off and watched her intently as she went back to moving dead wood. She was quite deliberately licking up termites. I recounted this to Orogai and asked him whether he knew if the other rhinos did this. He seemed astonished and shook his head and replied "faro mingi akili", "rhinos are very clever". I could not but agree.

When she was little I tried to show Samia what food plants to eat, but it certainly would never have occurred to me to show her how to eat termites. That was entirely her own idea and I only ever saw her do it during the drought and never saw any of the other rhinos eat them, but I should not be surprised if they did. During the drought Samia also picked up, chewed and licked old bones. She was most partial to those of a long-dead ostrich, and played with and chewed one particular thigh bone regularly. I could never determine if this was for minerals or for fun. Only bones that were very dry and had no scent interested her; she was afraid of and actually avoided anything that smelt of carrion. She would also eat dried dung, especially that of zebra and cattle. I was never able to discover if the other rhinos were also supplementing their sparse diet with dung and bones and perhaps carrion. They certainly would have had the opportunity, for in the huge die-off there were plenty of both lying about the sanctuary; but, when asked, Orogai and the other trackers shook their heads and thought it unlikely.

6

Mating and Breeding Behaviour

It is irrefutable that creation and creature are good even in the fact that all that is exists in this contrast and antithesis.
Loren Eisley

The purpose of this sanctuary is not simply to provide a haven for a few individuals of a very endangered species. It is, more importantly, to provide an environment in which they will reproduce, so that we will be able to help restock the parks and reserves if and when poaching is stopped so that restocking is feasible. It is also, to a lesser extent, to breed animals to exchange with other sanctuaries in order to extend the gene pool of each. Thus it has been of the utmost importance to keep breeding records. We have been very fortunate in being able, thanks to the skill and diligence of our trackers, to keep fairly close tabs on breeding in the sanctuary without in any way disturbing the rhinos. What has emerged is that both the black and, to a lesser extent, the white rhinos are remarkably individualistic in their breeding behaviour. Both species, however, make use of certain similar actions that are predominately, although not exclusively, associated with breeding behaviour. These are spraying, cocking the tail and making flehmen.

The rhino's habit of scraping its dung has already been mentioned. It also uses its urine for definite purposes of communication and, in particular, in connection with its sexual condition, and therefore has two very definite methods of urinating. The animal may urinate in a normal fashion or it may spray, shooting the urine out backwards in a series of blasts, usually at bushes or around dung heaps, and with such force that it may cover up to three or four metres. The female does this particularly frequently when she is in season, and in such cases she then rubs her hind feet in the wet soil. The male will cover the female's spray with his, which is shot out at an even greater velocity as a fine mist - his ability to sustain his spray on these occasions is most impressive. Although spraying is generally an adult, sexually-associated activity, our young hand-raised female, Samia, sometimes does it, and in her case I think spraying has to do with marking what she considers to be the core of her home range.

When sexually aroused, a female rhino will invariably cock her tail in a very specific fashion, lifting it and crooking it in a manner that makes it look as if the tail has been broken and then set badly at a curious angle. Making flehmen is an action characteristic of many ungulates, including rhinos. These species have a sensory gland at the back of the mouth and when using it, the upper lip is lifted in a very distinctive fashion. A male rhino in particular will make flehmen when it sniffs the rear end of a female rhino or the places where she has urinated. Samia did it from a very early age, after sniffing intently at certain objects. I could never understand why, as of course my sense of smell is most deficient, but her action was unmistakably that of making flehmen and not of simply extending her prehensile upper lip to feel something. However, making flehmen most typically has sexual connotations.

Black rhino males and matings

When Morani came to us we put him in one section of the holding boma. Shaba was in another section and she seemed quite taken by her boma-mate, for the day after she was released from the holding boma she re-entered it and went around spraying urine and holding her back arched and her tail up in a manner highly reminiscent of a bitch in season. So, after having tempted Shaba out of the boma once more, we released Morani and the following day, 26 April, 1984, I watched him approach Shaba. When she snorted at him he retreated to some bushes which she had just left, sniffed them and then turned and sprayed on them. Then both rhinos moved off down the valley and out of sight. The next morning they were together; whenever Shaba moved Morani followed and sprayed on each bush she had touched. Again, his behaviour was very much like that of a dog following a bitch in season. When he approached her she would cock her tail and he

Rhinos have been seen to mate up to eleven times in three quarters of an hour. (Gerry Ellis)

would nuzzle under it with his prehensile upper lip. During the afternoon he mounted her three times, but as they were partly hidden by bushes it was impossible to see what was happening. Thereafter they were together much of the time.

On 11 August when I saw them together in the morning, Shaba showed no sign of being in season, but in the evening Morani was seen to mount her briefly. He did this on and off for several months; the last time, again rather briefly, was on 7 December. Morani would often indicate his excitement not only by spraying but also by performing a dust-sweeping ceremony with his horn. Although I have seen Shaba watching this with her ears intently pricked, it is not purely a sexual ceremony, for he would also sweep the dust if he was annoyed by the presence of Makora or the donkeys.

Although Godot was the first rhino in the sanctuary it was not until the end of June 1984, and at a most awkward moment, that we first had a chance to view his sexual exploits. Karl had completed the building of our new house and we had arranged to have a house-warming party. As we were expecting about forty guests, I had told Errada that I would not accompany him on our usual rhino-ing expedition for I would be busy cooking. However, in the middle of the morning he suddenly turned up, very breathless, and said I must come as he thought that Godot was about to mate Rongai. Obviously such an exciting event had to take priority over cooking and the kitchen was abandoned. Errada installed me on a rock halfway down the west slope of the main valley, providing me with a seat in the front row of the stalls for the scene being enacted at the bottom of the valley.

Godot, Rongai and Kelele were all standing together, taking the odd mouthful of browse. A few minutes after my arrival, Godot and Rongai turned to face each other and stood nose to nose, gently sniffing each other's nostrils. Kelele stood by his mother's rump. Then, when she turned to present her rump to Godot, Kelele moved to her head. She cocked her tail, slightly arched her back and urinated. Godot mounted her but, however hard he tried, he could not penetrate her (she is a very big rhino, bigger than him) and liquid trickled slowly from her vagina. After ten minutes of abortive effort, Godot dismounted and took a minor snack from the nearest thorn bush, while Rongai lay down and had a nap.

Five minutes later Godot started moving round her at a very slow trot, his neck arched, his ears pricked and his head and tail held high. He moved on very elevated diagonals, as in the equine high school movement known as the 'passage'. In fact, he looked quite astonishingly like a Lippizaner stallion from the Spanish Riding School in Vienna. After this really elegant display, the two animals once more stood nose to nose, huffing gently. Then Rongai moved away, turned and backed towards some higher ground. Godot moved behind her, mounted and penetrated her with ease, having a violent orgasm that lasted a full five minutes until she moved forward and he fell off her.

Godot huffed angrily at Kelele who had been observing the performance with ears pricked and obvious interest. Then all three started to feed and soon after lay down. I was surprised not only by the gentleness and affection both adults showed towards each other, but also by how little aggression was shown by Godot towards Kelele who though sub-adult was also a male. Over the years Godot and Rongai were seen to mate on several occasions and she was clearly his favourite mate. However, this did not stop him considering all the female black rhinos in the sanctuary to be his.

Early on Christmas Eve of 1984 it was reported that he was mating Shaba. By the time I arrived half an hour later, the two rhinos were feeding side by side. Then Godot walked off, sprayed and scraped several times and then returned and moved around Shaba with his head and tail up, doing a beautiful passage. Later the two lay down side by side.

Godot did not always have it so easy, and sometimes his advances were firmly rebuffed. On 25 November, 1984 Errada and I were watching Stumpy and Solia, who were sleeping side by side on the west slope of the North Valley, when Godot came marching up the hill towards them. As he approached both females got up. Solia snorted, laid her ears back flat against her head, wrinkled her nose and let out a fearful roar. Godot, appreciably smaller than she, retreated backwards at speed, then stood his ground and scraped, defecated and scraped again violently. He then went to a bush and demolished it with savage sideways thrusts of his horn. He returned to Solia and the two rhinos stood nose to nose, he with ears pricked and gently huffing, she with ears flat back, mouth open and snarling. Stumpy then approached and as she

PREVIOUS PAGE

Samia (Gerry Ellis)

LEFT

Charging rhinos may reach a speed of 50 kph (Gerry Ellis)

The daily walk (Gerry Ellis)

Red-billed oxpeckers remove ticks and act as an early warning device when danger approaches (Gerry Ellis)

Samia and Samuel

Minor skirmishes break out when one or more rhino comes too near another. Fights between rival males over a female are more serious, and the loser may die of his wounds (Gerry Ellis)

Females have been seen to back on to a higher ground to aid penetration by a smaller male (Gerry Ellis)

did so Solia charged forwards at Godot who, turning fast, nearly collided with Stumpy so that she too jumped forward at him. Solia's very long, thin horn would have gone swiftly between his hind legs had he not clamped his tail down in time, hunched his rump and sprinted away.

Godot then turned and walked back and stood nose to nose with Stumpy. She also roared at him but without much conviction, unlike Solia she is a lot smaller than him. He merely stood there, ears pricked, swaying to and fro without moving his feet. Stumpy also started to sway, but her ears were back and she was making groaning noises. Eventually both animals fell silent, until Stumpy suddenly jumped at Godot. He stood his ground and their horns met with a clang. She growled at him, the ominous noise coming from the back of her throat. Then Godot raised his tail and made a small charge forwards. Stumpy stood her ground, Godot retreated and he continued to growl. He came towards her again, but then Solia emerged from the bush under which she had retreated and both females charged him, Solia again with her ears back and making fearful snarling noises. Godot cantered off in a big circle, head and tail held high, and then 'humphing' returned to Solia. She charged him again and he moved off so fast that he went head-first into a tree which rather unbalanced him, but he went on to return again and again. Each time one or both females charged him, but eventually his persistence wore them down and all started to feed near one another.

The following day Godot was seen to mate Juno, but when I saw them later on they were feeding, and, while I watched, lay down to sleep side by side, with no signs of any more mating. Early on 5 July, 1986 our trackers reported that Godot had been fighting with Juno and that she had blood on her hind legs. By the time I caught up with the embattled couple, they were on the Top Plains and he was mating her. When he had finished she stood, head and ears drooping, while he, head up and ears pricked, shifted his weight sideways and lifted his right front leg so that it was crooked over her spine in a most comically relaxed fashion. When he finally dismounted she lifted her head and trumpeted but made no attempt to depart. During the next three quarters of an hour he mated her a further ten times. Sometimes he shifted his weight on to one hind leg and rubbed the inside of his thighs against the outside of hers, but then did the same with his weight on the other hind leg. At last he dismounted and they walked off slowly together out of my sight.

Godot was a highly active animal, covering every bit of the sanctuary in his travels and keeping company with all the females regularly, and he probably mated them all. On 17 August, 1987 he was with Rongai and Kelele, on the nineteenth he was with Juno all day, on the twentieth he was busy masturbating on his rock, and shortly after dawn on the twenty-first I saw him with Solia opposite the house. She was chasing him and he was beating a hasty retreat; however, he then turned and they stood horn to horn. His ears were pricked and he swayed his body rhythmically to and fro without moving his feet. Solia looked really wicked, her ears flat back, her nose wrinkled and her mouth open and snarling at him. After ten minutes of this rather uninviting behaviour on her part, Godot's nerve broke and he rushed off and totally demolished a small tree with vicious sideways swipes of his horn. Then he returned to Solia and they again stood horn to horn while she snorted savagely at him. Again after some ten minutes he could stand it no longer and broke off, but this time instead of killing another tree he cantered around Solia in a series of circles and figures of eight. Each time he changed direction he changed legs like a well-schooled horse, it was beautiful to watch.

After this lovely display he returned to Solia again but he had not impressed her - she looked and sounded more wicked than ever. His courage failed him and he backed off and wrecked another tree. Solia then moved out of my sight and Godot followed her. An hour and a half later when I had got dressed and found Orogai to come with me, we came upon the two rhinos lying up together half a mile further south but there was no further action that day.

Every day from 24-28 February, 1987 Godot was with Stumpy and her calf Bahati, a male then two years old. On the twenty-eighth I received a radio call that Godot was mating her; and as I was not very far off with Orogai, it was only minutes before we were perched on a rock half way up the slope of the North Valley with the three rhinos below us. Stumpy is a very small rhino and a gentle, nervous animal; in every respect, both physical and mental, she is the exact opposite of Solia. Godot was right on top of her, with his front legs hanging down over her shoulders and she was sagging visibly in all parts, back, head and ears. When he had an orgasm his tail shot up in the air and he shuddered and moaned, while she stood motionless. An anxious nose peering out from a nearby bush was all that was visible of Bahati. When Godot finished he moved his body back slightly, withdrew his penis and then stood there, right front leg hanging down over her ribs, left front leg curved over her spine so that the underside of his foot was towards me, and his chin resting on the hump of her shoulders. He looked exceedingly pleased with himself.

Shortly afterwards Stumpy urinated and by pressing his chin more heavily on to her shoulders, Godot somehow or other managed to scrape it with his hind feet. Stumpy sagged even more noticeably. Eventually he dismounted and as soon as he had done so, turned and charged savagely at the unfortunate little female. They both circled at speed, snorting at each other and kicking up so much dust that for a few minutes neither was visible. When the dust settled they were standing side by side, but again Godot went for her and again they disappeared in a cloud of dust. He then emerged 'snort-breathing' and walked off up the valley, grabbing a few mouthfuls of grass as he went. Stumpy walked over to a pile of dung, defecated and urinated on it, scraping as she did so. She then went over to the bush under which her calf had retreated and he came out to join his mother. In the meantime, Godot had returned and was scraping away violently in Stumpy's dung heap, while she slowly walked off up the valley, Bahati at her heels. He was obviously very nervous of Godot who now followed close behind and moving thus they passed out of my sight.

On all subsequent occasions when Godot was seen to mate Stumpy, he was very rough with her. The day after the last mating he was captured to be translocated to Meru National Park. None of the matings took and Stumpy has not produced a calf by Godot.

After Godot's departure (and before the arrival of Osupat), the position of resident breeding male was taken by Kelele. He seems to have a very different temperament from Godot and to be much more solitary. This may be partly due to the fact that he is a lot younger and less experienced; he may also still be nervously expecting Godot to re-materialize and wallop him. The first indication we had that Kelele was approaching sexual maturity was in April 1987. Godot was with Stumpy and her calf Bahati in the East Valley when Rongai and Kelele arrived. Godot went up to

Rongai, and Stumpy and Bahati moved off with Kelele following and continually making flehmen. After walking about a kilometre, Kelele tried to mount Stumpy but she took exception to this and turned to chase him.

Kelele has never been seen with Solia but he is quite often with Juno, Stumpy, Shaba and his mother Rongai. While I was having breakfast on the morning of 20 May, 1989, seven rhinos became visible on the slope opposite the house - Rongai and Julali, Shaba and Jupiter, Juno and Juniper and Kelele. Juniper was only eleven months old and Juno was not showing any signs of being in season. Her vagina was not swollen nor did she spray, but that did not deter Kelele. He spent a lot of time sniffing under her tail and then making flehmen. When he first tried to mount her, he had his chin pressed against her rump and was scrabbling madly in the air with both front legs, but failing to reach her vagina with his penis. It was all I could do not to laugh, he was trying so hard and his efforts looked so ludicrous. He eventually mounted her with difficulty, only finally succeeding because Juno cooperated by moving so that he was facing downhill. He mated her twice, but each time it was only a matter of seconds. He has also been seen to mate Shaba but again only very briefly.

I do not think that any conclusions can yet be drawn about Kelele from these few observations, but some can certainly be drawn about Godot's sexual relationships. I have observed him with five different cows and have noted how very different his behaviour was with each of them. With Rongai he was definitely affectionate, with Juno indifferent, with Stumpy really rough and with Solia obviously more than a little intimidated. He spent much less time with Shaba than with the others and I never saw them actually mate. He visited all five females regularly just as he visited every part of the sanctuary regularly, but it was Rongai whose company he clearly preferred, and he spent more time with her than with the other four put together. Juno, Rongai and Solia were all bigger than him, but neither Juno nor Rongai tried to dominate him whereas Solia, with her domineering personality and her incredibly long rapier thin horn, definitely had the whip hand. Godot might have liked to have treated her as he did the unfortunate little Stumpy, but he obviously did not dare to. Instead he vented his wrath and frustration on the nearby vegetation.

If a dominant male can treat five different females in such very different ways, this is surely an indication of the complexity of the rhino's social organisation and also of its highly individualistic behaviour.

Black rhino females and breeding

To ensure the right conditions for successful breeding, it is extremely important to understand the behavioural patterns of the females. Yet I could not even find accurate information about the rhino's gestation period; zoo records indicate anything from 15-18 months. In an effort to get more accurate information, I have been careful to keep precise records, only recording matings where penetration has been seen by either Francis or myself. Obviously these observations are limited to what our rhinos are doing in daylight hours, while what happens at night is a mystery to us all. Tracks may show that a male and a female have been together but not what they have been up to. Determining the gestation period is further complicated by the fact that the female rhino seems to come into season and to mate even when she is several months pregnant. From what we have seen, we believe the gestation period of the black rhino to be 16-17 months, we cannot yet be more precise.

We have usually found that it is virtually impossible to determine whether or not a female is pregnant until the very last days of her pregnancy. Since she comes into season even when pregnant, mating or lack of it gives no clue, and the sheer bulk of the female makes her unborn calf imperceptible - an adult female black rhino weighs 1500-2000 kg, a full-term calf 35 kg. This has serious implications, for the several unsuccessful births have shown that the capture and translocation of a pregnant female is so traumatic that she is very likely to miscarry. The stress of drought, too, seems to cause a female to abort or abandon her young. If we could determine when a rhino was pregnant, we might be able to avoid such disasters by not translocating pregnant females and by giving supplementary feeding during droughts.

We were also intrigued to see how our rhinos behave with their young. Different species of animals have totally different patterns of behaviour as regards their offspring. Many antelopes hide their newborn calves in the grass or in bushes, returning only once or twice during each twenty-four hours to suckle them. The young stay hidden and motionless; and as they have virtually no scent, they are reasonably safe from predators until such time as they are old and strong enough to follow their mothers. Once I stumbled on a newborn eland and even though I had nearly put my foot on it, it remained motionless and virtually invisible in the long grass. I backed off, hoping my scent would not disturb the mother when she returned. Elephants, on the other hand, are intensely protective of their babies and never, ever leave them. I initially knew nothing of rhino behaviour, and there were so many questions to ask and so much to learn. Although we cannot yet answer any questions conclusively, the following descriptions at least give us some interesting information as a basis for further studies.

Rongai was released on 6 May, 1984 and on the evening of the 24 May we received a report that she had been seen with signs of fresh blood running down the insides of her hind legs. By the time we got the report it was nearly dark and we could do nothing. By mid-morning the next day Errada had located her lying up with Amboni and Kelele in some fairly thick scrub on a steep slope. Errada pushed me up a reasonably substantial tree and leaving me thus perched, disappeared. He then managed to place himself so that he could flick a pebble in front of Rongai's nose. She jumped up and turned round just as he had intended, presenting her rear for my inspection. Hanging down from my branch I could see that her vagina was very open and the pink mucous membrane within was clearly visible. Thick streaks of dark dried blood ran down the inside of her thighs. She had clearly aborted, due no doubt to the traumas of being captured and translocated - otherwise her health seemed quite normal. Waiting until all three rhinos had lain down again, Errada reappeared and helped me down from my perch.

Rongai was subsequently seen to mate with Godot, but, as seems to be normal with rhinos, there was never any visible sign that she was in calf, not even early on the morning of 29 January, 1986 when I saw her and Kelele together on the west side of the main valley. However, when I next saw her, at eleven o'clock that same morning, right beside her was a tiny and very wobbly calf and Kelele was some twenty metres away. We were watching from the top of the hill on the far side of the valley, so it was difficult to get a clear picture of what was happening, but Rongai appeared to give suck to the calf and then walked away from it in a large circle. The calf wailed a tiny bird-like cry and then staggered off into some shade. Rongai responded with a deep blowing sound that I had never heard a rhino make before and have never heard since.

For the next two days Rongai was always in the vicinity of the calf but very seldom actually with it. It cried much of the time and I was certain that something was terribly wrong but did not know what to do. On 2 February Rongai was not seen all day, nor was the calf heard. I was convinced that it was dead but we did not dare look for it until Rongai had been located. Early the next morning it was reported that she was up on Fumbi with Godot, Amboni and Kelele. We went in search of the calf at once, and found the pathetic-looking little thing lying dead under a bush. It was a tiny male, weighing only 22 kilos which was under the normal weight by a third. It was impossible to tell whether or not it had suckled.

Why had Rongai left it? Was the calf premature and she sensed that it did not stand a chance? If it was premature was that due to Rongai's system being upset by the previous abortion? Could I have done anything to save the calf? I have asked all these questions of myself and of anyone whom I thought might know the answers, but sadly none were forthcoming.

Kelele returned to his mother and for the next two years the two were together the whole time. In 1987 the sanctuary was stricken by drought, which reached a heart-breaking climax in February 1988 when a great many animals of many species died. Many of the animals that were still alive were pitifully thin. The rhinos were suffering, but to a lesser extent. On 16 February Rongai and Kelele were together as usual. That night Rongai calved. The next morning she was with the calf, which looked well and strong and was not crying - Kelele was not in the vicinity. We left some lucerne nearby, hoping that Rongai would find it before anyone else did. It seemed impossible that during such a severe drought she would be able to produce milk but, thankfully, she somehow managed to. During those first days she never left her calf, and we never once heard it cry. By the 19 February it was so strong that it was able to bounce all around its mother, although sometimes, slightly out of control, it would collide head-on with her hind leg. Sometime later we were able to determine that it was a female and we named her Julali, the Swahili for 'drought'.

Rongai was a wonderful mother and was giving her all for her calf. As Julali got fatter and bouncier, Rongai got thinner, despite our efforts to get a small ration of lucerne to her daily. Thankfully we received a small rain in March and another in April. It was not a lot, but enough to save the situation, for both the vegetation and the remaining animals recovered.

Juno's reproductive mechanism, like Rongai's, suffered from translocation. On 21 September I saw her sleeping calmly at noon. Late that afternoon I was called on the radio; she had calved. This was the first calf born in the sanctuary and we were all tremendously excited. We rushed over and managed to get within sight of Juno from the other side of the North Valley. She was lying down, and a tiny calf was just visible beside her. Ten minutes later it struggled up to a sitting position, its pearly grey skin looking almost transparent and its ears enormous. It staggered up and, moving along its mother's body to her head, pressed its nose first into her ear and then into her eye. It then managed to get astride her outstretched front leg and sat there. Later it fell off her leg and when Juno got up, we could see the afterbirth hanging out of her. She put her horn under the calf's stomach to help it to its feet and it disappeared under her belly. We all hoped it was nursing. The calf then lay down again and Juno defecated, scraping both her dung and the dangling part of the afterbirth with her hind feet. It was nearly dark by then so we left.

We went back early next morning and found Juno browsing on the opposite side of the valley, with the afterbirth still dragging behind her. There was no sign of the calf. Through my field glasses I could see her teats and they appeared tiny. If Juno had been a horse, the still attached afterbirth would have been a pretty major crisis, for mares die very quickly if they cannot get rid of it. With cattle it is not so serious. How was it with rhinos? I had no idea, but I was worried as Juno was obviously troubled by the huge burden dragging around behind her.

While watching, I heard the calf start to cry and was able to locate its position - it continued to cry for the whole of that day.

Meanwhile, Juno, while never very near it, was never far away. I was increasingly and frantically worried. Mid-morning the next day the Wildlife Department arrived in full force by helicopter. It was decided that I should take the calf and try to hand raise it, as it was evident that Juno had no milk. Apparently she should have eaten the afterbirth to stimulate milk production, but she obviously could not reach while it still dragged behind her. So we decided that if by the following day the situation had not improved, Dieter would have to dart her and deal with it himself. Luckily she was saved that additional traumas as she rid herself of the afterbirth that night.

In the meantime, the calf had been placed on my lap and we were driven home. She was pathetically weak and cold, but tried very hard to respond to me. I managed to get her to take a little of the milk mixture that Dieter prepared for her, and by wrapping blankets and hot water bottles around both of us I tried to give her warmth and comfort. In the early hours of the morning she died in my arms and I blamed myself bitterly for her death.

The trouble that Juno had with the calf and the afterbirth must have damaged her far more than any of us realized, for although she came back into season almost immediately she did not produce a calf. We almost gave up hope that she would ever breed again. Nearly four years later, on 24 June, 1988, Juno was up on Fumbi. The next day she disappeared and for the next four days we had no idea where she was. We could not even find her tracks leading to water. Had she died? I consoled myself that as there were no vultures flying around, she was presumably still alive.

At eight o'clock in the morning on 29 June Lesile called me over the radio to say that he had located Juno and that she had a calf with her. I rushed over to see. The calf was tiny but seemed full of bounce and we judged it to be already two or three days old. We watched it suckle and then follow close behind her when she moved off. For five days and nights Juno did not go for water; but for the next week her tracks revealed that she went down to the river each night, leaving the calf behind. We could usually see where she had parked it and I wondered how she told it to stay put. After a week the calf began following her to water.

As Juno favoured open and high ground, it was reasonably easy to observe her and her offspring and it was a constant delight to me to watch the calf play. It would bounce and rub round its mother's body and jump over her legs when she was lying down and she would gently and affectionately nudge it with her nose. None of us ever saw the calf more than a few metres away from its mother and none of us ever heard it cry. This relieved us greatly, for we had learned that a wailing calf was a calf in trouble. I named it Juniper, and Juniper remained 'it' to us for nearly a year, after which we were finally delighted to discover that she was female.

Solia, like Juno, was pregnant when she arrived, and she was the second of our rhinos to calve. She gave birth on the afternoon of 15 February, 1985, near the north fence. That evening I stood on the opposite side of the valley and watched through my field glasses. The calf was just visible in the long grass. It was, however, highly audible, giving little bird-like cries. There was no sign of an afterbirth anywhere and Solia was feeding and moving steadily away from the calf, taking no notice whatsoever of its cries. As dusk came down she was quite a long way from it. That night I slept at the holding boma on the roof of my Land Rover as Womba was there, and Solia wandered around us all night. She never again went anywhere near her baby, and from the look of her teats she had no milk. Presumably her instinct told her that she could not raise her calf and therefore she left it. Her behaviour, unlike Juno's, was so decisive that we were left in no doubt as to what had and would happen. I either had to leave the calf to die or attempt to hand-raise it - I opted for the latter. This calf was Samia.

Solia was obviously in better health than Juno had been, for within five weeks she was in season and mated by Godot. She was seen to be mated again on 11 April and 2 May. We do not know which mating was responsible, but on 9 March, 1988 Solia produced the lovely little female calf Zaria, and this time she proved to be an excellent mother.

Stumpy was also in calf when she arrived on 10 August, 1984. That year was the year of the dreadful drought and of all our rhinos Stumpy was in the worst condition by far. When on the morning of 22 March, 1985 I was told that she had calved, I received the news with more dismay than joy. Rongai had already aborted; Juno had given birth to a calf that died almost immediately; and Solia had abandoned her calf which I was hand-raising. Samia was then five weeks old and it was a day and night performance to keep her alive. The prospect of another dead or abandoned calf appalled me.

Stumpy had calved in the North Valley in a very open area - she was clearly visible through the field glasses. When I arrived there she was lying down, but when she got up I was horrified to see the afterbirth hanging out. She looked most uncomfortable, repeatedly getting up and lying down again. At noon the afterbirth came away; she turned to sniff at it but did not appear to eat it. The calf disappeared between its dam's legs and we could only hope for the best.

Next morning Stumpy was in the same area and the calf with her. It looked strong and was close beside her and not crying which was a good sign. Two nights later Stumpy left the calf and went to the river to water. The next day I had a very good view of her and saw that her teats seemed big and swollen, despite she herself being so thin. Indeed Stumpy proved to be a wonderful mother and the calf throve. We called him Bahati, the Swahili word for 'luck'.

On the night of the 28 March the drought was broken by a heavy rain. I welcomed it with joy, but was also worried. Samia still had a hopelessly subnormal temperature and it was an unending battle to keep her warm. How was newly born Bahati going to survive the cold and wet? How I still do not know, but with his mother's care there was no problem. The next day when I saw them, Stumpy was browsing on the top of a steep bank with her calf near by. Bahati wandered a short distance away from his mother, then suddenly slipped in the mud and whooshed down the bank and out of sight. Three times he reappeared, trying frantically to scramble back up the bank, but each time he was defeated by a tree root and slithered down again out of sight. After the third descent Stumpy turned round, peered down at her son, then walked into the valley by an easier route and eventually, to my relief, reappeared with her calf following close at heel.

Four and a half years later, Bahati was still with his mother. Although Stumpy weaned him after three and a half years, the two were never seen apart before Bahati's death. This seems to be normal. Kelele was weaned before he and his mother arrived here, yet he stayed with her until the birth of Julali, by which time he must have been about nine. No animal stays with its mother for such a long time without a behavioural reason. As my hours of observation mounted, I became increasingly convinced that the reason for this very lengthy period of close attachment is because the young animal has to learn the patterns of social behaviour, for the structure of black rhino society is a great deal more complex than I had been led to believe.

Shaba, my favourite rhino, was the first to give birth to a calf conceived in the sanctuary; although, like most rhinos, she kept her condition so secret that it was only a week before the birth that we had a clue that she might be pregnant. On 21 May Errada and I had a really good close up look at her and noticed that her vagina was swollen, and Errada agreed that she might be in calf. I saw her on 25 May, but then she disappeared for two days without a trace. Three days later I was with Errada when we heard that she had been sighted in the main valley and that she had a calf with her. When we arrived at the opposite side of the valley we could see both of them. Rongai and Kelele were there, too, only about forty metres away. The calf got up and started rushing at its mother's head. She got up and stood facing us and the calf suckled first from one side and then from the other. It looked so strong and bouncy that we were sure it was at least two days old. Unlike Juno and Stumpy, she never left it behind when she watered; tiny as it was, its tracks were beside hers by the river. From the word 'go' it was always far more playful than Bahati and used to produce some lovely little bucks and jumps.

When Shaba lay down the calf played games with her legs, had battles with bushes and clumps of grass, and was always falling down and over things. He was one of the most determined little animals I have ever seen, and none of us had any doubts as regards his parentage; he was a miniature replica of Godot. Many times when I watched the way he treated Shaba, I was duly grateful that Samia had not such a riotous personality. Yet, however many times he fell down we never heard him cry and we never worried about his health. Shaba has been a most excellent mother and although her son Jupiter is now nearly as large as she is, they are still inseparable.

Despite all our observations, it is not at all obvious when a female rhino is in season, but there are certain pointers. When Godot was in residence and the dominant male, we noticed that when he defecated he always scraped first with his hind legs, then defecated and scraped again, scattering the dung madly. The female normally defecates without any preliminary scraping, then scrapes her dung just two or three times, but when in season she scrapes as wildly as Godot. As we have already seen she also sprays and urinates with far greater frequency than usual.

We know too that the set of the tail is another indicator. Normally the black rhino, male and female, carries its tail hanging down; and then when alarmed holds it straight up in the air. But when in season, the black rhino female will carry her tail cocked and her back may appear to be slightly arched over the loins in a way similar to that of a bitch in season. This arching was particularly marked in Shaba, probably because, being young, she normally has a very straight back. The older females all have very sagging backs, presumably as a result of having carried a succession of heavy calves each for many months.

In my experience the straightness or sag of the back is also the only way in which a rhino can be sexed if the sexual organs are not visible, although this is only indicative of the sex of older animals. The size of the horn, of the foot, or of the entire animal do not give any indication as to its sex. I believe that the size of the foot, for instance, may have more to do with the type of habitat in which the animal lives, but this is difficult to prove.

I have watched all our calves suckle their mothers many times and they obviously do so whenever they feel like it. If the calf is very young and nudges the mother when she is lying down, she may just draw her uppermost hind leg back to give it access to the teats, but normally she will get to her feet. A rhino cow has two teats and usually the calf will suckle from one to four minutes from one side and then go round and suckle from the other. When the calf is about two years old, it will have reached a size that requires it to lie down to suckle. The calves are always very gentle when sucking; there is none of the butting that you see with cattle and antelopes.

The calf starts nibbling grass when it is between a week and ten days old, when very young it eats mostly grass and small herbs, although this varies. By the age of six weeks Jupiter had already started to eat wild asparagus and some of the less thorny browse. It is amusing to watch a calf trying to imitate its mother when she is consuming acacia branches, thorns and all. It is also always painfully obvious when the calf does not know how to cope with the thorns and its mouth is still very tender.

The white rhino male and mating behaviour

Judging from his behaviour in other respects, I suspect that the white rhino male is as individualistic in its breeding behaviour as the black male. But my experience has been limited for we have only one white rhino bull in the sanctuary; and although Makora has been with us since 1984, his three brides only came at the end of 1988.

Makora did not have too good a reception from his brides. The two larger females, Marembo and Sungari, behaved very aggressively towards him, which led us to suspect that they were already pregnant when they arrived. That left only little Gororika, the youngest, as a possible mate.

About four months after she arrived, on 16 April, 1989, I heard on the radio that Makora was mating Gororika. I was slightly surprised, for the previous day she had shown no sign of being in season, and Makora had spent most of the day several kilometres from the cows, in the immediate vicinity of my house. By the time I arrived on the scene some twenty minutes later there was no action; all four rhinos were just standing around. Then one by one they lay down. A quarter of an hour went by in this leisurely fashion, until Makora got up and went over to Gororika, rested his nose on her rump and made flehmen. This obvious sign of sexual interest seemed to annoy Marembo, for she got to her feet and went for Makora with her ears laid flat against her head, her nose wrinkled and her lips drawn back, making snarling noises. Makora backed off hurriedly and then stood flicking his ears to and fro. Soon both he and Marembo lay down again.

At midday I had just broken some eggs in the pan for lunch, when I was called over the radio. Leaving the eggs half-cooked, I rushed off once again to the scene of action. Makora was mounted on Gororika, and while I watched he managed to penetrate her. He remained aboard for half an hour during which time he had fourteen orgasms. Throughout Makora's lengthy performance, Gororika stood quietly with her head and ears drooping and with a very disinterested expression on her face. The moment he dismounted she lifted her head, pricked her ears and moved over to join the other two females. Makora ambled out of sight. The trackers reported that he mated her again in the evening. He also mated her a month later and again the next month, although none of us had seen any sign of Gororika being in season.

On 29 September the three white females were together as usual, but the following day only Gororika and Sungari were there, and Marembo was not seen. The next morning there was still no sign of her, but at three o'clock that afternoon I was called on the radio to be told that she had been sighted and that she had calved. I drove over and had a glimpse of the tiny newborn creature, with its oyster-grey satiny skin, staggering round Marembo's recumbent form. Our trackers named it N'juku, the Masai word for 'new arrival'.

When the calf was a week old Marembo met up briefly with Gororika and Sungari, but then moved apart again. She stayed on her own, her calf never more than a few metres away. At night she watered, and the tracks showed that N'juku was always with her; by day she lay up about a kilometre from the stream. She was clearly very protective of her calf and moved off at once if anything approached them, and to my surprise the calf always followed her closely to heel. I had read and been told that black rhino calves walk to heel, as they do, but that white rhino calves always walk ahead of their mothers. N'juku and Sungari's calf, Lari, only began to proceed their mothers when at least three months old.

7

Social Behaviour and Communication

Can it be that man is so locked in his own type of intelligence, an intelligence that is linked to a prehensile grasping hand giving him power over his environment, that he is unable to comprehend the intellectual life of a highly evolved creature from another domain?
Loren Eisley

Animal behaviour has always fascinated me. Some of the happiest hours of my life have been spent watching animals, bartering food and my time for information and understanding. Elephants, I have read and I believe, understand death and at least some dogs do too. For most animals, I suspect that the 'thought' process is different from ours, but I am convinced that animals do think, even if it is along very different planes. Animals live in an 'older' world and for most of them it is a world where scent and sound predominate and where sight is of less importance.

I also believe that when the human species developed the ability to speak and then, much later, invented the technique of writing, we became so totally adapted to these forms of communication and so obsessed by their possibilities, that we forgot there were other, older ways of exchanging information and, possibly, thoughts. But animals still use such methods and still find them adequate to hold their social structures together.

Before I moved to Ngare Sergoi, I believed what I was frequently told and had often read, that the white rhino was a gregarious animal and the black rhino very solitary. As our hours of observation mounted, I began to see for myself that the latter statement was not true. I also became increasingly certain that the black rhinos were communicating amongst themselves, although for a long time I could not work out how they did it.

George Schaller, an eminent animal behaviourist, defined territory as the area which an animal will defend from other members of its species. Within this definition, I do not think that any of our rhinos are territorial, certainly not the females. Godot possibly regarded the whole sanctuary as his territory, but not any particular part of it. A home range is an area which an animal normally uses but does not defend. Some of the female black rhinos seem to have a home range, others do not. None of them show any signs of aggression towards one another, unless they are in very close proximity and have small calves.

Whether or not a black rhino has a clearly defined home range it will always have 'houses', usually under trees and large shrubs, where it lies up during the heat of the day. Although they will at times lie up anywhere, all our rhinos have several regular 'houses', some shared by many rhinos, others used only by one or two. I have never seen an altercation ensue if one rhino found the 'house' it was heading for already occupied.

These 'houses' are never in the valleys but invariably on high ground where there is most likely to be a breeze, and we have noted that the rhino will normally lie up tail into the wind. We have also noticed that if the rhino is lying under a tree with a large horizontal branch, it invariably aligns itself with the branch in such a way that its shadow blends with the ridge of the spine, making the animal nearly invisible. I believe the sites are chosen for security, and with its tail to the wind and its ears pointing forward the rhino chooses the optimum position for making use of its ability to hear and to scent. If we know a rhino is in a given locality we can often find it by searching its 'houses', and conversely if we search the 'houses' and find no rhino we usually suspect that it has left the area. Of course a rhino sometimes makes a new 'house', and that will have us searching for a while. Unfortunately, while the use of such 'houses' makes it easy for us to find and observe them, it also makes it easy for poachers to find and kill them.

As already mentioned, I believe that rhinos, like dogs, use their droppings and urine to communicate amongst themselves, and that the piles of dung serve as information centres. All the black rhinos have special areas where they defecate and scrape their dung, but they do not invariably use them. Sometimes a rhino will go to another rhino's heap and just smell it; at other times he or

A rhino can spray with such force that its urine may reach three or four metres (Gerry Ellis)

she will add droppings and scrape the lot. As we have seen the female uses her droppings and her urine to inform other rhinos if she is in season. The way Godot covered up an in-heat female's droppings presumably told other males that she was his. I often saw him walking nose to the ground following the exact route a female had taken some time before. When a female in heat urinates and scrapes when there is a male with her, he will go to the urine, smell it and make flehmen, and then turn and scrape it with vigour, sending soil flying in all directions. Presumably the more often a female stops and scrapes, the easier it is for a male to follow her. A male scrapes more or less vigorously depending on whether he is dominant or not.

A calf will almost invariably defecate when and where its mother does. Sometimes the calf defecates at the same moment in a slightly different place; sometimes it waits until the mother has finished and then uses exactly the same spot. Two adults moving about together will also frequently synchronise their defecation, and I have read that elephants do likewise. The calf scrapes from instinct rather than by copying its mother, as I learned from Samia when she scraped the very first time she defecated. Since her first droppings were extremely loose, this made a fairly spectacular mess in the house. Some of my trackers have a different theory for the origin of scraping; they told me that it is because the elephant, whom the rhino respects, does not like to see any animal producing droppings resembling its own.

When we are expecting a new rhino in the holding boma, we go around and collect samples of droppings from all the other rhinos and place them in a row along one wall. When the animal is unloaded into the pen, one of the first things it does is to sniff at all these calling cards with great interest. We then collect samples of the new arrival's dung and put them around the sanctuary in various places to help to introduce the rhinos to one another before the newcomer is actually released, and it does seem to help reduce tension when the release takes place.

Rhinos also use body language resembling that of horses. Tail up means action of various sorts. Ears pricked mean interested and well-disposed. Ears flat back mean trouble. When the trouble is really serious, the nose is wrinkled, the lips drawn back and the mouth half opened. The nostrils and the ears are both more indicative of mood than are the eyes, which is what you might expect from an animal that lives primarily in a world of scents and sounds, rather than one of sights. This is a world difficult for us to understand, as sight is of such overwhelming importance for us. A glance at the dictionary will reveal what an incredible number of words there are to describe what we see, and how many fewer there are to describe sounds and hardly any at all to describe scents.

Poor eyesight is another reason for rhinos' eyes not being very expressive. Samia rolls her eyes when she is playing, and rolls them even more when she has knocked me down and I am remonstrating with her. She will then gambol around me, bucking and kicking, eyes rolling and mouth half open in what looks remarkably like a wicked grin, but she is just playing. When a rhino is really furious the eyes will be half-closed narrow slits.

Rhinos' social behaviour shows tremendous variation. Godot was far more socially active than Kelele is. Is that an individual variation, or will Kelele become more active as he grows older? I do not yet know the answer. For a female, the degree of sociability seems to depend almost entirely on whether or not she has a young calf, for then she becomes noticeably unsociable, having almost nothing to do with other rhinos. Shaba provides a good example. In a period of one month we noted that she was seen variously with Godot, Amboni, Morani, Solia and Juno - in fact, during that month we never saw her on her own - but since the birth of her calf, she has eschewed the company of all others until recently. However, in general black rhinos, although not truly gregarious, spend a good deal of time in one another's company, and meet with one another amicably. The following series of incidents, picked more or less at random from my notes, indicates both how interesting and how peaceful the normal interactions within a group of black rhinos are.

One day I was watching Kelele, Rongai and Amboni sleeping in the main valley. Rongai got up and wandered off, followed by Amboni, but Kelele continued to snooze. When he awoke he scrambled to his feet, looked frantically around and started to cry for his mother, who by this time was about half a kilometre away. She no doubt heard him but took no notice. Amboni, however, went back towards Kelele who rushed to greet him and they stood nose to nose for a while, then Amboni walked back to Rongai with Kelele following.

Another time I watched Amboni and Godot standing together nose to nose. The big dominant male gently pushed Amboni who took a step back, and then rubbed his head under Godot's throat. Godot then lay down and Amboni walked over to Juno who was lying under a tree about 25 m away. Juno heaved to her feet with a terrific snort and Amboni rushed back to Godot and the two stood nose to nose again. Once more Godot lay down and again Amboni advanced, but this time with greater caution. Juno stood looking at the younger male with her ears pricked but did nothing, and Amboni soon returned to Godot and lay down beside him, while the female backed once more into her bush.

Once Orogai and I were sitting on a hill watching two rhinos sleeping below us, hoping to be able to identify them. A herd of zebra was grazing peacefully nearby. Then Shaba appeared on the scene, walking towards them with Jupiter at heel. When she was about 15 m from the sleeping pair, she suddenly stopped, gave a terrific alarm snort and jumped backwards knocking her calf right over. From under her nose rose to view a very wobbly zebra foal, so newborn that its umbilical cord was still attached. The little zebra stood there, quite uncertain what to do. Meanwhile, with ears pricked, Shaba very cautiously stretched her nose out towards it and Jupiter - who had picked himself up - tip-toed over to inspect the baby.

On hearing Shaba's snort, the two sleeping rhinos had jumped to their feet and revealed themselves as Juno and Solia. With the utmost caution, they too advanced on the little zebra. It stood stock still, surrounded by rhinos, poking out its little muzzle first to one and then to another. Three years earlier, when I knew nothing about rhinos, I would have been convinced that the little creature would be massacred then and there. Now I knew better and watched happily and with interest. The zebra's mother suddenly realised that something was happening to her offspring. She detached herself from the nearby group, trotted into the middle of the circle of rhinos and trotted off again followed closely by her tiny foal.

The scene then became even more interesting with the arrival of Stumpy and Bahati. Orogai and I moved a short way down the hill in the other direction, but had not moved more than a few metres when Orogai signalled for me to get up a tree - and quickly. As soon as I was up I saw why, Godot was standing only metres away and with him were Rongai and Kelele. All our rhinos were within about fifty metres of one another and that included Makora, as we soon discovered when we started to extricate ourselves from the middle of them.

One morning we were watching Stumpy and Bahati sleeping together, when Godot walked up and pressed his nose against Stumpy's cheek. She took no notice so he put his large horn under her chin and hoisted up her head - she took the hint and got to her feet. He then walked around her, sniffed under her tail, made flehmen and, having assured himself that she was not in an interesting condition, strolled off, totally ignoring Bahati.

Whenever Stumpy and Shaba met, their calves would play, having mock fights. Although Jupiter is more than a year younger than Bahati, he makes up in determination what he lacks in size. Once Orogai and I were watching Stumpy and Bahati - walking across the plains. Some considerable distance behind them, Jupiter was trotting along with his nose on their trail while his mother Shaba brought up the rear. We had no idea that Juno and her month-old calf were also in the area until she suddenly emerged from a bush. She had let Stumpy and Bahati pass without protest, but confronted young Jupiter with a very angry snort. Jupiter got a serious shock, jumped backwards (which rhinos can do as well as forwards) and stood for a few second with his ears pricked forward and his nose stretched towards her. Then he wheeled around and cantered back to Shaba and they both turned and went away.

Since much of our rhino viewing has been from a discreet distance, beyond hearing range, most of what I have learnt of vocal communication I have learnt from Samia. But it took me a very long time to start learning, for the simple reason that I was not expecting her to try to communicate with me in any complex fashion and therefore did not notice it. Thus it was only later, when my ears were better attuned, that I became more aware of the vocal communications of the other rhinos.

Normally rhinos are rather quiet but they are also capable of making tremendous noises. When Godot and Wamba fought one night, one roared like a lion and the other trumpeted like an elephant - the sounds were most alarming. Rhinos also have several sorts of snorts. The anger snort is a long 'hummmmph' and usually accompanied by a change in facial expression. The alarm snort is short, like a sneeze. The startled "who the hell are you" snort is made with ears pricked forward in curiosity, but a cautious expression on the face and a slight wrinkling of the nostrils. I fear that it is meant to be as rude as it sounds, for that is the snort that Samia invariably makes when strangers come, something which does not please her much.

Fear of the unknown is expressed by a high-pitched 'wonk' sound. Even before I really knew what the sound meant, whenever Samia wonked I would respond automatically by becoming alert. I have heard other rhino calves make the same noise and seen the mothers quickly come to attention. Real terror is shown by a high-pitched scream. Samia used to make this noise regularly when she woke up to find herself surrounded by cattle. It was a sound that used to bring my heart into my throat and I would rush out to see what had happened to her. When in utter despair, Samia would wail unceasingly with a 'whaa whaaa whaaaa' noise. Thankfully she only really had occasion to do this once, when she was being flown to the Mara to meet the Pope.

Total contentment is expressed by a deep, resonant sound that comes from right down inside the chest, a kind of 'mmwonk' sound. I have only ever heard Samia make it - when she was young she used to make it when walking beside me when I held her bottle. Now she does it when she sees me bringing lucerne or horse nuts. If I am slow or stop to talk to someone, the sound becomes deeper and more resonant. Yet, however slow I am, she never tries to grab the food from me or push me about - she just goes on 'mmmwonking'.

The most common noise that all rhinos make is perhaps the most unlikely one, a squeak. It sounds like 'eeeak' but it has many variations. In the very early days when we had our first rhinos in the holding boma, I learnt that if I made the 'eeeak' noise, holding the last note steady, the rhino would respond and come to me. If, however, I raised the final note, the animal would stop and look around with varying degrees of anxiety. I thus realised that if the final note rises slightly, the noise means "who, or what, is that?". However, I now think it indicates curiosity rather than alarm, for since then I have often heard rhinos make this particular squeak while looking around in an interested rather than in an alarmed manner.

Samia produces the basic 'eeeak' in a wide variety of tones and intonations accompanied by different movements of the ears and nostrils. The combinations seem to convey a fairly wide range of feelings which frequently mystify me. There is one unmistakable 'eeeak' meaning "where are you?" which she used to make when we went out for walks and she lost me. If I did not respond she would make a stronger and higher pitched 'eeeak'. If I still did not reply and we were in an unfamiliar area, she would make a truly desperate high-pitched 'eeeak' which quite obviously meant "help, I'm lost". I have heard all the calves make this noise when they have lost sight or perhaps scent of their mothers. In fact, we have often only located a rhino after hearing this noise, which carries an incredible distance despite its small volume.

Rhinos also communicate by their breathing, but this is so subtle that I had been watching them for three and a half years, and raising Samia for two, before it dawned on me that breathing is a method of communication. I knew Samia had a particular way of breathing which she evinced whenever she came home, or when I was out walking and she heard, or scented, either me or the dogs. I recognised it as a greeting noise, reserved only for me. It is a very slight sound, yet it carries in a remarkable way. I can

Nose to nose, the rhinos communicate by their breathing patterns (Gerry Ellis)

hear it when she comes to the fence even if I am cooking in the kitchen or have the door closed.

Samia has a different way of breathing in answer to my call. Normally when she is out on her own I do not interfere, but there are occasions on which I need to call her and she always responds in this way. Again, it is a very small sound that carries a most remarkable distance. I think it means "I'm coming, I'm coming".

I became aware of two other sorts of breathing one evening when I was sitting in a favourite place on a rock above a little water hole. Samia was feeding about twenty metres away when a very large bull eland came down to drink. She both heard and scented him and with head raised and ears pricked she gazed intently in his direction. Then she ran to me and thrusting her nose into my face breathed hard in a series of short, strong, even breaths. She stopped to look back at the eland, then repeated the breathing again and yet again. I knew she was asking me "what is this, is it dangerous?" Using my intuition, I tried to reassure her by remaining calmly seated and breathing at her with long drawn-out breaths. It worked, for she at once appeared to be reassured, walking calmly off and starting to feed again. I had apparently successfully communicated to her that elands were not to be feared.

Since then I have become very attuned to this pattern of breathing and have heard many calves breathe in this way to their mothers when meeting other animals. If the mother is calm she will reply to the calf with a series of long drawn-out breaths, as I did. Perhaps I had registered this in my subconscious from earlier observations.

One evening soon after this episode, Juno was feeding on the opposite side of the valley from where I was walking with Samia and I decided to make an experiment. When Samia was engrossed in feeding, I slipped away quietly and hid myself. Shortly afterwards Samia looked up, realised I had moved and gave the "where are you?" squeak. I kept still and she repeated the noise. On the other side of the valley, Juno lifted her head and gave a very marked sequence of four breaths, "ho-hoo-hoo-hooo". Each time Samia squeaked, Juno made the same response, as if she were asking "who are you?" This was a totally different noise from the "who the hell are you?" snort. I had initiated Samia's first vocal communication with a wild rhino.

Another chance to experiment with rhino communication came at the end of the 1988 drought. Samia was safely locked up for the night and I was about to go to bed. It was a very dark night, with a light northerly breeze, and I walked out into the garden and stood beside a bush near the fence facing north. I think I sensed the presence of the rhino before I saw it and as he moved right up to the fence I realised it was Godot. I stood silently, he was only about three metres from me, just the other side of the fence, but I knew he could neither see nor smell me. Quietly I made the 'ho-hoo-hoo-hooo' breathing sequence. To my intense excitement he answered with an identical pattern of breathing. Twice I asked him "who are you?" and twice he replied. The third time I obviously should have said something else, for he put his tail in the air, gave an exasperated grunt and moved off to feed from the tree he had knocked down the previous night.

Since then, because my ears are now alert to it, I have heard this polite questioning noise many times. I am now so aware of the combination of breathing and body language that if I am watching rhinos together (and am close enough to see them well through my binoculars), and if they are standing nose to nose, when I see the tension lines of their nostrils I am sure, even though I cannot hear, that they are communicating by breathing.

Shortly after lunch one day, soon after the rains broke in 1988, there was a heavy rainstorm and I stood by the window facing north, watching the deluge with joy. Suddenly Samia came into sight, coming up from the Marula at a canter. She repeated three different sounds several times, always in the same order. First came the "where are you?" 'eeeak', followed by the breathing noise that meant "I'm coming" and then finally the squeal of joy, which I have only ever heard her give when it is raining and she can play in the mud. She had quite clearly said to me, "Where are you, I am coming. Please come and play in the mud." Not only had she produced a sentence but I had understood her. I rushed out to greet her, but with deep regret told her that I would not play with her. The only time she has ever played rough has been when it rains; the cool and the mud and her general excitement overcome her normal gentleness - and by this time she weighed nearly a ton.

The white rhino seem to be less vocal than the black. In fact the only noise I have heard Makora make is the greeting breathing. He makes the same greeting sound to me as he does to his cows, and it is identical to the greeting breathing that Samia makes. Makora also makes the same contact breathing with his cows as I have heard the black rhinos make.

The white rhino also seems to be more of a herd animal than the black. Most of the time our three white females are together, and Makora spends half his time with them. His behaviour has changed since their arrival in that he is spraying in a far more emphatic way than he ever did before and makes curious drag marks just after he has done so. When I first saw the marks I thought they were ordinary scrape marks such as the black rhinos make, but when I actually saw him make them I realised how different they were. I was driving along slowly when I came up behind Makora who was walking along a road by himself, going from side to side. He would stop and produce a tremendous spray backwards, then walk a few paces on dragging his hind feet and doing so with such force that he rooted up tufts of grass. Within a period of five minutes he sprayed seven times, shooting out small clouds of vapour with great velocity, and dragged each time. His distinctive toe drag marks can now be seen all along the roads in the sanctuary. As he sprays and drags when he is by himself, and not with any of his cows, the actions do not seem to be directly connected with mating. They seem to be territorial signs, either for the cows or, more likely, for any other male who might happen to come along.

In August 1989 a large sub-adult male white rhino spent a week in our holding boma. It did not take long for Makora to learn of his presence there and he was obviously outraged. He hung about the boma continually and made some very determined efforts to break into it. We were in no doubt either as to his intentions towards this younger and smaller male, or as to what would happen if Makora succeeded in getting at him. It astonished me that angry and upset as he clearly was, he was still gentle and responsive towards us and would even come towards me if I called him to try to get him away, although he would always go straight back again. Two months later he was still visiting the holding boma at regular intervals to check that no further outrages were being perpetrated against him.

More recently we have been considering a very important experiment - we want to find out whether it is possible to keep rhinos on Lewa Downs outside the sanctuary. Is our whole security operation good enough? Our idea is to make this experiment with a pair of white rhinos, which unlike the black can be owned privately, are less endangered and easier to keep tabs on as they prefer open ground. We could also experiment on de-horning them. To this end a pair of young white rhinos were purchased by a friend of Ian's and a benefactor of the sanctuary and placed in our holding bomas during the last week of November 1990. On 7 December the male broke out. Ian thought it was young enough not to provoke Makora, but I was somewhat fearful. However, there was nothing that could be done about it, as Ian was about to leave for Europe and Dieter was in Germany recovering from an operation. For three weeks all was well, until on Christmas day Makora came upon a dropping that the young male had scraped. He put his nose on the trail and followed him.

There had been shifta trouble in the north east that day and I had refused a lunch invitation and stayed on the sanctuary distributing Christmas bonuses. As Senanang and I came over the crest of a hill, we came upon Makora having the most terrifying battle with the new male. He was flinging him up into the air and then kneeling on him. Yelling at Makora to desist, I drove the Suzuki over some pretty rough ground and tried to ram him in the backside. But I kept on getting stuck on rocks and in holes and the rhinos kept moving out of reach in a running battle across a little gully. Eventually after about forty awful minutes, I managed to ram the car between them and to push the young one ahead with the bonnet. But he kept trying to turn round and whack it, while in the meantime Makora was having a go at the back. Luckily at that moment my frantic cries for help over the radio bore fruit and a driver appeared in the big Toyota and managed to drive Makora away, while I pushed the young rhino in the other direction.

The next day Dieter flew up from Nairobi and we managed to catch the young male. But alas he died on 28 December of a perforated stomach and heaven knows what other internal injuries. The Suzuki meanwhile could have been a lot more damaged were it not obvious that Makora knew well who I was and, although a bit annoyed at our interference, had no desire to cause us serious injury.

8

Samia's Diary

I love forms beyond my own and regret the borders between us.
Loren Eisley

The only justification for raising a wild animal is that it is done with the intention that it should at some stage be able to return to the wild and lead a natural life. Thus raising a wild animal is totally different from keeping a domestic animal. Domestic animals are kept for some human-oriented purpose, be it work, food or love and companionship. They are expected to fit into your way of living and can do so because, since they have been domesticated, they have been bred to do so. Wild animals by definition are not adaptable to human ways. Most raised from infancy may well be cute and cuddly when young but are disasters as pets when they mature, both for themselves and their owners. There are, of course, exceptions - occasionally an individual does adapt well to human ways or sometimes circumstances make it impossible to return an animal to its natural life. But by and large if you take on the responsibility of raising a wild animal, your goal must be to give it a natural life as soon as it is mature and ready.

Aiming for this goal requires the development of an entirely different attitude towards the young wild animal from that which you may have had towards any domestic animal. The wild animal must not be trained or disciplined to slot into your life. On the contrary, you have to use your intelligence and imagination to try to give it an upbringing as close as possible to that which it would have received from its own mother. In other words, you have to adapt your life to its, not vice versa.

The dumping of wild animals that have been kept as 'pets' back into the bush may satisfy the conscience of the owner, but it is likely to prove an unmitigated disaster for the unfortunate animal concerned. It is as brutal as dumping a pet dog on a public highway. An animal has to be prepared for independence by its surrogate mother to the very best of her - or his - ability. In Ghana I raised a great many orphaned animals, from mongooses to antelopes, monkeys and chimpanzees. So when I undertook to raise a newborn rhino I had no illusions at all as to what was involved. I realized that if I tried to hand-raise it, my life would not be my own for some time to come. Even so I had no real conception of the way my life would be altered by the advent of Samia.

Extracts from Samia's diary

1985

15 February
Between three and four o'clock in the afternoon Solia gave birth to a calf near the north fence and wandered away from it almost immediately. We could just see the long little ears poking above the grass and hear tiny bird-like mews. The mother wandered further and further away as dusk came down.

16 February
In the morning the calf was still alive and still crying, but Solia was feeding more than a kilometre away and taking no notice at all - she did not come near it all day. At five o'clock Ian, Francis and I took a bottle to it. We also took some of the mother's dung with which we hoped to disguise the scent of my hand when I touched the calf. I had filled the bottle with the formula given by Dieter for Juno's calf which we had attempted to save. This calf was female and she squeaked in fear and protest, but I got some milk down her and then crept away. That night a guard slept in a Land Rover parked about 100 metres away on the fence track to try to protect her from leopard or hyena. While I spent the night on my Land Rover beside the holding boma containing our newly caught wild rhino Womba, and Solia spent most of the night wandering around us. I could see that her teats were not swollen and had no sign of having milk.

17 February
Armed with Solia's very fresh dung, which she had deposited all around the Land Rover, I went and fed the calf at 6:30 am. She protested but not quite as violently as yesterday, mainly because she was colder and weaker. I fed her again at 11:30 am and at 2:30 pm. Solia was a long way off and giving no signs of returning, and at the after-

At two days old, Samia looked as though she might not survive.

noon feed the calf appeared weaker and was showing signs of dehydration. At 5:30 pm we decided that I should take her home. We wrapped her in a rug and she was placed on my lap in the back of the Land Rover. I tried to save her from the worst of the bumps as Francis drove us home very carefully; and from fear and desperation she turned to me for comfort as I held her.

Luckily I find it easy to love baby animals. You cannot pretend to them, for they sense it at once if you do not truly love them and, consequently, they cannot love you. Then when crises arise, as they surely will, they are much less likely to fight for their lives. However, when you do love them, you always have to remember that you are trying to give them their own lives. They are never yours to possess.

A stable was prepared with warm, dry grass for bedding and the calf was installed. She took some milk but was very cold and very weak. I wrapped us together in a blanket for the night but even so it was chilly and uncomfortable - and the mosquitoes were bad. At about midnight I decided it would be a lot warmer and more comfortable if I took her to bed with me - Karl was in Nairobi - but even in bed I could not get her warm despite blankets and hot water bottles. What worried me still more was her inability to shiver - a mammal's way of warming itself.

18 February
In the morning the calf produced a large puddle on the floor but her bowels still have not moved. Will it be constipation or diarrhoea I wonder? One or the other is almost inevitable, due to her having had no colostrum, which she would otherwise have received from her mother's first milk. The diet Dieter has given me is part skim-milk and part low-fat milk, with syrup and added vitamins. Rhino milk is low in fat and protein and high in lactose and certain trace minerals. I fed her five times during the day and she took the bottle without too much trouble. She is still very cold and dehydrated, and is not at all happy if I am out of her sight. However, although she is weak she is mobile.

I have named the calf Samia, a name concocted out of that of my beloved dog Sambo and that of her mother Solia. Karl returned and remained fairly calm at the thought of having to share his bedroom with a little rhino - luckily we have twin beds.

19 February
Her insides are still not working - she made a large puddle on the floor but that is all. I took her for a little walk in the evening. She hates being woken and fed in the middle of the night so I will not try that again.

20 February
She took all her feeds and produced a small, rather bad smelling dropping and scraped it. I took her for another tiny walk. She slept in the bed all night but is still terribly cold.

21 February
She seems a little stronger but is still cold and dehydrated, and looks very thin. She makes three different noises: a small squeak when she

follows me, a more desperate one if I leave her and a little 'huff-huff' if she gets stuck at the single step up into the house. The dogs are very gentle with her.

22 February
I am increasing her feeds so that she is now getting five of 900 cc each. She is very calm and affectionate. During supper, which we eat by the fire for her sake, she climbed on to my lap and then on to the table, causing a considerable crisis with the soup. She made a big mess during the night, her first proper output - Karl slept through this rather noisy event.

23 February
I took her for a slow walk down to the drift and she sat on my lap and crunched a blade of grass. She is taking her bottle well but is still thin and looks cold and dehydrated. There was a series of defecatory crises during the night.

24 February
I took her for another little walk and she nibbled the tiny acacia leaf I gave her. She is still taking her bottles well and clings to me trustingly, but her bowels are very loose and I am worried. The milk is never quite the same, even though we use the same cow and that cow is on a semi-starvation diet to cut down the richness of its milk. In the evening we got a message from Daphne Sheldrick. Daphne is the widow of the late David Sheldrick, famous warden of Tsavo East National Park. She is the first person who has ever succeeded in raising a very young orphan elephant and has also raised four orphan rhinos. She said that we must change the calf's diet completely and put her on Lactogen - Dieter agrees, especially as the zoo rhino calf whose diet I am using died. There were more crises during the night and Karl trod in one of them *en route* to the loo himself, which resulted in minor matrimonial complications.

25 February
I have increased Samia's bottles to 1200 cc each and we are trying to get the ingredients for Daphne's formula. She walked with me as far as the drift, and tried a taste of wild asparagus. A difficult night followed, with a lot of mess. Her diarrhoea is worse, like thick yellow custard, and smells foul. She is still really cold. I wonder if she will survive the diet change tomorrow.

28 February
I have changed over to Daphne's formula, adding Lectade for the diarrhoea. Dieter says we must not use antibiotics as they would destroy whatever good bacteria she has in her system – rhinos digest by bacterial fermentation in the large intestine. Her temperature is still low, only 35° C.

5 March
The course of Lectade finishes today and she is no better. I gave her one and a half tablets of Sulphaguanidine in the evening and am using boiled rice water to mix her formula.

6 March
She cut the middle tooth in her lower left jaw, but is terribly weak and has no appetite and her urine is yellow and bad-smelling. She had diarrhoea so badly and Karl was so upset that she and I slept in the bathroom. The mess I had to clean up in the morning was fairly spectacular. I dare not upset her by leaving her at all. I fear for her very much, but will not let her die.

7 March
Her temperature is up to 37°C and I think she is better. Daphne came up to see her.

9 March
Lots of yellow diarrhoea today. I have got her back in bed with me - Karl is sleeping in the office. She is very weak but wants to live and is trying very hard. However, I am very afraid she will not survive much longer.

11 March
Her tooth is nearly through. She seems a little stronger, and I am increasing her feed. I also had the idea of putting a rug on her, tied around the waist like a horse blanket. Thus warmed, she was installed in the dining room for the night. She made the most spectacular mess and scraped it all over the carpet and up the walls and rubbed her nose in it. By the time I had got her clean, the dog had rolled in the mess. By 6:30 am I had cleaned one rhino, one dog, the carpet, the walls - and was in tears. A bad day.

13 March
In my effort to stop her diarrhoea without using antibiotics, I am adding kaolin and rice water to her formula. She seems a little

stronger. I gave her a hose-down with warm water after her 2 pm feed and she loved it. She cut another tooth.

14 March
She is a little better. We walked to the drift and she played with grass and a leaf, gave two bucks and fell flat on her precious nose. When I sat down she came round behind me, and put both her front feet up on my shoulders.

18 March
She is much better, playful and bucking. I have moved her into the stable to sleep with her rug on for part of the day. I have to sit with her until she goes to sleep and then she is alright and does not move if I leave. I have learnt to differentiate between two of her cries: they sound rather similar but one means "I need you" and the other "I want you". Young as she is, I must leave her on her own some of the time and get her to be less stressed by my departures.

19 March
She seemed fine at her 6 am and 10 am feeds, but did not want her 2 pm bottle. She was very uneasy and kept scraping but nothing happened. She took her 6 pm and 10 pm bottles and produced a very evil smelling yellow diarrhoea again.

20 March
A visiting vet from Milwaukee Zoo said Samia was dehydrated and that I must increase both glucose and water. I am glad she is not constipated, for it is apparently very dangerous to give a rhino an enema as there is a flap of skin behind the anus. I discovered the flap when I took her temperature, you have to open it very gently with a finger and let the thermometer follow the finger, not just push it up as you would do with a dog or a horse.

21 March
She is much better and bucked and kicked and even tried to change legs when she cantered in circles, but made rather a mess of it. We walked a bit further than usual and spent the whole afternoon out.

29 March
I have had to keep her in as it has been raining. Her temperature is still not normal. She is fine as long as she can get into the sun and run around, but if she gets wet she goes straight down. As soon as we get

back from our walk at 6 pm, her rug goes on and stays on until 7 am by which time the sun is well up.

30 March
She has diarrhoea again. I think she got cold yesterday, so today, which has also been cool and rainy, I kept her in the house with her rug on.

1 April
She seems well and frisky again. We walked up to Top Plain where she ate some grass and green herbs and took her first mud wallow, which she loved.

12 April
I am increasing her food ration steadily, and she seems well and happy. She still has only two teeth but they are very sharp. She has got used to the stable and last night spent her first night in it. I can now recognize six distinct noises. 'Eeeak' means "where are you?" Another sort of 'eeeak' when waiting for her bottle means "please hurry". A loud 'eeeak' means "I'm lost". 'Huff-huff' means "I'm coming". A snort means "what's that?" and the funny little noise which she always makes when I put her rug on, means "you're troubling me".

15 April
She is two months old today. Her insides are more stable but her temperature regulating mechanism is not right yet. We are still not out of the woods.

21 April
She seems well and happy and has cut two front teeth and is eating a lot of grass. At lunch she heaved herself right up on to my lap and very nearly on to the table. She had her first shower for a week (it has been too cold to chance it) and really enjoyed it. She now also has a very wee front horn and I am getting rather bruised legs.

4 May
She is definitely getting stronger and more stroppy. I have started taking her over rough ground as she has to learn how to handle it and it also calms her down. Sambo is very good with her and she has learned to respect his growl and treats him with a lot more care than she treats me. Today she ate a little browse for the first time.

9 May
She galloped down the hill and had a terrible fall, scraping quite a bit of skin off her side. She stood and trembled but did not cry out, although she did want to sit on my lap instead of going exploring.

18 May
She put her nose in water for the first time, looked really surprised and rolled her eyes like mad. Her front horn is really through now and she has twelve teeth and digs up and eats small grass roots, soil and all.

25 May
I took her up the valley to where Rongai and Kelele were last night. Instead of trying to graze she went over to their tracks and did a lot of interested smelling and snorting. Then she came back to me, put her front feet on my leg, her nose close to my face and with ears pricked, produced a series of variations on the 'eeeak' theme which I have never heard before. I had little doubt that she was either asking or telling me about the strange scents and large footprints.

26 May
Her brakes are becoming more effective and she can now do some quick stops and sharp turns without falling over so much - although she is still incredibly clumsy with her big feet.

27 May
We encountered one of Morani's droppings. I knelt down and sniffed it and then scraped it with my feet in the hope that she would defecate on it, but instead she made a little chirping noise, rolled her eyes and ate some of it. Dieter says I must let her eat what she likes, for she knows better than I what she needs to get her intestinal bacteria right.

28 May
Today I was able to compare her droppings with those of Bahati. Although five weeks younger, his are already like a miniature replica of his mother's, whereas Samia's are still very loose and very smelly. She now has fresh cut grass and a little browse in her stable every night, but although she eats the grass she still does not know how to handle thorns. I blow on them and pretend to eat them but she is not deceived. She now has four different sorts of snort-snuffs: "I'm a little afraid"; "please love me"; "what is that?"; and "this is fun".

5 June
I had to go to Nairobi for the day and on my return she greeted me with great affection, but sniffed me all over and seemed none too pleased with the strange smell of traffic and exhaust fumes. When I sat down she scrambled up on my lap, stuck her nose in my ear and told me a long and complicated story which I did not really follow.

9 June
Samia was absolutely terrified when I sent for help to shoot a big cobra which I had found in the bantam house, and rushed off into the bush. I had to follow her and calm her down. Was this just fear of a loud noise or an inherited fear of guns? I have now decreased her feeds to three a day, but have increased the amount of each.

14 June
Samia went quite mad on our walk, spinning round in tight circles until she was so giddy that she fell over and then got up shaking her head. On the way home we met one of our trackers. Samia stopped, crinkled her nose and gave a perfect "who the hell are you?" snort. She is eating a lot of grass and also a good deal of cow, zebra and rhino dung. I have noticed that she has different sorts of ticks in different places, but Dieter says she must have some ticks in order to acquire all the necessary immunities. I therefore de-tick her but never remove them all.

17 June
I took her for a walk up the valley. She gets over rocks with more agility now and with fewer anxiety huffs. She played with and moved quite a fair-sized rock with her nose. She then trod on a dead branch which popped up and hit her and she made flehmen and chewed it. Coming back she raced up and down the road and raised a real dust storm.

18 June
We walked home in a drizzle - it was very light but enough to get Samia chilled. While we were walking she took the tips of my fingers between her lips and held them.

23 June
On a walk in the valley a bird suddenly erupted in a most startling fashion from just under our feet. Sambo, Samia and I each showed the response typical of our inheritance - carnivore, herbivore and primate. Sambo went into instant forward action, Samia leapt back-

wards and I, the curious primate, stood and stared. She is eating a lot of grass, flowers and herbs and is increasingly playful, her toys being bits of wood, rocks and, above all, my feet.

12 July
Samia is eating well and getting stronger and more riotous daily - while out walking we met a herd of cows and she fled in terror and had an awful fall down the hill. However, I am afraid that all her progress is going to be put at risk for an absurd publicity stunt. She has to go and meet the Pope - orders from on high. The Pope cannot come here; she must go to the Pope. I am not even permitted to go with her, for I am the wrong sex, colour and nationality.

15 July
Today she ate a little acacia on her own and without my encouragement. She had her lips pulled back and a really comic expression on her face as she tried to manipulate the thorns. I gave her a tiny bit of lucerne mixed with her grass at night and she loves it.

22 July
While out walking we met more cattle and this time Samia stayed to heel instead of flying, although she gave some very anxious huffs. She also had great fun at a mud hole, pawing at it with first one front foot and then the other and splattering mud all over her belly - she also got a great scoop of it on the end of her nose. She then managed to follow me up a very steep bank, making some frantic 'eeeaks'. She seems to rely on her hearing and not on her nose or eyes to find me. Daphne came to see her and says she is still very underweight for her age.

27 July
I gave her her lunch and supper bottles in the crate that has been made for her to travel in to meet the Pope. I also had her spend time in the small boma we have built for her with Kiptamoi, my gardener, who will accompany her (he is the right sex, colour and nationality). She does not appreciate being cooped up. Dieter came and gave her a trial dose of the tranquillizer Azaperone. Instead of calming her down it made her so upset that she went for him and then Francis and Kiptamoi in succession - clearly that drug will not do.

4 August
Samia knocked both the crate and the boma to bits. I had no idea how strong she is when she is upset - and how furious it makes me to

have to upset her and for such an idiotic reason. All this upset has made her insides loose again. She is now having to stay in her boma all day, except for her walk - it is like being in prison for her. She was, however, taken for a drive in her crate in the back of the Land Rover, but did not appreciate the outing much.

10 August

By this morning I was not only nerve-wracked but furiously angry. It was only last month that I really started to hope that Samia would pull through. Now for the past two weeks this ordeal with the Pope has been hanging over us. My orders from Nairobi have changed almost daily, with people flying up and down bearing sealed instructions, most of which contradict each other and none of which show much care for the welfare of the little rhino herself. Apart from being locked up at night and for a very few times during the day, she has only ever had minimal restrictions placed on her freedom. Now she is locked in a tiny boma almost all day and kept cooped up in a crate for hours. I am desperately afraid this may affect her behaviour as well as her health.

At 6 am this morning I fed her half a bottle. She was crated at 8 am and received the other half of her bottle in the crate. This was then loaded on to the back of David's pick-up and Kiptamoi and I sat in the back beside it, trying to calm Samia down. We managed to reach the Isiolo airstrip without mishap. Fiona Alexander, a friend of mine and one of Kenya's most experienced bush pilots, arrived with a plane, a photographer and the vet Paul Sayers. The plane looked far too small for the crate but somehow we managed to load it. Then Fiona, the photographer, Paul, Kiptamoi and I got in - a very tight fit. Samia wailed desperately and plunged to and fro in the crate, banging and bloodying her poor little nose. I tried to calm her, but she was so terrified my efforts were to no avail. Afterwards David told me that he stood on the runway with his heart in his mouth, unable to believe that the plane would ever get off the runway; and Fiona said that she had seldom been so worried as when Samia was crashing to and fro in case she shifted the balance of the plane. Luckily I was too afraid for Samia to realize there were any such serious dangers to the plane and all of us.

Fiona had to go a rather long way round to the Mara, as she did not think she could get the heavily loaded plane over the Mau Escarpment. However, we eventually reached Keekorok airstrip where we were met by Sam N'gethe of the Wildlife Department and his team and driven to the little boma that had been erected for Samia and her papal meeting. Orders were that I was to hand her over to

Samia on her way to meet the Pope, a reluctant star attraction.

Sam at this point and to fly back to Nairobi with Fiona. But Samia had got badly overheated and dehydrated and her insides were not working properly. It was suggested that she be given an enema, but because of the oddities of a rhino's back end this could be very dangerous and should be done only as a last resort. So Sam and Paul agreed that I should not leave until Samia had defecated.

I had carefully packed all her 'luggage', bringing food, milk, some of her favourite flowers, lucerne, bottles and sterilizing equipment but foolishly I had not thought to bring a bag of her dung with which to establish a loo. I stayed with her all afternoon and evening. She settled down well with Kiptamoi and ate and drank and urinated, but defecate she could not. The last plane for Nairobi left and I had to book myself into Keekorok for the night while Kiptamoi stayed with Samia.

11 August

I went back to Samia at dawn, but still nothing had happened. I felt frantic and told Sam that I was sure I could get her to defecate if I took her for a walk and found some rhino droppings and scraped in them, for then she would almost certainly do likewise. But he informed me sadly that there were very few rhino left in the Mara and none in the vicinity of Keekorok. I said I would try to make do with

zebra droppings if he would give me permission to take Samia for a walk and most considerately he agreed to this, warning me to keep on open grounds and near the roads, as there were lion about - so Samia and I set forth. At every pile of zebra droppings I got down on my hands and knees and sniffed it and scraped it. Very obligingly Samia copied me - but still nothing happened. I soon had a large convoy of minibusses following me with interest, but I was quite past caring what the occupants must have been thinking.
At last, after two hours of walking and scraping, Samia functioned. I gathered the proceeds up in a plastic bag and we returned to her boma where I established her loo. Then feeling a real traitor, I left her to Sam and Kiptamoi and flew to Nairobi and from there on home to worry about her.

17 August
I flew back to Nairobi and went directly to see Fiona. We sat in her office until we heard that the Pope was airborne and then immediately took off for the Mara. This time Dieter came with us and we traveled in a considerably larger plane with another pilot, Dick. When we landed we found Samia already crated in Sam's pick-up by the airstrip. Dieter gave her a small shot of Rompon which calmed her and the flight home was, thankfully, uneventful. She is very affectionate and very happy to be home. She has lost a lot of condition but otherwise does not seem to be seriously the worse for her adventures.

19 August
She got both front legs on the table up at the stable and broke her bottle. When I went to mix a new one, she stood on her hind legs, opened the catch on the small front gate with her prehensile upper lip and marched into the kitchen. She then opened the catch on the big front gate and let herself into the garden. Every time I bundled her out, she did it again until I blocked the gate with the Suzuki. On neither gate did she attempt to use force; she knew exactly what and where the latch was, from watching me or perhaps from scenting my hand on it.

24 August
Since her return she is much less independent. She gets really upset when I leave her and does not wander off on her own as she used to. Her blanket slipped in the night and she made an awful noise until I went out to her and dealt with it. At least I now know that she will tell me if anything is wrong. She has also learned to use me to rub off the flies that trouble her, with disastrous results to my balance.

26 September
Something frightened Samia in the middle of lunch she came galloping home screaming. I dashed out calling her and she rushed up to me, then calmed down quickly. I have no idea what scared her. She is now keeping herself warm at night without her rug and is drinking a lot of water in addition to her bottles.

29 September
We received Presidential orders that Samia is to be sent to the big annual agricultural show in Nairobi - tomorrow! I, of course, am once more *de trop* and Kiptamoi is to go with her.

30 September
This morning the Wildlife Department lorry arrived to take Samia to Nairobi, but by no stretch of the imagination could she fit into her old crate. Luckily Peter Jenkins came to take charge and went to the Wildlife Department at Mweiga to have another crate made, and also, at my request, to alert Paul Sayers to stand by should anything go wrong. At 10:30 pm the lorry returned with the newly made crate and Samia walked trustingly into it. By midnight the crate was loaded and roped down, and the lorry disappeared into the night - Samia's pitiful wails of woe becoming fainter until I could no longer hear them. Again feeling that I had betrayed her trust most terribly, I returned to the house.

6 October
The Wildlife Department lorry returned this morning, having been on the road all night - both Samia and Kiptamoi showed obvious delight in being back. Samia has been kept in a cage for five days and it has not improved her health. She has a cough and a drippy nose and all her beautiful bounce has gone. Kiptamoi has apparently been quite wonderful. He never left Samia and never let anyone else feed her, and as a result her insides have not been upset. He guarded her faithfully and protected her from being too molested by the crowds - I am so grateful to him.

8 October
Samia's cold and cough are better but she is still very lethargic and has lost lots of condition. Once again she does not want to wander off on her own as she should, and does not like to let me out of her sight. Before this episode I never restrained her except at night - from a few weeks old she started to make little solo expeditions which gradually got longer. Now she stays and cries by the garden gate which is

currently barricaded in a way that has, so far, defeated her attempts to open it.

28 October
I am now walking Samia between two and three hours a day, although this 'walking' includes much time spent eating. She had her first encounter with giraffe today. They were overwhelmed with curiosity at this odd combination of black dog, small rhino and me, and tiptoed round some thorn bushes to peer at us with their huge dark-lashed eyes wide open. However, they suddenly came within range of Samia's short-sighted eyes, and with a shattering snort of alarm she sought refuge between my legs and swept me clean off my feet. Then, as she could not get under me, she sat on top of me huffing and puffing her consternation.

3 November
Samia is still spending most of the day crying and trying to get into the garden. If there are any more of these publicity stunts it will be really difficult to get her to be independent. Francis has put a low voltage electric wire round the garden to keep her out.

7 November
Samia burnt her nose on the wire and was most upset, but went on to burn it several more times during the morning. In the afternoon she saw me fiddle with the adjustment. In the evening she got braver, and after about half an hour managed to get her front feet on a rock and unhook the wire with her horn. We repaired it. She unhooked it again - taking only five minutes this time. Half an hour later she unhooked it at once and we conceded that she had won that round.

18 November
Two giraffes came and peered at us on our walk and Sambo gave an alarm bark to which Samia responded instantly by giving her alarm snort and galloping over to me. There can be nothing instinctive about a rhino responding to the alarm bark of a domestic dog.

19 November
I have been trying to teach Samia to put her nose down and track me, with no success at all. Today I went and hid up the road. She called me several times and I did not answer. She stood on her hind legs and opened the gate; and although she could not get through it herself because of the barricade, she succeeded in letting the dogs out. They ran straight to me and she followed in hot pursuit. On another

occasion when Samia lost me on a walk, she went to Sambo, who had gone off on a private investigation, and prodded him in the rear with her horn until he gave up and came to me, with her following close behind. It is no longer possible to regard this animal as anything but highly intelligent.

22 November
I still have to be careful that Samia does not stay out in the rain, for although she can now shiver efficiently, she still gets chilled very easily. She is eating about 80% grass and 20% browse - this is a much higher proportion of grass than Bahati seems to eat.

25 November
Samia really loves the horse nuts and has developed a new very deep grunting noise which seems to mean "nuts, please". She is one of the very few young animals I have ever had who never pushes or demands food roughly. She stands by my side and asks for it. Even if I get delayed talking to someone, she just continues to ask, never pushes. She is never rough except in play or when afraid.

18 December
I still do not know how I differentiate between Samia's alarm snort and an ordinary sneeze, but I do and so do the dogs. Sambo in particular responds at once to her alarm signal, barking and looking and smelling all around. A young oryx came down to the house to visit and put Samia in a real panic. The longer I live with these rhinos, the more I realize that aggression and bad temper are not normal aspects of their behaviour, and that being nervous and highly strung are.

29 December
While on our walk, I went down a very steep bank and Sambo took a longer way round. Samia surveyed my descent with trepidation and then, for the first time, put her nose to the ground and followed Sambo's trail.

1986

2 January
Samia got very excited when we found a mudhole and started to dig in it like a dog, her eyes rolling and her two front legs working alternately like mad, sending mud flying on to her belly and sides and all over the place. She came bounding over to tell me what fun it was

and got me plastered. Then she went over to Sambo, trod on his tail and got nipped on the nose for her pain - there was more eye rolling and her feelings were clearly very hurt.

28 January
As Samia gets bigger and her balance improves, she also seems to be getting more gentle. She tries to avoid touching me with her horn and I am now much less bruised than I used to be. She is careful with Sambo - she seems to realize that he is getting old and frail. But today it rained and she went quite mad up on the Top Plain, knocking me over three times. The third time I batted her over the nose with a blade of grass and cursed her. She rolled her eyes and galloped in tight circles round and round my prostrate form until she was so giddy that she fell down with her legs splayed out in all directions.

15 February
Samia is one year old today. She now has over twelve variations on the 'eeeak' theme, but the meaning of many of these defeat me. I wish I could in some way record her ever-increasing variety of vocalizations and breathing patterns. Now I know that when she breathes heavily she is not out of breath but is telling me something, although stupidly I cannot understand. When she finds a good smell and rushes between it and me breathing in a very distinct fashion, what is it she is trying to tell me?

18 February
Samia is starting to spray around the stables which I think means she is marking it as the core area of her range. We walked up on to the Headquarters North Road and were returning back through the bush when I walked round a tree and virtually into Juno. I gave my very best alarm snort and set off as fast as I could. I do not know if Samia also saw (or smelt) Juno, but she responded at once and shot between my legs for protection, so that I suddenly found myself perched on her back. Terrified by this unexpected turn of events, she bolted under the nearest wait-a-bit thorn bush. I became wholly entangled and fell off my charger, parting company with both my spectacles and my teeth in the process. Samia then trod heavily on Sambo's long-suffering tail and he smartly turned and bit her on the nose. I groped around for spectacles and teeth, found both and then tried to calm both animals down and get them out and away. In the meantime, about twenty metres off, Juno was huffing and puffing

her perplexity at the goings on, but thankfully let us slip away without further ado.

As soon as we got home, I made tracks for the storeroom. Karl found me vodka bottle in hand and inquired why I needed such a strong drink at such an early hour. I told him of our encounter and his only query was why I had not dispatched Errada to look for my lost possessions. The idea of explaining to Errada what he had to search for in my execrable Swahili, was quite mind-boggling.

9 March
Samia is getting really agile and did some lovely half and full voltes without falling over. While she was eating her horse nuts, I walked away to look at something and she made the most incredible trumpeting noise, a sound she has never made before. She was, apparently, expressing her frustration at being torn between the nuts and following me, for as soon as I came back she stopped trumpeting and went on eating.

31 March
Godot roared from across the valley, and Samia came tearing back to the house huffing her "I want to be comforted" huff. She stayed close to the house all day. I am sure Godot and Rongai and Kelele heard her, as all three stood looking towards the house with their ears pricked.

1 April
She is now eating a lot of browse but still very little acacia, unlike Bahati who eats very thorny things. I am certain he does so in imitation of his mother and I try to show Samia how to do it, but I am sure she detects that I am cheating. She is very perceptive, and apart from when it rains and she goes crazy, she is as conscious of my mood and as sympathetic to it as Sambo.

7 April
I climbed a tree to look at Juno at the waterhole some distance away. This totally disconcerted Samia who stood on her hind legs with her front legs on the tree trunk and made desperate efforts to heave herself up after me. I had to forsake my observations and return to earth. Later during the same walk, Samia and the dogs all disappeared. It did look funny when I called and three dogs and one rhino came galloping out of the bush abreast.

10 May
We walked across the Top Plain and on the way back I noticed Shaba walking along about twenty metres in front of us. I called Samia and she came to me full gallop, then, seeing Shaba, gave a terrific snort which the other rhino heard. Shaba stopped and snorted back, then trotted south for about forty metres with her tail up in the air. She then stopped again and watched while we ran home down the hill. Little rhinos are a lot more obedient than dogs. I think this holds true as a comparison between most wild animals and domestic ones, for in the wild the price of disobedience to your mother is often death.

19 May
Samia dug up some roots to eat, using her horn and her front feet alternately - digging with her horn to loosen the soil and then moving the loosened soil with her feet. Behaviour such as this is instinctive, for I have never tried to teach her that. Her whole range of behaviour is a most complex and fascinating combination of instinctive and learned or thought-out actions. No animal would stay with its parent as long as a rhino does if there were not a large range of learned behaviour and social interaction skills for it to acquire. This social interaction aspect of Samia's education is very difficult to deal with. For the present I have to teach her to fear other rhinos if we meet them, although I do not actually have to 'teach' her since she is immediately receptive to my fear. At the same time, she has to get used to them, for one day she will have to join them. The only way I can think to help her is to encourage her to defecate on their already established dung heaps, so that she gets accustomed to their smell and they to hers. Now every time we come across rhino droppings, she either eats them or defecates on them or does both.

31 May
I was sitting above the drift while Samia was feeding nearby when I heard a rhino coming around the corner. I was frozen with fear, for I was certain it was Godot. The big fig tree would have given me perfect shelter but I could never heave Samia and Sambo up it. As I was trying desperately to think what to do, the rhino hove into sight, revealing itself as Makora. Samia snorted what sounded like different breaths at him (what I later learned was the "who are you?" breathing pattern), but he merely glanced up, drank and moved on.

1 June
I tried using Trilk, a calf formula, instead of the much more expens-

Baby rhinos are suckled by their mothers for three years. For Samia this meant three years of bottles.

ive Lactogen which is designed for human infants. It was a disaster, just the one feed has given her terrible diarrhoea.

6 June
Samia has been off colour all week but is now back on Lactogen and skimmed milk and is well again. She spent a long time chewing on an old cow bone, perhaps to help cut her teeth or for the bone's mineral content.

11 June
For the first time since the near-disastrous Trilk experiment, Samia played. Daphne uses Trilk for her young rhinos without any problems, so Samia must still have a rather delicate digestion. Her temperature control mechanism is still not normal either.

1 July
On our walk this evening Samia smelt something that worried her very much. She made a large variety of moans, snuffs and 'eeeaks' and stayed very close to me. Sambo was not very happy either - leopard perhaps? The walk then became rather hectic, as there appeared to be rhinos in all directions. In her excitement Samia

knocked me down twice and sat on me once. Rongai and Kelele heard her and stood on the other side of the gully listening intently.

7 July
I climbed on a very high log and Samia got her front feet on to it and very nearly succeeded in climbing it too. Her tripartite pads can curve over rocks and logs and her toe nails can really dig down into the cracks. She also managed to get a front leg trapped in a crevice between two fallen branches. She had it in such a position that she could have easily broken it, but extricated herself cleverly and carefully. A horse would have panicked.

15 August
Samia is now eighteen months old and has at last started to put on weight. She looks good, eats well, is strong and very playful and affectionate. She is 120 cm at the shoulder, and her foot is 20 cm in diameter. She is going up and down steep, rocky slopes really agilely now and is starting to get to know what will be her home range. She has to learn all its dangers as well as its potential, hence we spend three to four hours in the bush every day.

25 September
She galloped home screaming and in a real panic and had to be calmed down and reassured. I do not know who or what she can have met. She now makes it very clear if she does not want to walk in the direction I am taking, but sometimes I refuse to indulge her because of having to avoid other rhinos.

1 October
I saw oxpeckers on Samia for the first time; she seemed a bit startled by their walking all over her hunting for insects.

9 October
Samia 'helped' Karl with some carpentry work, taking all the bits of wood he was trying to use in her mouth like a Labrador retriever and carting them off. Eventually Karl became vexed and I had to lock her up and then pacify her with some lucerne to atone for such an outrage. Hugh Lamprey joined us for our afternoon walk and Samia has never behaved so badly. If she was not jealous she certainly put on a very good show.

20 October
From the other side of the valley, Rongai and Kelele made the "who are you?" breathing pattern at Samia and she responded.

27 October
Samia opened the Suzuki's back door and very nearly succeeded in getting in. Her repeated efforts to take carriage exercise are not improving the appearance of my unfortunate car which is becoming more than a little battered. Later she followed me half way down a steep muddy slope, then tried to back up it. She had nearly reached the top when she lost her balance and slipped the whole way down finishing up draped around my neck. Luckily there was grass rather than rocks at the bottom, so neither of us was the worse for wear. In the evening, I went to retrieve the Suzuki which I had left up on the Top Plain and Samia followed me up there - then played madly around it, honking wildly, and eventually galloped home down the hill, keeping ahead of it all the way to the house.

12 November
She quite definitely responded to the alarm call of a bird the way I have seen her mother do. Would Samia respond to the alarm call of, say, an Australian bird, I wonder?

18 November
The barricade has been strengthened. As fast as my labour force dug holes for the posts, she filled them in again by scraping the loose dirt back with her horn. She is using her horn a lot for lifting things, testing them and digging; although she has managed to break the tip during her attacks on the barricade. Luckily the men all thought it was funny, but eventually I had to take her for a very early walk to distract her, otherwise nothing would have been done. She looks fatter and generally well now, and is eating real thorny browse such as acacias and mayternis.

28 November
On our way home we saw Makora - I tried to by-pass him but he trotted after us. I hoped Samia would run for home while I tried to drive him off, but when I turned towards him she decided to charge him. So I had to run away with her beside me and Makora trotting behind. Luckily he gave up when we reached the bottom of the drift. How brave Samia is to try to take on a rhino at least sixteen times her own size.

Samia's gentleness and affection belie the rhino's reputation for ferocity.

30 November
We encountered Geri, the hand raised female warthog which Ian introduced into the sanctuary. Samia looked very shocked and huffed, but backed off when Geri stood her ground. When we got to a muddy slope Samia came tobogganing down in a sitting position like a dog, looking wholly absurd and obviously thinking it was the greatest fun. I am not sure whether the slide was accidental or intentional.

9 December
My horse got a fright during my early morning ride. She reared up, slipped and fell on me and as a result I was very lame. Samia stayed close to my side and was very gentle and would not play at all. She always seems to know when I am injured or suffering from malaria and responds accordingly.

10 December
I was away all day so Samia occupied herself by obliterating Karl's workbench. Later she got across a big log which she has never man-

aged before, and then had a wonderful mudhole digging operation - sending mud and water flying in all directions and rolling her eyes wickedly the whole while.

27 December
Her neck must have grown longer, for she can again open the gate through the barricade - today she let all the dogs out.

1987

4 January
Twice today Samia nearly succeeded in clambering on to the bonnet of my Suzuki - heaven help it when she gets bigger. It is starting to look all too much like a baby rhino's favourite toy. She now knows the difference in sound between the two Suzukis; she always comes when she hears my yellow one but takes no notice when I drive up in the blue one. In fact she looks really startled when I emerge from it. Later another car gave her a fright when we were up on the Top Plain and she rushed to me, trying to dive between my legs which is what she used to do when she was smaller. She is now 135 cm at the shoulder and her foot diameter is 23 cm. I took a real header but luckily my specks survived. She reacts totally differently to cars coming to the house and to those met with outside; the former she accepts with interest, the latter scare her.

18 January
Whenever she hears me go to feed the bantams, she comes and lies down just outside the fence and breathes at me. Her breathing on these occasions is much too irregular to be just a coincidence - I do not know how to begin to describe it. It is such a very small noise and yet it carries in an amazing fashion. But this afternoon, because I had someone here with a tape recorder, Samia was, of course, silent.

2 February
It is now several days since I forgot to put her lucerne in her stable at night, along with the grass and cut browse. But ever since that day she has gone inside to check up on her fodder before accepting her bottle prior to being locked up for the night.

23 February
I ran a small experiment, intentionally omitting the lucerne from her

night's fodder. She inspected the pile and then told me in no uncertain way that the lucerne was missing.

8 March
She sniffed with great interest at Shaba's tracks; I had not had to show her the trail. And judging from other tracks, Samia must also have been very close to Rongai and Kelele down in the Marula earlier today.

1 April
She broke the barricade again this evening, not really by force but just by leaning on it. As she never, under any circumstances, uses her strength against me, it is only when she does things like this that I realize what an incredibly powerful young animal she is. Later she looked highly offended when, after a mud roll, I refused to let her sit on my lap.

6 April
Samia can now scramble up the steep hill from the Marula much faster than I can, so today I grabbed hold of her tail and she gave me a pull. We came back early as it rained and she was outraged at our early return and rushed up and down outside the garden fence squealing for me to come and play. I now refuse to walk with her in the rain, it is too hazardous for both Sambo and me - but as long as it is dry, she is very careful not to hurt me. Once recently, while I was sitting on a rock with her beside me, Samia decided she wanted me to smack flies on her off side. She could easily have walked over my legs, but instead backed off and walked round me.

2 May
We had to come home early because Godot was nearby and as usual Samia did not appreciate having our walk curtailed. She has an excellent internal watch. I have raised enough animals to know that you can cut down a lot on the inevitable stress factor involved with hand-raising if you are fairly regular in your habits. Later Orogai saw Godot going towards the house. So at his suggestion I mixed a bucket of water with Samia's manure and tipped it over her to disguise my scent on her. She seemed to sense my uneasiness about Godot, for she stayed very close to me and made no attempt to play.

6 May
While walking up the hill to the Top Plain I decided to stop and push my shoulder-bag containing notebook, camera and so on under a

bush and retrieve it on the way back. Samia was following me but turned back, went to the bush and re-emerged with the strap in her mouth and, to my total and absolute amazement, brought the bag to me. I praised and petted her and she cavorted around in circles huffing and puffing and terribly pleased with herself while I could hardly believe the evidence of my own eyes. What will my little rhino teach me next?

21 May
I took Samia down to the Marula by the very steep path. She hesitated at first and cried a bit, but when I took no notice she managed it well. She licked various rocks, played in the pool and made a series of noises which, accompanied by her expression, sounded remarkably like complaints about the dryness of the vegetation. We have had very little rain during this so-called rainy season, not enough to do any good. Samia is now making a habit of stopping at the bottom of the steep hill on the way home and holding out her tail for me to grab for a helping heave up. I utilized her tail thus five or six times before she got the idea, but now she has caught on, she always offers me her help.

28 May
She followed the car when I went up to the East Gate, but stopped at the drift. She must have waited there and then heard it coming back down, for she came racing up to meet me. I had no idea she was going to be there and we nearly had a collision coming around the corner. I jammed on the brakes, covering her in dust, and she then thrust her whole head in through the window and blew excitedly at me. She can stop and turn in the most beautiful way and could make a top class polo pony look downright sluggish.

11 June
Juno has been seen just to the north of the house and I think Samia must have met her, for she came racing home in a state of great excitement. She pranced up and down the fence and told me a very long story which I suspect was about Juno. A few days ago, when Samia heard the noise Rongai and Godot were making about mating across the valley, she also came racing back home - this time for reassurance.

19 June
When I fed Samia and let her out in the morning she behaved as if afraid and disappeared back into the stable. A few minutes later I saw

Godot just below the garden fence; the wind was blowing directly from him to Samia. The boma she sleeps in is now having to be strengthened because of him, I hope it is strong enough to keep him out. Once more she delayed operations by filling all the post holes as soon as they were dug, and had to be locked up under protest. She ate the hose pipe yet again.

27 June

I climbed a tree (to look for rhinos) via a large 4 m dead branch that was propped against it. I tried to adjust the branch a little but it was too heavy for me to move, so I clambered up anyway. Samia reared up on her hind legs to try to join me, making a series of frantic 'eeeaks'. When I would not come down she started working on the branch and eventually got it away from the tree. She manoeuvred it between her forehead and her upper horn until she found the point of balance, then carried it off quite a fair distance until it got hitched up on a bush. I had to jump down.

2 July

We decided to vaccinate Samia against tetanus and I have been keeping the drug in the fridge as per instructions. However, I had not realized that it should be given a chance to warm up before being used. When Dieter injected Samia with the Tetonal it was so cold that she reacted very angrily.

12 July

I moved Samia into her new stable; it is at the end of the row and has her night boma attached. I hope the boma is strong enough to keep Godot out.

13 July

Samia smashed the door into the fodder room and got herself locked in. She ate the leather flap off my saddle and what else I do not know. Ian came and designed a rhino-proof barricade for the door which was completed by evening. He also sent a message to Dieter to stand by in case Samia develops colic, but she appears to be perfectly alright. I think rhinos are more sensible than horses about not giving themselves colic. She now seems quite warm in the mornings; at last she is big enough for her temperature control mechanism to be working effectively.

27 July

Orogai walked with us today as no one knew where Godot had got to

- and Samia was very naughty and chased him up a tree. She knows both him and Karl perfectly well and is very nice to both of them at the house, but does not agree to either of them walking with us. Fortunately she behaved beautifully for Prince Sadruddin who is a VIP in the World Wildlife Fund.

13 August
Some tourists wanted to photograph Samia having her evening bottle outside the stable and I foolishly agreed. Having had it, Samia then refused to go into her stable. I temporarily gave up trying to persuade her and went to have a bath, thinking I would bribe her in later. I was alone in the house, lying in the bath, when I heard the bedroom door quietly opened and yelled out, "who is that?" "Hoo-hoo-hoo", came the answer, "I'm coming, I'm coming", and Samia trotted into the bathroom and put her front feet on the edge of the tub. I think she would have come in on top of me if I had not got out at high speed. Needless to say, she had got the barricade down again and opened the garden gate and the bedroom door.

16 September
I am cutting Samia's milk down, but not the other supplements as it is terribly dry and she is on the thin side. There is food available, both grazing and bush, but the protein content is very low. Samia made it very clear that she wanted to go into the Marula but as there were buffalo there I insisted we go up the hill. She balanced quite a big log on the end of her nose and brought it to me. I accepted it with gratitude but still refused to be bribed into going into the Marula. So with a most reproachful sigh she lay down beside me for a good quarter of an hour. She then got up and put her horn under first one of my feet and then the other, lifting them up and putting them back down. When I still did not move she went round behind me and prodded me in the rear with her horn. She could not have made her views more clearly known had she the power of speech. I could not, alas, make her understand about buffalos being dangerous for me even if they did not bother her.

22 September
Samia was very happy because we could go into the Marula today. She decided to demonstrate her ever increasing strength by putting her horn under the log upon which I was sitting and lifting up both log and me with seemingly very little difficulty.

26 September
Samia espied some green leaves and, with a certain amount of hesitation, managed to clamber on to a rock from where she was just able to reach them. If I were not giving her plenty fodder she would be in real trouble with these drought conditions. She eats a lot of papyrus and wild date palm fronds but neither are of much food value. There is roughage in abundance but protein is in very short supply, almost all the animals are starting to get thin.

2 October
There was a major uproar in the middle of lunch, as Samia, having broken the barricade again, had got her horn stuck in the wire of the fence. Luckily I was able to lay my hands on the wire clippers and she understood and kept still while I freed her. In the afternoon I took her down to the Marula. She must have had a fright down there recently as she will no longer go on her own and shows great caution when she follows me. I wonder what it was. Today she was quite unnerved when the baboons had a noisy family dispute, but remained calm when a pair of kingfishers used her back as a perch.

13 October
Prince Bernhard of the Netherlands paid us a visit and to my relief Samia behaved perfectly. VIPs may be no more fragile than anyone else, but if they get tipped over by a little rhino it would be bound to make front page headlines and would not do the rhinos' reputation much good. She also behaved beautifully for some TV people who came to include her in a film they are making about poaching.

3 November
There is so little for Samia to eat in the bush that she spends much of her time standing by the garden gate complaining. She is losing weight, so I have increased her ration of horse nuts and lucerne and the gruel content of her bottle.

22 November
Samia somewhat unnerved me by gently lifting the British High Commissioner off his feet, but to my relief he took this demonstration of her affection the right way. She is far from affectionate with the little abandoned eland that I am trying to hand-raise. She refuses to have anything to do with it and snorts angrily at it and behaves as if she were very jealous. I dare not leave them together, which means the eland has to be locked up in the stable the whole time.

25 November
She found a nice big log and tipped it over and started to lick under it. Alas, the residents were not termites but black ants which swarmed up her face and bit her. To my astonishment, instead of rubbing her face against her legs to get rid of them, she picked up first one front leg and then the other and rubbed them down her face the way a dog or a cat would do. I do not know if this is natural behaviour for a rhino, or if she has copied my dogs.

30 November
We were charged by a very irate Geri who, I fear, has lost all her off-spring. Samia backed off from the warthog, who is a quarter her size, with some very startled grunts.

23 December
Samia bashed in the door of the little eland's stable - I am sure she did it out of jealousy. Later she did a very good balancing act with a log on her nose. I wonder if a rhino could be trained to handle timber the way Indian elephants do.

1988

19 January
I had some guests to lunch and Samia made a fearful uproar in the middle of it - why do crises always occur when we have guests? This time it was only Masikio the giraffe who had come to call. Samia calmed down as soon as I went out to her and when I walked close to him she followed to heel - this looks rather absurd since she is now so much bigger than me. Masikio peered down at us from his vast height with his huge, long-lashed eyes, quite unperturbed by the commotion he had caused.

22 January
Samia was out by herself all day and according to Orogai went a couple of kilometres to the north. She did not come back until nearly six in the evening, and when she did return, she came galloping down the hill to greet me. I was very relieved to see her home again.

3 February
Godot spent the night with us. He had another tree down and a go at the reinforcements around Samia's night boma. I was very thankful that the men had done their work so well and that everything held.

5 February
Samia went to the water tank to have a mud bath in the overflow. She then had great fun banging the lid up and down with her horn - that really takes some strength. It takes six men to lift it off and I cannot even shift it one centimetre. Rhinos really do enjoy making a noise when they find something good to bang about.

7 February
Godot nearly got into the night boma last night and I had to park the Suzuki outside. I do hope that he does not flatten it before the reinforcements arrive.

9 February
Again Samia was out all day, and I joined her in the afternoon. She urinated on a rock and I noticed that her urine was very thick, cream-coloured and strong smelling. She sucked it up with a rather revolted look on her face (with which I could only agree) and then made flehmen. I have noticed her do this several times and know there must be a reason for it, but cannot think what it might be. It probably concerns territory or sex.

15 February
Samia celebrated her third birthday by eating my hat which was not quite what I had in mind as a rhino birthday cake.

18 February
We finally had rain, albeit very little. Samia celebrated by going crazy and heaving boulders around with her nose, including the one I was sitting on. I wish I could devise some way to measure her heaving capacity, it must already be considerable.

22 February
Godot arrived at the house at 2 pm and Orogai reported that Samia was about a kilometre away to the northwest, near the buffalo boma. This was a potential crisis, for I am fairly certain that Godot will bash Samia up badly if they meet. So Orogai was installed in the poultry run behind my house to watch Godot's movements and report on them with his hand-held radio, while Francis drove me to look for Samia. When we found her, she trotted straight to me when I called and followed me to Francis' Toyota. I jumped in the back and called to her again and Francis drove off with Samia galloping behind. Orogai radioed to say that Godot was close to him and the bantams. Meanwhile, Samia galloped all the way home after the Toyota and I

got her safely locked up, virtually under Godot's nose. It was a close call.

26 February
Reports of the endless crises with Godot reached the Wildlife Department. So Dieter came up and surveyed the damage he has caused and agreed that it would not do. He said he would arrange to have Godot translocated. Sad as I am, I also feel very relieved, for sooner or later he is bound to cause a major catastrophe if he stays here.

5 March
We walked up to the Top Plain where Samia ate dried grass and twigs and zebra droppings. After our return she broke the barricade and once more opened the gate and got into the garden. She came to find me in the kitchen and got wedged in the dining room doorway. A rhino has a peculiarity of design - which is presumably due to its great weight - it cannot bend its spine the way most animals do, nor can it turn its head to look over its shoulder. Therefore if something behind it alarms it, it will do quite a remarkably quick jump around, reversing its direction. Under normal circumstances this causes no problem, but when Samia does it she can knock me over if I am standing beside her and do not move quickly. In the house it is a recipe for total disaster. Luckily she had the sense to stand still while I grabbed a gallon of cooking oil, poured it over her and then backed her out. If she had not had the sense to stand still until I came to the rescue, I think she would have pulled our little wooden house down over both our heads. She was then very good and followed me up to the stable and agreed to be closed in until I had her supper ready.

9 March
Samia's mother, Solia, calved today and I tried to tell Samia she had a sibling, but I suspect I did not succeed. On our walk I crossed the marsh in a new place and she followed me with the utmost caution, testing every step in the mud before putting her weight on it - whether she actually realises how much heavier she is than me I do not know. Zebra droppings are forming an appreciable part of her diet at present. I wonder if this is because zebra have a less efficient digestive system than, for instance, the eland, and so excrete more usable matter?

13 March
We have had three days of rain and it has sent Samia quite mad. With eyes rolling she tipped a huge boulder into the middle of the road

and there it will have to stay until someone comes along with the strength to move it. I cannot even begin to budge it.

27 March
I have had to keep Samia locked in for the past six days as Godot has been here the whole time. She resented it bitterly, and I spent as much time as possible sitting with her to keep her calm.

3 April
Dieter captured Godot who is now safely parked in the holding boma - so Samia is free again. I have started to wean her and cut lunch out today.

10 April
As part of the weaning process, Samia has to learn to stay out at night on her own. We have had fair rains hence the vegetation is good, and Godot is safely out of the way. So tonight is Samia's first night of freedom. I am 'sleeping' with the bedroom door open, clutching a hay rake and an electric cattle prod ready to go to her rescue should her wails of outrage change to genuine fear.

11 April
I went out at dawn and Samia gave me the most rapturous welcome. She does not seem to be cold or in any way physically affected by having spent the night out, although she spent the entire time wandering up and down the fence using the whole range of her very considerable vocabulary to voice her distress.

12 April
Samia wailed again during the night but only until about midnight. She must have gone off, and then come back just before dawn, and is none the worse for wear whatever adventures she may have had. I think I was more nerve-wracked than she this time.

13 April
Last night she did not complain at all but was very tired this morning.

14 April
Orogai reported that Samia was in the Marula last night, and so were both Juno and Kelele and the buffalos. We do not know if Samia actually met up with any of them, but their tracks were in the same place.

15 April
This morning Samia seemed really cold for the first time since she has been out at night. There is no doubt that she has been a bit stressed and has lost weight in this weaning process, but the browse is now good and I will not do anything unless she deteriorates further. On our walk she ate some dried skin off a long-dead eland and also chewed on a leg bone for some time. She then made the most determined efforts to get on my lap but this will not do - she must weigh over three quarters of a ton now!

21 April
Today Samia was totally weaned. There were loud complaints but I refused to weaken. I know Stumpy is still nursing Bahati but Samia must be independent before I go to Europe to put Karl, whose health has deteriorated badly, in a nursing home next month.

22 April
Good rains enabled Samia to have a wonderful time playing in the pools and mud. Mud and water flew in all directions accompanied by great eye rolling and some fairly persistent efforts to get me to join in. Her ears are cold and she has a drippy nose and looks thin but is happy and full of bounce, so I will not do anything about her sniffles.

2 May
More rain - the drift is a real river. I waded across and at first Samia screamed with fear but as I took no notice, she followed and then discovered that playing in the river is wonderful fun.

9 May
We walked up the valley and I sat on my favourite rock watching the kudu and then turned to see behind me a large rhino backside. My first thought was, "surely Samia can't have grown that big" - and then in the next second I realized the backside was Makora's. In the same moment I saw Samia, flanked by a dog on either side. This absurd trio was stalking the vast behind. I did not dare call out because I knew that all four - two rhinos and two dogs - would rush to me. Eventually the backside realized it was being stalked and Makora turned round, gazed at the crazy trio, snorted and walked off leaving them all looking a bit abashed and me vastly relieved.

14 May
I took Karl to Europe leaving Samia properly by herself for the first time since she was born.

4 June
I returned home and was told that Samia had not been near the house for at least two weeks. Orogai knew where she was lying up, about a kilometre southwest of the house, and we drove up to see her. We parked the car and walked to within about thirty metres of where she was lying. Very quietly I called her name - she gave two tremendous snorts and jumped to her feet. Then after hesitating for a few seconds, she came to me at full gallop, with ears pricked forward and making the greeting 'huff-huff'. As she reached me I crouched down and she jammed on her brakes and pressed her face into mine while I held her nose between my hands and gave her my greeting 'huff-huff'. She then proceeded to smell me all over, pressing her nose gently against me. When I got up she walked back to the car at my side and then galloped after it back to the house. For the rest of the day she stayed near the gate, calling me continually. In the evening we went for a walk and she stayed really close. It was not until dusk that she wandered off on her own again. She has lost quite a bit of weight in my absence but is obviously well. Orogai said she had met up with some of the female rhinos - Juno, Rongai and Shaba. I was delighted at the wonderful welcome she gave me.

5 June
Samia came home soon after dawn and called me. She was very affectionate and obviously pleased that I went straight out to her and petted her, for she responded with a variety of 'eeeaks' and much blowing in my face.

6 June
Today Samia did not come to the house until late afternoon and then came for a walk with me and the dogs. If she is anywhere near the house she comes home at full gallop as soon as she hears the dogs barking, as this precedes the excitement of our daily expedition. Today she followed me as usual, but then somcthing gave her a bad fright and she galloped off and then came galloping back again. She was badly upset and stayed close to me, trembling for nearly an hour before calming down. The dogs, however, were not upset by whatever it was.

10 September
Orogai reported that Samia had been in the Marula at dawn with Rongai and Julali, Stumpy and Bahati and Shaba and Jupiter. At 6:30 am she was opposite the house with Shaba and Jupiter. When they moved off to the south she came home to greet me.

4 October
On my evening walk I heard Samia's breathing greeting long before I saw her. She came trotting over to join me and the dogs and gave me a beautiful welcome. It is very dry again and she is looking thin, so once more I am giving her a little lucerne and horse nuts for I do not want her to be undersized. She is, I think, a little bit smaller than Bahati despite the fact that her mother is a good deal larger than his.

17 October
I was feeling depressed and Samia quite definitely reacted to my unhappy mood to the most astonishing extent, pressing against me and laying her head on my knee, not wanting to play at all. I am increasingly convinced that the power of telepathy is something much stronger in many animals than in us. The way in which Samia responds to my moods has happened too often for it to be coincidence.

4 November
I was hosing Samia and the car down together, when the former unexpectedly turned her head right towards me and I sprayed directly at her nose - but before the water touched her she clamped both nostrils tightly shut. I have never seen her do that before. I have seen hippos and camels do it, but few other animals can close their nostrils. In the hippo it would seem to be an adaption to living in water, in the camel to living in areas of sand storms. What would have caused a similar adaption in rhinos?

5 November
I spent the whole morning at a meeting where we discussed the pros and cons of de-horning our rhinos in view of the current shifta - a big gang has just massacred all the Meru Park rhinos. When Samia joined me down in the Marula I told her about the discussion. To my surprise she rolled her eyes wickedly and then proceeded to give me a lengthy demonstration of just what a little rhino can do with her horn if she really tries. Oh, to have had a video camera with me.

14 November
Samia had a good go at both the Suzuki and the barricade today and nearly demolished both. She had both front feet right up on the top post of the barricade and when she does that she now towers over me and looks enormous. She weighs over a ton.

Samia loves being hosed down, but has also been known to eat the hose.

1 December
While I was out walking I heard Samia's "welcome" breathing and turned. The wind was blowing directly from her to me so I knew she could not have scented me. When she came into view, moving along at a smart trot, I saw she had her nose down to the ground. This is the first time I have seen her track me.

4 December
At long last Samia has managed to open the rear door of the Suzuki. She has tried many times but only now is her horn long enough to succeed (it is 16 cm). Of course, she promptly removed the sack containing the horse's lucerne, standing on her hind legs to do so. I rewarded her with the lucerne but removed the sack from her possession.

10 December
In the late afternoon Samia came galloping home from the north. As she rounded the corner of the fence she started her greeting breathing. She rushed up to me in great excitement and then went on up the hill stopping twice to turn and 'eeeak' at me. I did not follow so she trotted back to me, put her head between my legs and did her very best to push me up the hill. I refused to be pushed. Why she wanted me up there I do not know.

12 December
There was something big in the Marula this afternoon. Whatever it was, was hidden in the papyrus and I did not see it; but Samia stood up three times, putting her front legs on my log, peering forward intently and towering over my head. I suspect that it was either a buffalo or another rhino, in either case I felt very safe with Samia there. Later when my dog Buffalo suddenly stopped and growled with all his long, shaggy hair on end, Samia came straight to me and stood in front of me in a very watchful manner. Nothing materialised, but again I felt very safe.

24 December
Samia broke the barricade and the lights on the Suzuki and tried very hard to join my small Christmas Eve party.

1989

1 January
Samia put her head right under water in her pool and then gave a huge hippo-like snort which sent the water up in a fountain. Perhaps the rhino's ability to close its nostrils is an adaption to an originally riverine environment? She still uses me as a fly swatter, and I always carry a paper or magazine with me to use as such. The friend to whom I pass on my copies of the 'New Scientist' has commented on their being somewhat bloody.

25 January
A camera crew came up to film a TV commercial starring Samia. Her behaviour was perfect - she walked between a tent and a vehicle as required and has very much earned her cheque which is a more than welcome contribution towards the running expenses of the sanctuary.

28 January
Samia's vagina seems very slightly swollen and she is spraying more than usual. Can she be coming into season for the first time already? Dieter inspected and said she could be.

8 February
I have had a new barricade made for visitors' cars. The two compartments are closed by very heavy metal pipes over six metres long. Samia found the point of balance on them and carefully removed all three, one at a time, poised on her nose.

9 February
Another TV crew arrived, this time to film Samia for the BBC, with Desmond Morris. She behaved beautifully, it was me who was nervous.

15 February
Samia is four years old today. She is big, in lovely condition and very beautiful.

28 February
I heard snorting last night. In the morning I examined Samia carefully and found she had a small cut, about 4 cm long and 3/4 cm deep, up beside her vagina. It does not seem to hurt her. Senanang said that Kelele's tracks were below the house in the gully, I wonder if Samia met him during the night?

12 April
My beloved Sambo was put down today at the age of eighteen years and four months. For the first time in nearly a year Samia spent the whole night at the front gate, and throughout the night I heard her gently calling to me. If she did not stay because she knew I was deeply upset, then it was a most remarkable coincidence. The evidence that she had been there all night was quite obvious, and was remarked upon by all my household staff.

13 April
Samia spent the whole day near the house and when I went for my evening walk she joined me. She stayed very close and made no attempt to play in the mud and water. I do not believe this was coincidence. She left after dusk.

15 May
Samia heard me and the dogs in the distance and followed us part way, then lost us. She then went and waited under one of my favourite trees. I saw her there on my return, and she gave me a lovely welcome. Although she is not very good at tracking, she does at least have a very good memory for all my favourite haunts.

During my life I have had dealings with many and varied animals, as varied in character as in species. Four of them have had outstanding personalities. In Ghana there was an Akun eagle owl called Heavenly Horace. He was a bird of charm, humour and intense curiosity who flatly refused to return to the wild. He was my friend for eight years, from the time he was brought to me as a fledgling until he died. The second was a chimpanzee called Berta. When she was sent to me by the Ghanaian Game Department she was almost dead with terror, pneumonia and diarrhoea. Raising her to the stage when she could join a group of young chimps to be rehabilitated to the wild was a real battle, but one of the most rewarding experiences I have ever had. Berta taught me so much in the seven months I had her. Then there was my dog, the beloved Sambo, who was my friend for eighteen years and who literally saved my life three times. Samia is without doubt the fourth outstanding animal personality in my life.

When I brought the newborn rhino calf home on that fateful day in 1985, I had no illusions as regards the time, worry and expense that would be involved in raising her. I wanted not only to give her her life but also a chance to live it freely within the 10,000 acres of the sanctuary. I wanted her to live as naturally as possible, not as an adjunct to my life but as part of the social structure formed by the other rhinos. I was not hoping for any reward other than the satisfaction of seeing her live and become self-supporting and independent.

She has, however, repaid me a thousandfold for all my troubles and anxiety. She has given me her love, her trust and her friendship. I have increasingly noticed that our roles are now changing. If something alarms her she no longer hides behind me but has a tendency to stand in front of me. She does not visit me daily, sometimes two or three days lapse between visits, but when she comes to the house she comes because she wants to, not because I

Samia is now completely independent, but visits the house regularly
(Gerry Ellis)

go in search of her and call her in. There is no higher reward for raising a wild animal than this.

For once we have had very good rains, and Samia is at last putting on a lot of condition and growing fast. On one of her recent evening visits she made a breathing pattern I did not understand. "No more horse nuts", I said stupidly. When she realized I did not understand, she spread her hind legs out and lowered her backside into the position she takes when I de-tick her tits and private parts. It was very obvious what she was asking me to do and needless to say I obliged. So I am still of some use.

A wholly unexpected bonus that she has given me is that by raising her and trying hard to understand her, I have also been given an insight into the intelligence, the gentleness and the methods of communication of her much misunderstood species. Despite her very poor eyesight and despite the fact that her manipulative ability is limited to her upper lip and horn, her intelligence, her ability to work out problems that have nothing whatsoever to do with instinctive behaviour, her sense of fun which goes beyond mere playfulness, and her extreme sensitivity to my moods, have all combined to make me deeply aware of what a remarkable animal the rhino is and how horribly maligned it has been by humans.

On 13 December, 1990 the event I had been fearing since she was very small occurred - she met the new breeding bull Osupat. She should of course have met him in the company of her mother who would have protected her if necessary and also helped to introduce her. Instead she had to manage on her own. I was told over the radio that they were both in the valley south of the house and fairly near to each other. When I arrived on the east side of the valley, they were on the west side and Samia was carefully stalking Osupat, ears pricked, step by cautious step. I watched with my heart in my mouth, but as she approached him he lay down - it was quite obvious that he did this on purpose. Very carefully she sniffed him and he got up. Terrified she shot off backwards. He turned his back to her and let her creep up again. Alas they were too far off for me to hear how they breathed at each other, but when I left them they were feeding side by side.

9

Life in the Sanctuary

Do not forget your brethren, nor the green wood from which you sprang. To do so is to invite disaster. Loren Eisley

Lewa Downs is an area of great natural beauty but too harsh to be described as pretty. It is an area of upland grass plains, dotted with thorn trees and bushes and divided by deep wooded valleys. In all directions the views are vast and are dominated by distant mountains. To the south is Mt. Kenya, glittering with the snows and glaciers that feed all our springs and rivers. During much of the day the peaks are hidden in cloud, but in the mornings and evenings the grand solitary mountain is a splendid sight. To the north, the land falls steeply down to the Samburu Reserve and the semi-desert that stretches to Ethiopia, its flatness broken by occasional mountains. To the northwest rise the ragged peaks of the Mathews Range, to the northeast is the great flat-topped mountain, Ololokwe. To the west several ranges of tree-clad hills run north down to the flat lands, to the east the Nyambenis do likewise. Wherever you look there are mountains and sky, an infinity of space.

Although not as arid as the Samburu lowlands, the climate here is dry. In a good year we may receive over 500 mm of rain; in another year none, or at least not enough to bring forth adequate plant growth. Such drought years bring disaster to both cattle and wild animals, and ranching is not easy. In 1984 the rains failed. Ian had to kill all his new-born calves - a heart-breaking job to any rancher. He would pass the house with the back of his pickup loaded with pathetic little bodies, and would drop one off for my dogs.

In 1985 there were good rains and although many of the cattle died of a viral pneumonia, the wild animals flourished. In 1987 the rains were scant and there was a major die-off of both cattle and wild animals. The kudu and eland got thinner and weaker and one by one disappeared. Zebra, still looking fat, dropped down dead; not only the Burchell's but also the more drought-resistant Grevy's. Warthogs faded from fat bustling little dynamos to listless near skeletons. Even the baboons lost the weaker members of their troops. Only the Grants gazelle and the giraffe seemed unaffected and the vultures flourished and so, to my surprise, did the bush-pigs which I came also to suspect of feeding on the plentiful carrion.

Because of the altitude we are seldom too hot, and certainly not when I recall Ghana. The days are usually warm and windy and are almost always sunny. The glare, the incessant wind and the dust sometimes drive me nearly crazy - but the nights are beautiful, cold, clear and still. It is a real desert climate. Often, after the generator has been turned off, I go out into the garden alone with the stars and the loveliness to listen to the night.

Sometimes the silence is broken by my unseen neighbours. Zebra come down to drink, making the characteristic noise that is between a bark and a bray. The baboons in the Marula have loud nightmares, no doubt amply justified as a leopard lives there too - when his strange rasping cough breaks the stillness, the whole world seems to wait and listen, for all other sounds suddenly cease. Occasionally I hear the spine-tingling roar of a distant lion. Loud snorts are common, for the rhino and the buffalo that make them come right up to the garden fence at night. Sometimes the dogs create an uproar and I wonder what they are hearing or smelling. Frequently, especially during full moon nights, I overhear on the radio that the alarm on the fence has gone off. Then I wait unhappily and worry. Is it shifta or merely two giraffe bulls having a *contretemps* over the top of the wire? Or a tortoise wandering along the fence line, touching the lowest wire with his shell? This last is not easy for the people on night duty to identify.

Life here is gloriously full of the unexpected. No two days are ever alike, no one day is predictable. Each morning I get up and wonder what crisis or adventure the day ahead will hold. Even the events that are a bit unnerving at the time can make me laugh later. One thing unknown here is boredom.

The rhinos themselves, the focus of the sanctuary, are an unending source of incident and interest. In the early days when we were house-building, Morani found that much of our equipment was to his liking. He was an animal of musical tendencies and delighted in the noise he could cause with his horn on our old Land Rover. He would give it a mighty wallop and then, with ears pricked and evident joy, would stand back to listen to the splendid reverberations.

In those early days I had my horses in the stables just above the house, where Samia later had her home. One night I awoke to the most alarming crashes coming from that direction. Fearing the worst, I grabbed sandals and a torch and ran in my nightgown to see what disaster had struck - but when I got to the stables all was quiet and the horses were both intact. I shone the torch around and the beam alighted on the horn and nose of a very large rhino. I was paralyzed with fear until I realized that it was Morani. Then I spoke to him gently and he gave me his greeting huff-huff. In the light of the morning I saw that the commotion had been caused by his playing drums on the cement mixer - it was newly designed with some very distinct dents. During the 1984 drought Morani spent much of his time close to the house. He wrecked two wheelbarrows and several buckets, and invariably chewed up halters and ropes when I forgot to hide them. He also consumed vast quantities of horse manure.

Neither Morani nor Makora like horses or donkeys, and Morani chased my little mare Topsy several times, not only when she was alone but also when she had me aboard. Far more frightening, though, was the ostrich hen with chicks who chased us every time she saw us. I had the fear of God put into me several times as Topsy hared off over appallingly rough, boulder-strewn ground with the wretched, long-legged fowl in hot pursuit. One memorable morning after she had chased us, Topsy and I then managed to have close encounters with not one or two or even three, but four rhinos. Returning home to breakfast somewhat shaken, I quite clearly heard my father's voice saying, "Well, you have been warned." The next day I asked Francis to build me another stable up by the East Gate. From there I could ride outside the sanctuary and, with luck, avoid encountering so many hazards.

The dogs, especially the large black hairy hound known as Buffalo, could sometimes be excessively foolish concerning rhinos. Once, up on the Top Plain, Buffalo took off at full speed after Juno, circled her twice at a gallop, and then came racing back to me. I watched with my heart in my throat, but although Juno looked very perplexed she made no attempt to retaliate. Had it been the irascible Godot, the incident could have had a more dramatic ending. On another occasion, Remus the little collie was chasing some yellow-necked spurfowl through long grass and ran right over what he might well have thought was a large rock. It was a recumbent rhino, but fortunately only the placid Morani who merely got up in a bit of a hurry and did not take umbrage. I had not realized he was there until he emerged. Rhinos can be both noisy and conspicuous when they wish, but also, like elephants, can move incredibly silently and can do the disappearing trick in a most uncanny fashion.

When we started the sanctuary, Peter Jenkins cheerfully remarked that we would probably have a few vehicles bashed up by the rhinos. So far we have been very fortunate. Neither Morani, Makora nor Samia have improved my Suzuki, but their jousting has all been in the nature of good fun, rather than malice aforethought. In fact, they are remarkably considerate of my little car.

Once, in a terrible hurry and driving far too fast, I came downhill round the sharp bend towards the drift only to meet Morani walking up towards me at the sharpest part of the corner. I jammed on the brakes and did a smart skid. I did not touch him, but I did cover the poor animal with dust and must have given him a bit of a fright. When the dust cleared, he was standing just in front of the bonnet. The only way I could extricate myself was by going forward first, which meant bumping Morani. I apologized to him and he calmly backed down the hill, so that I could straighten the car. Then I backed up the hill and out of his way.

My next encounter around the same corner was with Godot. This time the positions were reversed. He was coming downhill and I was going up slowly. We were not more than five metres apart when I saw him. I slammed into reverse and retreated as fast as I could. Godot gave a furious snort and took one jump towards me. Then, to my great relief, he thought better of it and turned away.

Both Makora and, more particularly, Morani took a great deal of interest in the generator which lives in a little cement-block house outside the garden enclosure. My household staff, Henry, Benjamin and Kiptamoi, take it in turns to switch the engine off every night. One night it did not go off as usual. I went on reading not thinking much about it until nearly midnight. Then I decided that I had better investigate as I did not want the engine to run all night. I went out of the garden gate and, walking towards the generator house, called out to ask why the engine had not been turned off. A very unhappy voice replied out of the darkness that the engine could not be got at because a rhino was blocking the doorway. Sure enough, the beam of my torch revealed Morani's large backside sticking out of the little hut.

By the end of June 1984 Karl had finished building our new home and we invited some of our neighbours to a house-warming party. I started getting things ready in the morning, but my cooking operations were badly disrupted by having to go and watch Godot mating Rongai - one rarely gets the opportunity to see rhinos at it. However, by eight o'clock all was prepared. The dogs were locked up, the front gate open and our guests started to arrive. I was handing drinks around when I noticed that quite a few cars were parked up on the road with their headlights still on. When I went out to investigate the cause of the hold-up, I found Morani standing in the middle of the open gateway looking hopeful. I shut the gate quickly in his face and he backed off. Then I re-opened it and our guests drove in, while Morani stood to one side looking reproachful.

On the whole human visitors are few. The Craigs' tourist camp, Wilderness Trails, has the capacity for sixteen people and another company, Ker and Downey, has camping rights on Lewa Downs - both bring their guests to the sanctuary. During the tourist months, mid-December to the end of March and mid-June to the end of September, we may have as many as four visiting vehicles a day. Other people only come by special arrangement with me or the Craigs.

However, many animals other than rhinos and cattle live in the sanctuary. All those that lived here before the fence was erected are still here - with the exception of the elephants which we intentionally fenced out, and the lion and spotted hyena which Ian tries to keep out. Wild animals have an extraordinary ability to get through any fence except chain link. If a leopard or lioness jumps through the fence without touching the ground *en route*, it will not get a shock. My attitude towards such predators is coloured by my experiences in Ghana and is therefore different from Ian's. With every conceivable justification, Ian does not appreciate it if predators eat too many of his cattle. Lions amongst

Grevy's Zebra

cattle are rather like foxes in hen houses, for at times they appear to go berserk and kill far more than they can eat. One night, lions killed sixteen cattle and ate only part of one. Marauding lions cause financial losses above and beyond the cattle they actually kill or even maim. Their attack on a boma terrifies the whole herd, so the cattle scatter to the four winds; it often takes several days and many man-hours to round them up again and in the meantime they will have lost much condition.

Once lions have learned how easy it is to kill domestic stock, which is so conveniently penned up at night, they will ignore the wild animals and ransack the bomas instead. In just one month in the middle of 1989, one pair of lions making the rounds of Lewa killed over sixty of Ian's cattle and several camels as well. No rancher can take this sort of loss, even a tolerant one such as Ian who appreciates that lions have to kill, and who is willing to 'give' them a cow now and then. Yet who are we to condemn the lions even for their occasional apparently wanton slaughter? We humans are guilty of far worse and lack the saving grace of necessity.

A lion's brain and body have evolved with the idea of killing and with the skill to kill. But they only kill out of necessity, because as carnivores they have to kill to live.

We humans have not evolved as such specialised killers; yet, driven by insatiable greed, we have developed killing techniques which both in scope and brutality surpass those of all the natural killers a thousand fold. Gone are the days of simple spears and arrows. We now mow down whole herds of elephant with machine guns, even mothers and calves, just to have their tusks to carve into wholly unnecessary ornaments. We massacre herds of zebra by driving them on to stretched-out blades of artfully concealed band-saws, so that the agonised animals, their legs sliced off, drop down by the score, just to supply the meat markets of large towns. Who are we to condemn lions as wanton killers?

It is not only the lions that cause crises. Both the spotted hyena and the leopard can also wreak havoc with domestic stock, generally sheep and goats. During my twenty years in Ghana I saw all these predators become virtually extinct. Leopards are not difficult to trap, and in Ghana they were caught regularly and, so that their valuable skins should not be spoiled, were killed by having red-hot metal rods thrust up their rectums. The agony they must have suffered before dying still haunts me. In Kenya, leopards which have become a 'nuisance' are also trapped. But since they are legally protected here, they are not killed but are translocated to safer places. Since neither sheep nor goats are kept in the sanctuary, many such trapped sheep-killers have been released here.

In August 1990 an unusually large male leopard which had been making a nuisance of himself up at the Mt. Kenya Safari Club, was translocated down here by the Wildlife Department - I was not consulted. One evening I was in my bedroom, three of the dogs were in the house and Caspar was on the verandah outside my door. Suddenly I heard him scream and rushed out, slipped, lost my footing and took a header. I must have landed virtually on top of the leopard, I never really saw him but I gave him such a shock that he dropped the unfortunate dog. Caspar lived through the night and survived the plane trip to Nairobi next morning, but died in the car on the way to the vet.

The leopard, fully aware that he had made a kill and regarding the poor dog as his property, returned next evening to search for his supper. The other dogs were under lock and key, but I managed to shine the torch in his face quite by accident - he made the most awful noises at me and gave me a terrible fright. He was just a few feet away and looked more the size of a lioness than a leopard. He then proceeded to terrorise me for the next few evenings and nights - I could hear him snarling on the verandah. Eventually, to my vast relief he left the sanctuary and went some miles to a village where it appears that to date he has consumed some thirty dogs and nine sheep and is far from popular.

Even though leopard are legally protected, this does not necessarily mean that their survival in other areas of Kenya is wholly ensured. If, as in West Africa, their wild prey is killed by man so that there is nothing left for them to eat but domestic stock; and if they are consequently snared, trapped and poisoned with the consummate skill and relentless purpose that the West Africans bring to the task, then the leopard might become extinct here too, and it could happen in a frighteningly short space of time.

We had some spotted hyenas in the sanctuary who were killing calves. I used to love hearing them howl at night but I knew they were doomed. Ian tried and failed for many nights to shoot them. Sadly he told me that the only alternative was to poison them, by poisoning the carcass of a calf which they had killed and to which they were likely to return. I knew he hated to do this and that it really was a last resort. He promised that his head tracker would follow up and remove any poisoned hyena so that their corpses would not in turn poison the vultures or other carrion eaters. I heard him issue instructions that the corpse when recovered should be dumped down his brother William's old long-drop (an outside lavatory consisting of a seat over a twenty foot hole). William at that moment was in London getting married and would shortly be returning with his young and beautiful bride, and a new long-drop had already been dug.

Several days later I heard that a hyena had taken the poisoned bait and disappeared, presumably to die, but that no one could find its body. A few evenings later I was tracking Godot with Shambaini at the bottom of the main valley. We crossed the stream and there, very well concealed in the middle of the stream, was the horribly bloated body of the culprit hyena. I had no idea what poison Ian had used but the body, which looked as though it would burst that very night, was certainly a hazard to man and beast. Some of our guards were living in a small camp downstream, and the rhinos and many other animals drank from the stream. I felt something had to be done, and there was not much time to do it as dusk was starting to fall. Together Shambaini and I lugged that dead hyena up the very steep bush-covered hill, heaved it into the car and then drove off in search of the correct long-drop. The thought of the reaction if the hyena went down the wrong hole was most unnerving.

Cheetah come and go in the sanctuary, for the fence is no great barrier to cats. Although the spaces between the wires look small, even the big cats can leap through them. At the time of writing we have a pair of these lovely, long-legged cats. I sometimes see them and when I do it always brings a great joy to my day. Recently I was driving up towards the East Gate with Remus racing in front of the Suzuki. Suddenly a cheetah jumped out of the long grass on to the road just ahead of him. Remus slammed on his brakes and so did I. The cheetah hesitated and then continued loping on its way. While Remus and I were still recovering our wits, a second cheetah arrived in the middle of the road, and again looked at us and departed. When I related this to Senanang the next morning, he remarked that it was lucky for Remus that it had been cheetah and not leopard, as leopard have a notorious liking for dog meat.

Alas, the cheetah began killing quite a few calves. Since Ian had just lost over a hundred head of cattle to one pair of lion he became, most understandably, exasperated. I became very nervous on the cheetahs' behalf but, since in Kenya they are also 'protected', I know that if the worst comes to worst they will not be shot but translocated. However, I would still fear for them, for cheetah are delicate animals to handle and thus difficult to move and, most selfishly, I should miss them and their graceful beauty.

Buffalo had been in the sanctuary area but moved out of their own accord during the fencing operations. Soon after the fence was completed, a big bull buffalo broke through it and moved back into the sanctuary. We were pleased to have him back. At night buffalo can be very dangerous to people on foot and are generally more feared than lion. We thought that to have buffalo in the sanctuary would be good added protection for the rhinos - especially buffalo like the old bull who had just joined us, for he had a rather bad (or, from our point of view, good) reputation for chasing people. To keep our new bovine guard content, Francis and Ian captured a few buffalo cows and released them inside the sanctuary. We now have a nice herd of twenty-six.

One day when I was out rhino-ing with Orogai, I heard over the radio that a buffalo was en route to the East Gate. In due course she arrived, lying sedated in the back of a pick-up. Shortly after she was driven through the gate, a helicopter appeared. From its lower regions descended a rope and at the bottom of the rope dangled a small black object. To my intense astonishment the helicopter hovered overhead and deposited one baby buffalo in a net at my feet. It was then explained to me that the gift of mother and child was the result of a combined military operation. Ian had persuaded the British Army that catching buffalo would be good training for its helicopter pilots. Thanks to these various efforts we soon had a nice little herd, and several calves have been born here. Sadly some cows and calves died in the 1987 drought, but the numbers are already recovering.

After rhino and elephant, giraffe are my favourite animals. To me they are the most lovely and elegant creatures, and the reticulated giraffe of northern Kenya, with its wonderfully patterned, rich russet coat, is surely the most beautiful of all. To our great relief they adapted to the fence reasonably well. Bulls have even managed to fight over the fence, bashing their heads against one another over the topmost wire. In contrast the eland have not adapted to being fenced either in or out and regularly cause crises by trying to get through the wires.

Giraffe, however, can cause crises too. On one occasion in the early days I was on my way to the horses up at the East Gate, when I heard over the radio that a giraffe was entangled in the fence up on Fumbi, the area to the north. I drove there as fast as I could, the bags of horse food still in the back of the car. Ian called me over the radio to tell me that if the animal was down I must see that the head was kept above the level of the body, or it would die.

When I arrived at the scene of the disaster, I found the giraffe, a big male, lying prostrate outside the fence with his hind legs badly entangled and his head and neck stretched out on the ground. I am not very agile at getting through fences but with a certain amount of pushing and pulling I made it, and then asked that the sacks of horse food should follow me. I sat on the sacks and managed to pull the giraffe's head up on to my lap. The giraffe was not too happy about this so I had to keep a very firm grip on his ears to try to make him keep still, hoping that the elevation was adequate to keep him alive.

I was just about organised when the fence gang arrived on the scene with tools to cut the wire. Although they had only the best intentions, their arrival thus laden was too much for the unfortunate animal who now struggled frantically and managed to free himself. However, I did not realise he had done so. Everyone was shouting at me in Swahili but I did not understand what they were saying, for I was far too busy trying to control the giraffe's head to pay attention. Although horribly encumbered by me, the poor creature eventually managed to lurch to his feet. It was not until, clinging to his ears, I was hoisted a metre or more into the air that I realised what had happened and let go - returning to earth with a bump. Luckily the giraffe had no serious injuries and cantered away while we all had a laugh at my slightly bruised expense.

The next crisis with a giraffe occurred the following year, when I received a message telling me, to my great surprise, that a giraffe had disappeared down a hole. I could not visualise anywhere on the sanctuary a hole that could be big enough, but Gilly who was with me assured me that I had heard correctly. We drove straight over to the North Valley to see what on earth could have happened. Sure enough, the tips of two giraffe horns were visible just above ground level. We looked down and saw a very exhausted-looking giraffe wedged in a narrow erosion gully. The poor beast must have been stuck in there all night, for he appeared to be in a bad way.

Francis, at this crucial moment, was on his way to Nanyuki so we had to send frantic messages over the radio for him to come back. In the meantime we had to do what we could. I remembered that I had a very long and strong rope at the house and sent for it, and then managed to knot it around the giraffe's waist. By then about fifteen people had arrived and with my knot in place we all started to heave on the rope. Alas, the knot came undone as we were pulling and as the rope came free we all shot backwards down another equally deep hole which was so hidden by long grass, none of us had noticed it. I landed right at the bottom with about six people piled on top of me. They all scrambled

Giraffes at Lewa Downs

out with their usual agility but I, who even when young was not very agile, had to be hauled out. I then went headfirst back down the first hole, Errada and someone else holding me by the feet and dangling me in the vicinity of the giraffe's waist where I tried to improve on my previous knot. We then all pulled again. This time the knot held, but our combined strength was not enough to shift the huge animal. Eventually both the tractor and Francis arrived and, with his customary efficiency, Francis took charge of the rescue operation. Slowly the giraffe emerged. Luckily he stood still, but trembling, while Francis untied my knot and then he gingerly moved off. For a few days he did not look very happy and his ears drooped so sadly that our trackers called him 'Masikio', the Swahili word for 'ears'.

A surprising sequel to that adventure has been that from that day on Masikio has shown no fear of people. It is as if he knows that we saved his life. He visits both my house and Francis' regularly and it was always Masikio who caused crises with Samia by making himself at home in what she considered her domain. He used to peer over the fence with interest at my bantams too and they would be shocked into making such an uproar that on several occasions I rushed out thinking that they were being devoured by a herd of mongooses. Eventually they got used to being studied by a giraffe, and even Samia has become used to him.

The reticulated giraffe, with its rich red-gold coat divided by white lines, formerly ranged throughout Somalia, parts of Ethiopia and the north east corner of Kenya. Now, due to heavy poaching and civil wars, it is extinct throughout most of its range and a very reasonable proportion of the surviving population is here on Lewa Downs where we now have an estimated seven hundred plus. Eighteen months ago in a game count in the sanctuary we counted 79 of these giraffes. In January 1991 that figure had risen to 172. Something has to be done as they have started debarking the trees, causing serious die-off - particularly of the seyal acacias - and these trees, especially in a semi arid area, are vital for the black rhinos to which we must give priority.

We are not allowed to cull them, and anyhow the thought of killing these beautiful and gentle creatures is appalling to us all. Instead the idea is to translocate them to the Meru National Park. This park had its game virtually wiped out by shifta but now that Peter Jenkins is back there as Park Warden, the situation is improving. We are all very keen that our surplus giraffe - about four hundred - should go there. The only problem is money - we estimate that it will cost us in the region of US$ 127,000 to move them and somehow or other I have to find this money.

I have mentioned our trackers many times. All of them are Ndorobo, to me the most remarkable people. By tradition they are hunters and gatherers and they have an incredible wealth of knowledge of the forests and the plants and wild creatures which they contain. In the old days the Ndorobo hunted many of the animals, but always within the productivity capacity of the ecosystem. Now they no longer hunt, but they still gather honey and many wild products. To make a livelihood in rapidly changing Kenya many of them now seek employment outside their forest homes and some from nearby come to work in the sanctuary. I am happy that they are able to make use of their traditional expertise in a modern enterprise. To them, and in particular to Errada, then Orogai and now Senanang, I owe all I know of this area. As we go round the sanctuary they tell me the names and the uses of all the plants; which trees, bushes and herbs are eaten by which animals; which are poisonous and to which species; which (a most surprising variety) can be used as medicines and for which ailments; and which can be eaten by humans and how. I am sure that with any one of our Ndorobo I could walk unprovisioned from here to Lake Turkana - a month's walk through arid thorn scrub, mountains and desert - whereas by myself I would be dead in a few days.

Watching the Ndorobo track an animal is a whole experience in itself. Each leaf, stone and blade of grass tells them a story. They see things which I would never notice and can tell from the most minute signs what animal has passed, and when and at what speed it was travelling. Without doubt they must think that I am impossibly unobservant and clumsy but never once in all these years have I seen them show the slightest annoyance with me. Amusement, yes, but that is fair enough.

I remember once trying to follow Errada up a dry waterfall. I had nearly reached the top when I slipped and tumbled down in a cloud of dust. I can still see the mixture of concern and amusement on Errada's face as he peered down at me. Another time Orogai and I were trying to get a good view of Shaba and Jupiter who were at the bottom of a very steep wooded valley. I skidded and went whooshing downhill. The noise of my descent startled both mother and calf and they galloped off down the valley. Fortunately I got hitched up on a tree *en route* which brought me to an abrupt halt. Poor Orogai did not know whether to laugh or cry as he came to give me a hand back up the hill.

Another time, again with Orogai, we got too close to Juno and her calf before he saw them. He started me up the nearest tree and then scrambled up another himself as Juno came to her feet with a sudden snort. In the meantime, I had got myself into a real mess. My hair, hat and the string on my spectacles were all so tied up in the thorns that I could climb no higher. Nor, with my spectacles dislodged, could I see what I was doing. Juno emerged from her bush, snorted at my feet with disgust and then trotted off, tail in air and calf at heel. Orogai had to use his knife to disentangle me.

Compared with the enormous rewards of living here, the hazards are small. The worst, as far as I am concerned, are Ian's bees. Ian, like the Ndorobo, is a bee-keeper and I am terrified of bees. This is a source of constant amusement to all our trackers, for the Ndorobo love bees and their products. They use the honey to make mead, and also eat it and the wax, the pollen-filled cells and the dead bees inside them - the whole comb thus providing them with a very balanced and nutritious diet. Traditionally honey served as a medium of exchange, and formal gifts of honey are still essential to Ndorobo rituals. Our trackers have the most astonishing empathy with bees, not only their own bees at home, but any bees. When a swarm arrived in my bantam run I locked myself in the house while Senanang came to deal with them. He handled them with his bare hands and with no form of protective clothing; bees crawled all over him and not one stung him. Had I not seen it (through a tightly closed window) with my own eyes, I would not have believed it.

The other hazards to my peace of mind are snakes and scorpions. The snakes are nowhere near as numerous as they were in Ghana, but we do see some. Egyptian and spitting cobras are inevitably attracted by the rats that follow human settlement and infest grain stores, but these quick-moving snakes usually slither rapidly out of the way when they feel human footsteps approaching. Puff adders are more dangerous because their superb camouflage and lazy habits make it easy to step on them inadvertently. The scorpions are tiny compared to the huge glossy green and black horrors we had in Ghana, but they pack a far more powerful wallop. They also have a very disconcerting habit of arriving in the bath via the plug hole.

However, the joys of living here far outweigh such minor inconveniences. When Karl and I were wondering where to site our house, David told us of a place that was, in his view, magical; a place he called the Marula. When we saw it we could only agree. It is a deep, hidden and wholly unexpected gorge. Although we made our home directly above it, the gorge remains hidden. Below the house you climb down to a waterfall shaded by a huge fig tree. Only three times since we have been here has the water actually flowed over the fall. When the river does run, it floods and it is wildly exciting. But even when there is no water, there is a permanent pool at the bottom of the waterfall, a deep, dark, beautiful pool on which the sun never shines. It is fed by a spring and so never dries up. Sometimes I see big silvery fishes glinting in its depths. On very rare occasions I have seen the lovely curved form of an otter playing down there - but usually the pool is still and silent. Below it is an area of papyrus swamp, edged by yellow fever trees and wild date palms. In the gorge it is always cool and green and quiet, blessedly far away from the dust and wind and glare above. It is a very special place for both me and Samia.

In the very early days I used to sit on the edge of the waterfall and look down and wonder who, apart from the noisy, conspicuous baboons, lived there. I had not yet plucked up courage to go down and explore, when one evening I heard the most appalling crashing noises, followed by loud splashes. Quite obviously some very large animal had arrived in the swamp at speed. I was convinced that it was either one of the rhinos or one of Ian's beautiful Boran bulls, but whatever it was might be in trouble and I had to investigate since no one else was about.

I clambered down with difficulty and started to explore - it was all was very quiet. Then I saw a big male waterbuck looking wet and breathless standing near the pool. A few minutes later two large brown eyes and a wet black nose came into focus near my feet. It was a second big male waterbuck, and this one seemed to be stuck and half-drowned. I said "shoo-shoo" hopefully, but although the beautiful big eyes blinked, there was no further response. Obviously stronger action was required. I managed to wade out into the mud and water behind him and, groping around, discovered his tail. I heaved at it with all my strength, shouting at the same time. With huge sucking noises he came unstuck and managed, with a parting heave from me, to get up on to the bank. For a few moments he stood there, dripping and trembling, then slowly moved off. The other waterbuck had vanished.

Another time as I sat on the edge of the waterless waterfall, Remus, the little collie, somehow managed to fall over. Luck was with him and he missed all the bits of rock he could so easily have hit *en route* and plunged straight into the pool. For what seemed an eternity he disappeared from my sight, but in due course surfaced looking none the worse for wear but clearly very frightened.

I started going down to the Marula regularly when Samia was old enough to negotiate the steep slopes that enclose it. The dogs always came, too. They knew they were totally forbidden to hunt and slowly the other occupants of the area came to accept us. A pair of grey-headed kingfishers decided that Samia could be a useful adjunct to their insect-hunting operations and they often used her back as a perch. Very occasionally, if I managed to sit still enough, they would use me. Once, taking off from Samia's back, one of the kingfishers plucked a pale pink scorpion, 5 cm long, from behind me, right from the log I was sitting on, and battered it to death on a rock. One evening the male captured a huge insect and took it to his mate who was perched on a nearby branch. As she accepted the bribe he grabbed her by her top-knot and mated her, talking volubly all the while, and when he had finished he flew off leaving her to devour her supper. Another evening I saw the male catch and eat, in a little over an hour, three small lizards, one scorpion, two grasshoppers and six assorted small insects. Where such a diminutive bird put it all I do not know.

My greatest pleasure in the Marula has been my acceptance by the greater kudu who visit it regularly. The largest and most spectacular of the African antelopes, they stand over one and a half metres at the shoulder and the males may weigh up to three hundred and twenty kilograms. Both sexes are greyish brown and marked with 6-10 vertical white stripes. The male has huge spiral horns. I make a point of never trying to hide, of never staring at them and of always moving slowly. Sometimes I speak to them or to Samia and sometimes I read out loud to them. After a while they just look at us and then carry on with their normal affairs.

My most astonishing encounter in the Marula took place just after Christmas in 1987, when I was down there with Samia and Buffalo. Samia was browsing behind me while Buffalo sat on the log beside me. He was trembling but I thought this was only due to the big bull kudu who was feeding no more than twenty metres away. Then there was a sudden small movement in the papyrus in front of me and I found myself looking into the beautiful, hate-filled eyes of a big male leopard no more than four metres away. For a long time we just stared at each other. The great cat must have been lying there concealed in the reeds for at least half an hour, perhaps waiting for the baboons to return from their daily foraging expedition. (Francis and I once heard a leopard kill a baboon in the gorge and the noises were fearful.) Whatever he was doing there, my presence must have been a sore trial to him. Slowly he rose to his feet, turned and then vanished from my sight into the papyrus. By then both Buffalo and I had the shakes. Samia, however, was quite unconcerned. Either she had not scented him or else she realised that she was too big for a leopard to tackle. A few weeks later, a leopard killed a young zebra above the house. I went out the following dawn when he had returned to his kill and had a magnificent view of him outlined against the eastern sky. I suspect it was the same leopard.

I enjoy our evening walks as much as the dogs and Samia do. I try to avoid rhino and buffalo (by that time of day I generally know where they all are), but there are always other animals and many birds to watch for and learn about. Slowly the dogs have acquired some 'bush sense' and know that baboons and warthogs are not to be chased. One evening we unexpectedly met a porcupine and they wisely refrained from tangling with him as well. However, on another evening Buffalo dived under a thorn bush from which there immediately emerged awful sounds. I grabbed him by the tail and hauled him out. To my horror he appeared with a tail in his mouth - a fluffy white tall. The owner, and I had no idea what it might be, was still under the bush making dreadful noises. I got Buffalo to sit and extracted the tail from his mouth, then with it in hand and no clear plan in my head, I crept into the bush. There I met the owner - a zorilla, a sort of African weasel, black and white and fluffy, and with all the courage of his kind. Apart from the loss of his tall he did not appear to be injured but was so enraged that there was no way I could have handled him to check. Some weeks later I saw a zorilla without part of its tail and presumed that it was the same one alive and well.

One particularly beautiful picture, the last frame in an evening walk, remains most clearly in my mind. When Samia and I were walking down the hill towards the house, I heard Karl starting to play the piano - he played beautifully before his health went. Samia stopped, ears pricked, to listen. Beyond the house, across the valley, three rhinos were browsing. All stopped, pricked their ears and looked towards the house intently.

10

The Future

Extinction is an act too great for man, he bungles it by obscene malice. Mass death should be left to mountains, left to glaciers, it should be left to the sand that covers the boasting of fratricidal kings.

Loren Eisley

In an ideal world the future for the African rhino would be to roam unmolested in the wilderness areas of the continent where for forty million years the species have evolved, and in numbers large enough to ensure the continuation of genetic variation. At first glance this seems possible, in Kenya at least. To the north of the sanctuary right up to the border of Ethiopia there appears to be a perfect wilderness area. It is an arid land of thorn bush, mountains and desert inhabited only by the semi-nomadic pastoral peoples who, with their cattle and camels, goats and sheep, have shared the land with the rhinos for centuries. Fifteen years ago Karl and I travelled through this area, over to Lake Turkana and up to the Ethiopian frontier. My diary records all the larger wild animals we encountered: elephant, giraffe, zebra and antelopes of many species.

Alas, today the wilderness full of wild animals is only a vanished dream. Now, wherever you travel in this vast area, you see few wild animals. The human population has increased and will continue to increase. The number of men carrying guns has also increased, primarily because of the shifta problem. The shifta are incredibly well armed with highly sophisticated weapons and the local people, fearful of attacks by these bandits, have responded to the threat by increasing their firepower. In this conflict the animals are the losers. Any rhino released in the area would not stand a chance. For instance, Tsavo National Park, which is over 20,000 square kilometres in size, once had what was estimated to be the highest population density of black rhino in the world.

Now there are so few left that a sanctuary had to be built in which to gather a few of the scattered remnants of the once huge population, in the hopes that they may meet and breed.

Rhinos are easy to kill, for they tend to be creatures of habit and, having few natural enemies, sleep heavily. They can cope with the complications of their normal existence but they cannot cope with man's killing skill. The Africans have always been adept at devising clever methods of killing by using traps, poison and snares. Now they have guns as well and not just rifles, but submachine guns - due to the iniquitous trade in arms, Africa is full of such weapons. The few rhinos left are now worth a fortune to their killers and still more to the dealers and traders. Most Africans are short of money, many are hungry and some are insatiably greedy. The temptation to kill rhinos and elephants for their horns and ivory is overwhelming. The actual killers in the field, the people who take the most risks, are the least to blame; for in many cases they are employed to kill and only a relatively small proportion of the profit goes into their pockets. It is the dealers, few of whom are African, who are really to blame for this vicious trade, and the people who use the end products, none of whom are African. Unless people like Esmond Bradley Martin can prevail upon the governments of the world to stop the trade in horn and ivory; and unless enough people become aware of what is happening and concerned enough to join him in this action, I see no future for the rhino except in well guarded sanctuaries.

The sanctuaries should be as big as finances permit, but at present security is of paramount importance and size cannot be bartered for it. To a certain extent animals within a sanctuary must be managed, but they must be managed for their own welfare and this must be the only consideration. By management I mean that during drought periods it may be necessary to supplement their feed. It may also be necessary to exchange breeding males in order to avoid inter-breeding and to ensure genetic variability. I most adamantly do not mean that rhinos should be 'farmed' for their horns or herded like domestic animals so that they loose their independence, intelligence and natural immunity to the diseases endemic in the area. Man is all too clever at breeding animals to suit his own purposes. In order to make them easy to handle he breeds from the more docile individuals, reducing the native intelligence and sense of fear of the species. Man is not very good at letting animals breed to serve their own purposes, the evolutionary processes of adaptation and mutation and the continuation of the species.

One sees this wrong sort of breeding in zoos. Because zoo animals are kept in confined spaces and have to be handled, the individuals that breed most easily and the ones the zoos prefer to breed from are those least stressed by noise and the presence of large numbers of people and those that are quiet to handle. None of these characteristics may help the animal to survive in its natural setting, nor are they the traits best suited for the perpetuation of a stock of wild animals. In areas of West Africa where lion had been exterminated, some governments - wishing to increase their tourist potential and realising that in Africa national parks without lions are not tourist attractions - imported lions from zoos and safari parks in Europe and dumped the unfortunate animals in the middle of newly gazetted national parks. The lions, used to receiving daily handouts, were quite unequipped to hunt for themselves, so very naturally moved to the nearest human habitations and helped themselves to goats, sheep and children. George Adamson's legacy to the world is that he has proved, and left all the relevant documentation behind him, that lions can be rehabilitated into the wild and taught to kill for themselves, but that the process is both lengthy and costly.

Some zoos of Europe and America have been reasonably successful in breeding the white rhino but far less successful in breeding the more endangered black species. No one, to my knowledge, has yet attempted to rehabilitate a zoo-bred rhino back into the wild, and such rehabilitation might prove very difficult. The black rhino is an incredibly versatile animal, and, given the chance, could continue to be a great survivor. It can endure extremes of both heat and cold, from the deserts of Namibia to the montane forests of the Aberdares. It can live in plains, swamps and mountains. In each area it knows what to eat and how to survive the stresses of that particular environment. However, much of its behaviour is learned, rather than instinctive. I believe that if the Namibian desert rhino were to become extinct (and there are now well under a hundred left), it would not be possible to reintroduce rhinos from a very different environment into that harsh habitat; they simply would not have learned the skills from their mothers that would enable them to survive. Surely it is much more sensible to save the black rhino *in situ*, and in much of Africa this means in sanctuaries.

At present sanctuaries are necessary not because of a lack of space - there is still mountain, desert and thorn scrub enough to support tens of thousands of rhinos. Sanctuaries are only essential because of security. Only man can protect the rhino from man. The loss of rhinos in all of the national parks in Kenya, despite the goodwill and good intentions of the government, has proved that only special sanctuaries, be they state-run or private, can afford the rhino the degree of security necessary to ensure its survival. Only when - if - the price of rhino horn drops dramatically, will sanctuaries perhaps no longer be necessary.

The whole matter of the trade in rhino horn and elephant ivory has been dealt with at great length in books and articles by Dr Martin, and I strongly recommend them to all who are interested in this aspect of the subject. Dr Martin sets out every use man has devised for rhino horn in great detail, from status symbol dagger handles in the Yemen, to cups in China which will cause any liquid containing poison to froth when poured into them, and medicines for almost every conceivable ailment.

In order to thwart poachers, many people have suggested that rhinos, at least those in sanctuaries, should be darted, relieved of their horns and then left to go about their own business again. What effect would that have on the rhino? The most obvious use of the horn is for fighting, both aggressive between rival males and defensive, such as the protection of the young. But apart from this, and especially during periods of drought, the horn is much used as an aid to feeding. Branches, otherwise out of reach, can be hooked down with it and whole bushes can be battered. In the 1987-88 drought, Juno was particularly active in this respect and much devastation followed in her wake. The horn is also a useful instrument for digging - I have observed both Morani and Samia digging up bulbs and roots to eat on many occasions. Samia also uses her horn to debark dead trees and turn over logs. Although I only saw her doing this in the 1987-88 drought when she was uncovering termites to eat, I should not be surprised if other rhinos sought such protein supplement in times of acute stress.

Male rhinos make much use of their horn in mating - which

unfortunately adds fuel to the rumour that powdered rhino horn acts upon humans as an aphrodisiac. I have seen both Godot and Morani use their horns in the splendid dust-sweeping ceremony that precedes mating and when generally excited. Samia, with her little horn, does exactly the same thing in moments of intense excitement. I have also watched Godot use his horn to send trees and bushes flying in annoyance when Solia was forcing him to keep his distance. It was obviously a displacement activity, a means of working off his frustration. He used his horn both in affection and anger; I have seen him use it to caress Rongai, and to punish both Juno and Stumpy. Samia sometimes caresses me with her horn and also prods me with it to try to steer me in the direction she wants me to go. I have seen Kelele do the same to Rongai - although he prodded his mother with considerably more force than Samia has ever used on me.

The argument, both verbal and written, as to whether or not to de-horn the rhino has raged in Kenya ever since I have lived in the country; and people more eminent than I and vastly more experienced take opposite sides. Having watched the various uses to which rhinos put their horns, I used to be much against the idea. It seemed to be both an abuse of the animal and an admission of failure on our part. However, since the massacre of the Meru rhino in October 1988, I have changed my mind. I would prefer our rhinos to be de-horned and alive rather than reduced to stinking heaps of carrion.

I am convinced that the rhino is sufficiently intelligent to adapt its behaviour to managing without a horn, although in a few instances it might need help. In bad droughts, for instance, we might have to supply some fodder to compensate for the animals being unable to hook down branches and dig up roots and bulbs. Moreover, we would have to make sure that lion and spotted hyena were few, for these predators would be dangerous for young calves whose hornless mothers would be unable to protect them. Ngare Sergoi could be used as a testing ground for observing the effects of de-horning on rhinos. We have enough detailed observations on mating to make at least an informed guess as to whether or not de-horning upsets the rhino's breeding behaviour; and many other questions about the effects of de-horning could also be answered. The advisability of the policy on a large scale could then be decided on the basis of observations here, rather than on the basis of hypotheses and guesses. Only one aspect of de-horning brooks no discussion. If you are going to de-horn at all, you must de-horn all the rhinos in a given population.

What clinched the argument in favour of de-horning in my mind, was the danger factor. The sanctuary was my idea, and as such not only the animals in it but the other people involved are, to a certain extent, my responsibility. Ian and Francis and our men would be facing large gangs of shifta armed with submachine guns, while themselves armed only with a half dozen old rifles. Were they to be mown down, I should feel to blame. The shifta have never come on to Lewa Downs. Like us they have a good intelligence network. They know that, despite our inferior fire power, we have a plane, field glasses and radios, and our people are well paid and hate and fear the Somalis. They also know that if they come here, whatever they do to us or the rhinos, some of them will die in the process. In the past we have heard shooting to the north below the escarpment, but that is as near as they have come.

However, after the Meru massacre we all met and decided that to avoid a similar disaster in Ngare Sergoi we should de-horn our rhinos, but since all wild animals in Kenya technically belong to the government, we had to ask the Wildlife Department for permission. The department turned down our application. Since then we have planned to experiment with de-horning two white rhinos, which can be owned privately, and releasing them outside the sanctuary - but as I mentioned earlier, the death of one of these rhinos after a fight with Makora has caused a setback.

The question of 'ownership' of wild animals is a sensitive one. In Ghana in the old pre-Nkrumah days, the land belonged to the various tribes. It was administered by the tribal chiefs and elders for the benefit of their people. The land, trees and animals were harvested on the basis of sustained usage. The rivers were sacred, as were the forests that grew on their banks and the hilltop forests - and trees could not be cut down. The old religious taboos protected the rivers, the soil and the forests. The animals were hunted but within the limits of their breeding potential. They were protected at certain times of the year and in certain places. The hunters of each tribe were men appointed by and responsible to the chiefs and elders.

Then came 'progress' and a thirst for power by western-educated politicians. The whole tribal system and the chiefs stood in the way, so both had to go. The idea of land as a form of capital was accepted. Profit became the prime motive and for profit the land was raped. The forests, the soil, the rivers and the animals all disappeared at the most alarming speed. I saw it happening during the twenty years I lived in Ashanti. When the tribes still owned the land, the land was cherished. When it became either private property or state-owned, it was exploited for the quickest possible gain with a total disregard for the consequences. As the average soil cover in Ghana is only about 10 cm over hard laterite, disaster was the almost immediate result.

For nearly thirty years now I have believed that the whole concept of land as a form of capital, be it public or private, is wrong. Land should not be merely regarded as a commodity from which to produce income, but as something infinitely more valuable. It is not ours either to rape or over-utilise, but should be held in trust for future generations and utilised only within the limits of its regenerative capacity. Until people and nations develop a trust concept, as so many African tribes used to have, the present rate of depredation will not merely continue but will accelerate, leading us all to disaster. This, I believe also applies to the wild creatures that live on the land. Unless the trust concept is paramount, state ownership all too often results in a free-for-all grab. In countries that hold to the concept of private property, it is perhaps more practical to encourage the trust concept in individuals. If the animals belong to the land-owner or occupier and are seen by him to be of benefit to him, he may take the trouble to protect them. Of course many landowners are greedy and will continue to kill the animals and cut down the trees to reap short-term profit; but there are other kinds of landowners, people like the Craigs of Lewa Downs and many of the other ranchers in this area. They are people who love their land and wish to leave it richer, not poorer, and who are already putting into practice a form of trust concept.

Such people are prepared to tolerate a certain amount of financial loss for the sake of wild animals. If the wild animals belonged to the ranchers and they were free to utilise them - within the limitations laid down by the government for the protection of endangered species - for the maintenance of a constant yield, these ranchers would encourage more wild animals on their lands and would be content to keep fewer cattle and goats. Cattle are better adapted to lusher environments and when overstocked can damage arid lands badly; a changeover from cattle to wild animals would benefit both the soil and the vegetation of the arid ranch lands. Studies on 'game ranching' have shown that, without doubt, decreasing the number of domestic animals and increasing the number of wild ones in arid areas not only benefits the land itself, but also benefits people: it makes land that is unsuitable for agriculture more productive and hence more profitable.

Increasing the number of wild animals not only increases the biomass that a given area of land can well support but also brings another economic benefit - tourism. Holiday-makers are usually not willing to take expensive trips to view cattle and goats, but every year hundreds of thousands come to view wild animals. Combining tourism with ranching makes maximum use of semi-arid land as well as bringing foreign exchange into the country. In Kenya tourism is now the major foreign exchange earner and also one of the biggest sources of employment in the country. This multiple use of land has proved to be very successful both in Zimbabwe and in South Africa. In South Africa there are now more wild animals than there have been since the turn of the century. They are bringing more profit to the people who own land in the arid areas than cattle alone ever did.

Many people are now aware and increasingly worried about the rate at which plants and animals are becoming extinct. Although extinction of species has always been part of the evolution of life in this world, the rate of extinction has increased greatly in the past decades. Almost all recent extinction has been due to man's activities. Often a species becomes extinct because man destroys its habitat, but in some cases all the members of a species are simply killed. This is what is happening to the rhino.

To my way of thinking, to drive any species over the brink to extinction is a crime, and just about the worst crime that man can commit, for it is irreversible. Many organisms are disappearing before we even know they exist. These are the tiny plants and creatures that live in one area of the world only, each in its own ecological niche, perhaps on an island, or a patch of forest, or some small underground cavity. Their passing is deplorable both in itself and for ourselves, for loss of knowledge and potential in science and medicine. All living things are important, and in the whole fragile structure of life on earth we do not know which things by their passing could upset the balance of the planet's life support system.

At the moment we must develop, temporarily I hope, an 'ark' concept of conservation. This means we must do our utmost to conserve areas throughout the world which can be protected and where small pockets of wild animals can be reasonably free. These pockets will need to be managed, not only for security reasons, but also to ensure genetic interchange - but they will not be glorified zoos. These scattered arks - national parks, reserves and private sanctuaries - will safeguard species from being pushed into the abyss of extinction. The day may come when the human population explosion is brought under control, and a time may even come when our species deserves the name it has, in all arrogance, given itself – *'sapiens'*.

The rhino's passing would not upset the balance of life on earth, but it would deprive the world of a magnificent and intelligent animal, the likes of which we would never be able to see again. Its passing would be for no good reason, for it is not dangerous to man nor does it compete with him. It is being exterminated simply out of greed and this is a wholly deplorable crime.

People sometimes ask me why I fight for the rhino and not for some other species. The answer is very simple, by coincidence. When we retired to Kenya in 1976 I very soon realised that the rhino was in serious trouble. My life in Ghana and my work with the Game Department there had made me very aware of how quickly man can exterminate animals. I believed that every one who cares about life on this planet must try and act to save it. I had some money and decided that I would use it to try to help save this animal that was the closest in my immediate neighbourhood to being exterminated. By coincidence I met the Craig family, people deeply aware and sincerely committed to conservation. They were brave enough to agree to an experiment to provide a refuge for an animal I knew nothing about except that it desperately needed help. From what everyone told me I was prepared to find the rhino a dangerous animal, and a dull one compared with the chimpanzees with whom I had done much work in Ghana. I discovered I was wrong on both counts.

For many years I have believed that all life is one. By itself each living particle, from a cell to an elephant, may be unimportant, but each is part of our magnificent living planet. Our human species has evolved as just one part of the whole - but we have developed such means of destruction that we now hold the future of this intricate and glorious world in our hands. We now have the power to destroy the world. We also have the power, if we can hold our greed in check, to let the world continue.

We talk endlessly about our rights but very little about our duties. I believe our most important right is the right to give, I do not believe we have any right to grab. I have lived much alone, and some modern priorities seem strange to me. I do not understand why physical possessions should be regarded as important and take priority over mental wealth.

I have also thought much about boundaries, the narrow lines that divide yesterday from today and today from tomorrow and the lines that differentiate one life form from another. How does one species during the passage of time evolve into another, while other species remain unchanged for millions of years? What divides our brains from the brains of other creatures? How do their brains work? Is understanding between us possible? Many creatures live in a world of scent and sound and possibly other and older methods of communication. We live in a world expanded but also limited by speech and language. The spoken and written word has made us what we are. It has enabled us to store and to share knowledge, to convey the most profound thoughts. It has made us powerful in the extreme, but it has created a chasm between us and all other forms of life. Safe in our presumed superiority we forget that other living creatures may be different and older than us, but not necessarily inferior. In our constant search for knowledge I fear that we are in danger of losing other qualities - wisdom and compassion. Knowledge alone can be a very dangerous weapon.

We may think that we are communicating with an animal when we issue it with an order and it obeys, but this is only a one-way system: we command, the animal obeys, or gets punished for disobeying. If the animal tries to communicate with us, ninety-nine times out of a hundred we do not notice, and the hundredth time we do not understand. Only a few people, those who live in sympathy with and close to animals - like George Adamson with his lions, Dian Fossey with her gorillas and untold 'ordinary' people, from little old ladies with poodles to nomadic herdsman with cattle - try to communicate on a two-way basis, endeavouring to understand what their animals are telling them. The potential for communication is there. One day - if we do not blow ourselves up first - perhaps a wiser, more sympathetic and gentler race of man may arise. He may be able to surmount the communications barrier that exists between us and all the other species of animals on earth. What a breakthrough that would be, and how infinitely more exciting than landing gadgets on the moon and Mars.

However, for this breakthrough to happen, animals must continue to exist. Of particular importance is the survival of the great mammals, who possess well developed brains and whose thought processes are closest to ours. As they live in a different world from ours, much of their intelligence may be beyond our present comprehension, but of their intelligence there is no doubt.

During the twenty years I spent in Ghana, I had a great deal of experience handling and raising a wide variety of animals, domestic as well as wild, including antelopes, monkeys and chimpanzees. I have always had a strong suspicion that few animals are stupid except for those domestic species the brains of which have been bred out of them to suit our convenience. When an animal seems stupid to us it is usually due to a lack of comprehension on our part, combined with a lack of interest as to what does go on in the mind of a creature that lives in a world quite different from ours.

While in Ghana I did a lot of work with primates, especially chimpanzees. A creature like a chimp is so like us that it takes no degree of imagination to recognise its intelligence. We can see it in the chimp's eyes, in its expressions, in its manipulative ability, in the way in which a young chimp, like a child, is intensely curious and tries to copy behaviour from others. It is relatively easy to 'understand' a chimp, and the crowds in front of the chimpanzee houses in zoos indicate that the average city dweller feels some sort of sympathy with and interest in the animals. But when we are confronted with a rhino, a creature with bad eyesight, that lives in a world of which we know nothing, understanding - and hence sympathy - is not so easy.

All five species of rhino are at present being so hunted that they are galloping headlong towards extinction, bounded out of this beautiful world for no better reason than human greed. If enough people cared and understood, this would not happen.

At home with Samia (Gerry Ellis)

The slaughter could be stopped. It is in our power to save the rhino, a glorious animal in its own right, and a delight and source of inspiration for future generations of mankind.

In September 1986 Morani was taken from the sanctuary to the orphanage in Nairobi. There he was held until early in June 1989 when he was transferred to the newly created rhino sanctuary on the Ol Pejeta ranch. While the boundary fence was being completed, Morani was kept in a well-guarded 100 acre paddock. At, the end of June I had to go to Ol Pejeta and I was asked if would like to see him again. When we went to his paddock he was feeding some way off. He lifted his head, pricked his ears and slowly walked towards me. As he drew near I dropped to my knees and made the greeting breathing. He stepped nearer and then, gently avoiding touching me with his horn, pressed his nose against my face. It was enough.

11

And the Years that Followed After

It is now five years since *Rhino* was published, five years of births and deaths, of progress, set-backs, disaster and learning all intermixed. My husband, Karl, who had suffered a stroke just as I was beginning to write the book, died four years later in hospital in Switzerland. Francis Dyer, who has been with me since the very beginning as manager, and his wife Bimbi, have had two handsome sons, Harry and William. The boys have brought much joy to all our lives and I am sure that when they grow up they will ensure that our work with rhinos carries on. The Lewa Wildlife Conservancy has come into existence and by absorbing the Ngare Sergoi Wildlife Sanctuary has vastly increased its scope and future potential.

My beloved Samia proved that a hand-raised rhino can adapt to a wild environment and become a successful part of a wild rhino society. She not only mated but also produced a calf, the birth of which must have been the most exciting and satisfying moment of my life. She successfully raised her calf for seven months and their tragic death was devastating to me personally. But it also was astounding proof of the impact she had made on people. The hundreds of letters I received from friends and total strangers, beautiful and caring letters, helped me so much to handle her loss and to continue to work for her species.

Other rhinos have died; others have been born, their deaths bringing us sorrow and their births great joy. More rhinos have been brought in, some have been moved out. Here is a brief summary of the main events of the last five years (1991-1996) on Lewa Downs.

Samia and Anna

The creation of the Lewa Wildlife Conservancy

Already by the close of 1991 it had become apparent that even 4,000 hectares was not adequate for us to breed genetically viable populations of black and of white rhinos: these huge mammals need space. Thus it came about that early in 1992 the Craig family made the enormous decision to turn the whole of their Lewa Downs ranch into a rhino sanctuary. When this decision became known, the Kenyan government requested that the 6,500-hectare Ngare Ndare Forest Reserve that lay up on the lower slopes of Mt Kenya to the south should be included. This meant an increase in size from 4,000 hectares to 25,000 hectares.

We were very pleased at the suggestion, for access to the forest would be of great benefit to the black rhinos in particular, and especially during periods of drought. But the inclusion of the forest involved several important things. Firstly, it was no use giving the rhinos all this space if their security was thereby decreased. We had to erect over a hundred kilometres of new electric fencing and to more than treble our security force and our expenditure thereon. Secondly, as the forest was Government property, to put rhinos there and to protect them meant opening up a new realm of co-operation between the public and private sectors.

Most important of all would be the benefit of the new electric fence to the agricultural people who lived on the slopes of Mt Kenya to the south of the forest boundary. Most of these people possessed only two-hectare plots, on the produce from which they and their families were dependent. A single elephant could destroy their entire livelihood in one night. And elephants were not the only, though by far the worst hazard for those people. Assorted antelope, pig and buffalo could also wreak devastation. The erection of this fence, 110 kilometres long and 2.5 metres high, made possible thanks to the generosity of the American Association of Zoo Keepers, the British High Commission and many wonderfully generous individuals, would thus be of huge benefit to the local people who are our immediate neighbours.

All of us have appreciated for many years that no major conservation project is going to succeed if it does not have the support and goodwill of the local population. In a poor rural area this means that the project must be of immediate benefit to them. People living on or close to the poverty line are not going to think about what is going to be of benefit to future generations, they have enough difficulty in keeping themselves and their children alive and fed. Therefore whatever is done must not only benefit them but also do so in a direct and obvious manner. This the fence did. The increase in our security operation was also of direct benefit to all the local people. Employing some 160 people directly and a further one hundred indirectly, we became the largest employer of labour in the Meru District.

Wildlife conservancies are well known in South Africa and other parts of the world but the creation of the Lewa Wildlife Conservancy was a new concept for Kenya. The Conservancy, which included and absorbed the Ngare Sergoi Rhino Sanctuary, came into being in 1993 (although it was not officially registered as a non-profit organization until February 1995). Its objects are many. The primary ones, of course, are to breed and protect both species of African rhino, and to protect all other wildlife on Lewa Downs with particular reference to the highly endangered Grevy zebra, of which more than sixteen percent of the world population is on Lewa Downs.

The Conservancy is also to prove that cattle and wildlife can co-exist and that multiple land use of the arid rangelands of East Africa benefits the land, the soil, the wildlife and the people. Another important aspect of the Conservancy's work is education. It has been instrumental in raising funds for the building of four primary schools on the periphery of Lewa Downs and in raising money for a few scholarships from these schools to secondary schools. In 1996 another long-time ambition was achieved thanks to the Rhino Trust of Guernsey and various donors; we were able to build a small health care clinic which offers medical care not only to our own staff, but also to many of our immediate neighbours who otherwise had to face long and difficult journeys to the nearest clinic.

The Conservancy wishes to go beyond supporting educational efforts for local children. We also attempt to explain to our own guests what we are trying to achieve and why we consider it to be so important, so that people come as tourists but leave as ambassadors for our work, determined to fight for the rhino's future existence on earth.

Probably the most important thing the Conservancy has done to date has been to promote the idea of communal wildlife management amongst two groups of the pastoralists who live to the north of Lewa Downs. These people have seen that rhinos and other wildlife co-exist on Lewa Downs with cattle. They have seen that this is a combination that attracts tourist revenues and they are starting to realize that wild animals may be of benefit to them instead of being in competition with them. They are realizing that revenue from wild animals can act as a buffer against the devastation caused by drought to their flocks and herds. As a result, they have already created two organizations, the Il Ngwesi Trust to our immediate north, and the Namunyak Trust in the Mathews Range beyond, to enable them to protect and benefit from the wildlife in their areas.

With funding from the Kenya Wildlife Service (KWS) and help from the Conservancy, a small lodge was built at Il Ngwesi and opened for Christmas 1996. This is the very first lodge of its kind in Kenya, built by, owned by, operated by and for the benefit of the local people. A similar small lodge is planned for Namunyak. The Conservancy maintains close contact with the two Trusts and helps with the training of their staff. We also have a radio link, to be able in an emergency to give assistance if requested. We are rewarded by seeing that in both these areas, wild animals are returning owing to the protection they are now receiving from the local communities.

We believe that it is through projects such as these that the wildlife of those areas will continue to flourish and, equally importantly, that the people of those areas will be able to continue in their own way of life, maintaining their heritage and retaining their identity. And eventually, if the trade in rhino horn can be controlled and security is adequate, the offspring of our rhinos may be able to return to the lands across which their forebears roamed in vast numbers only a century ago.

The rhino's intelligence and social structure

All life is precious and the loss of any plant or creature is a loss to the diversity of life and its ability to continue evolving. But to lose the world's second largest land mammal, the forty million years of evolution that the five remaining species represent, and the intelligence they have developed throughout the course of their evolutionary history, is more than a tragic loss, it is a crime against humanity and our beautiful and unique planet Earth.

Most of the people whom I meet seem to be surprised when I talk about rhino intelligence. I am certain that the reason for this is the difficulty we humans have in appreciating intelligence in a creature very different from ourselves and operating within different constraints. I fully acknowledge that without my eleven years with Samia, and to a lesser extent Makora, I could have spent my fourteen years in the sanctuary learning little except details about their eating habits and similar obvious behaviour.

Samia had metaphorically to knock me on the head to open my eyes to her mental capacities because so often if you do not expect something you do not see it. In a zoo, a very large animal like a rhino has severely restricted space and lacks most forms of mental stimulation. Usually a baby rhino is taken from its mother at far too young an age, and its social contacts with other rhinos are also limited. So, being both bored and frustrated, its mental capacities are not likely to develop. Yet despite this, it is really only among zoo keepers that there is any appreciation of the rhino's capacity to learn.

Anna Merz walking with Samia and Samuel

I am going to relate a story about Makora, our white rhino bull, that convinced me, and I believe will convince you, beyond any shadow of doubt, that he was possessed of great intelligence. I have kept horses all my life and learnt from painful experience how totally panic-stricken they become if entangled, even slightly, in wire. One morning I was in my Suzuki with Senanang watching Stumpy and her calf when we noticed Makora slowly approaching us. The wind was blowing from us to him so he would have scented us. Thus his approach was intentional. The nearer he came, the odder was the appearance he presented until we both realized to our horror that he was completely entangled in a whole roll of fencing wire that he had collected from heavens know where.

As he drew level with the Suzuki, he stopped and gave what I call the greeting breathing. It was obvious as he stood there, trembling from head to foot, that he was asking for help. But what could we do? I had never actually touched him before and I had no wire clippers in the car. Slowly we both got out. While I slipped my hanky between his eye and the strand of wire pressing on it, and then my shirt between his penis and the strand of wire binding him there, Senanang found a flat stone and, using that to cut against, took his big knife and started to cut the wire around the rhino's hindquarters. As he cut the wire I talked to Makora and moved round him, disentangling the wire as Senanang cut it.

The whole performance took some forty minutes and Makora stood motionless the whole while, but for the violent tremors that shook his huge body. As the last strand of wire fell free he moved off slowly, leaving both of us totally convinced that we had been helping an animal of the most amazing intelligence. Had he panicked, his own death, not to mention ours, would have been certain.

For many years it perplexed me why there is such a very long period of togetherness between the black rhino, and to a lesser extent the white, and its calf. Rhino 'childhood' usually lasts at least four years, even longer if no other calf is born or if one is born but dies. This is a long period in the life of an animal that only lives some thirty years and there must be a good reason. And the reason is surely not because the calf needs all this time to know what to eat or where to find water.

Now I believe that the social lessons that a rhino has to teach her calf must be the reason for this. Unlike the elephant, the rhino does not grow up as part of a herd with a devoted group of 'aunties' in attendance. But this does not mean there is no social structure among a group of rhinos; there is, but a very different one from amongst elephants. Apart from the cow-calf bond, I believe that the most important relationship is that of friendship between two or more adult females.

When a new calf is born, the mother will drive away her older calf and this can be the most dangerous moment in that young animal's life. It is neither mature nor in a position to defend itself from the possibly violent attentions of mature bulls. Invariably I have found that within some forty-eight hours of a new calf being born, the older calf joined up with an adult female with whom its mother had friendly relations, providing that she had a calf of her own, at least six months old or older, with her. The cow would then protect her friend's child against bull rhinos and other dangers, until such time as she herself calved again, when, frequently, the young animal would return to her own mother with the friend's calf in attendance. Thus if I saw a cow rhino with two or three calves of different ages, invariably the youngest and the oldest would be hers, and the middle one would be her friend's calf.

This bonding between adult females and their calves I believe to be the basis of rhino society, a situation which is wholly different from elephant society but every bit as fascinating.

Samia's life and tragic death

As Samia continued to grow and mature and become wholly independent of me, so she learned to spend more of her time with the other rhinos who lived in the vicinity of my house and whose home ranges overlapped hers, in particular Juniper, Julali and Shaba. But still, to my unending joy, she remained my friend and occasional companion, visiting the house at intervals and joining me and the dogs in our evening walks whenever she was nearby and heard us. During those years the relationship between us changed. Her intelligence informed her of my physical limitations compared with hers and she also learned to sense my fear and would act as my protector should need arise instead of coming to me for protection.

One evening in particular stands out in my memory. I had been delayed and was walking home as fast as I could with the dogs, as dusk was fast coming, when Samia, heavily pregnant at the time, joined us. Onto the track just ahead of us strolled three white rhinos, all of whom Samia knew well and all of whom were about twice her size. Her acute perception informed her both of my fear and its cause and entirely on her own initiative she trotted forth, ears flattened to her head, and snorting aggressively. The three rhinos stopped, obviously astonished at her unexpected behaviour, then beat a hasty retreat back into the bushes whence they had come. Satisfied, Samia trotted back to us and escorted us nearly home, then rubbed her nose against me and departed about her own affairs.

Above I mentioned that Samia was pregnant. Yes, it finally happened! If the huge, gentle male, Osupat, had lived and become Samia's mate as I had so hoped, this story could have had another and happier ending, but such was not to be. Rhinos do seem to be accident-prone animals, and Osupat and the bull Kikwar met and fought one dark night and both leapt to their deaths over a low cliff.

Thus it came about that Samia was in due course and on several occasions mated by the wild and savage bull Kenu (I will tell you

Samia with her baby Samuel

later how we came to have him). My trackers saw them mate and once I too witnessed it, from the top of a tree up on Fumbi. Unlike with Godot and Rongai there was little sign of affection between them, but as both were small rhinos and well matched in size, Samia appeared to be well able to stand up for herself.

Thereafter followed some amazing episodes because not only were Samia and Kenu quite frequently together in various parts of the sanctuary, but when she came home to visit with me he not infrequently followed her. This was a serious added complication to my life. Once walking the dogs near the house in the early morning I met Samia and was greeting her, when Kenu erupted out of a nearby bush with murderous intent. With the speed always so astounding in such a heavily built animal, Samia planted herself between me and Kenu, enabling me to escape home. That she would defend me against her own mate was sufficiently amazing, but that she would act thus in defense of my staff and guests with whom she had no bond at all was even more astounding, though the reports I received left no room for doubt that she had acted quite intentionally.

On another occasion I saw Samia at the garden gate and went to greet her, not realizing that Kenu was near her. As he charged she jumped between us and I froze. For nearly forty minutes I stood there, only the flimsy garden gate separating us. I could clearly sense his rage against me but she stood between us breathing in an intricate pattern of sounds that clearly controlled him and when she moved off at last he followed and I was able to creep back to the house, aware once more that I owed my life to her.

The birth of Samia's calf in April 1995 was one of the happiest events in my life and the wonderful culmination of ten years of care and love. Above all things I had wanted to prove that a hand-raised rhino could be successfully rehabilitated and this meant not only living with wild rhinos but being able to raise her own calf. I was fully aware that for a rhino to be a good mother involved being intensely protective of her calf against all the world which, even for Samia, could include me. My trackers had warned me of the dangers of the situation and I was fully expecting that the bond between us would finally break and was happy that it should be so.

For two days Samia had not been seen but this was not unusual and I was preoccupied with other things. Early that morning I had been watching Shaba and her well grown male calf opposite the house, when Kenu suddenly appeared and attacked the young male. Shaba in turn attacked him and there was an uproar. This was Kenu's second fight within two days, the previous one he had attacked Makora and would no doubt have paid for his foolishness had not Makora been dehorned and had there not also been a helicopter at the time to help separate them. This morning there was no helicopter, so it was up to me to try to separate them with a car. This was something which I would not have attempted in the Suzuki, but by now I had a big Land-Rover which was fairly rhino-proof. But I was not successful and merely got entangled with bushes and rocks. Finally Francis came to the rescue in the Super-Cub to dive-bomb them. It was in the midst of all this confusion that I was called over the radio and told that one of our trackers had found Samia, just north of my house, and that she had a baby with her!

With both joy and terror I crept through the bush behind Joseph until we could see Samia feeding quietly. We peered around: in the long grass nearby we saw just two tiny rhino ears. There was no sound but Samia munching. I knew from previous experience that baby rhinos cry when they are in trouble, so I took the silence as a good sign. About half an hour later the calf staggered to its feet, thrust its little nose into Samia's flank and started to suckle. Samia stopped feeding and stood quietly while the calf drank first from one teat and then the other. There was no doubt that she had milk and there was also no doubt that her child was a son. Having nursed he lay down again and carefully she lowered her great body to lie at his side. Later in the day Samia left him for a short time to go and drink in the valley but she returned at once to where he lay, sniffing him carefully before starting to browse. That evening when he got up to suckle, he already seemed stronger on his feet, distinctly less wobbly.

That night I felt very fearful for them both. Would Samia, hand-raised and protected until she was big, realize that the great predators of the night, the lion, the leopard, the spotted hyena, who were no threat to her, posed a serious threat to her baby? Would she know how to keep him away from elephant? A huge herd had recently moved into the sanctuary area and with them a particularly vicious bull of whom not only I, but most of us were terrified and with very good reason. To keep the elephants at bay, Ian and Francis had erected a high electric wire round my house and the core of Samia's territory. Would she stay within this area?

On the morning of the third day of the calf's life, I was watching him and Samia with one of our trackers and was so absorbed and fascinated that I failed to notice the wind had changed, so she got my scent. Ears pricked, she came towards me. I knew how protective rhino mothers are of their calves and how solitary they are during the first year of their babies' life. I realized I should retreat, but my knees were shaking so much, that instead I sat down. Samia came right up to me, her baby at her side, so tiny and perfect and so like her when I first knew her, big ears and feet, blunt nose and oyster-satin skin. Gently I told her how clever she was as she laid her great head on my lap and I knew that she was telling me not to be afraid.

As the calf grew in strength, it became obvious that Samia was

The young Samuel

being a perfect mother and my pride in her knew no bounds. Most mornings she would come to the garden gate at dawn and call for me almost as if she knew how nervous I still was for her at night. One morning she came and when I went out to greet her, I could not see the calf. Fear was in my throat. Then he awoke from under a nearby bush and finding himself alone he cried for her. As a complete reflex action she knocked me out of her way and rushed to him, leaving me where I had fallen in the grass. Finding he was unhurt she trotted back to me and thrust her great nose into my face, obviously perplexed at what she had done. Then, as so often in the past, she turned and offered me her tail for a pull up.

So the magical months followed each other. Samuel, as I called the calf, grew in strength and beauty. I never attempted to touch him but he learned to accept my scent. Not only did I myself learn so much about them during this period, but a documentary film was made about them by Jack and Pauline Bellamy of the BBC. They were not only skilled photographers but, even more important, people who cared deeply for the rhinos and never upset them and they completely earned Samia's trust.

It was on a moonless night in November 1995 when Samuel was seven months old that disaster struck. When Samia did not come to visit me at dawn I went down the valley with my tracker to look for her. The valley was lovely, I had spent so many wonderful days there with Samia. Now I found her lying there, dead.

She was lying on her back below the forty-foot cliff from which she had obviously fallen. Her back was broken and death must have been instant. Samuel lay crying some few yards away. I tried to help him but could not do so, so sent Patrick to call for help. A leopard grunted nearby, but I did not see it.

When Ian came he realized what I had not, the baby's back was also broken, just above the tail. A merciful bullet ended his suffering, and the most beautiful days of my life.

The other rhinos

I am sure my readers wish to know what has happened to the other rhinos too, so I will bring this book to a close by bringing all their affairs up to date.

The bull rhino Kenu was, without doubt, the cause of more trouble and grief than any other rhino we have had. He was the last of the wild rhinos we captured and introduced into the sanctuary. For several years, we had been hearing rumours that a solitary rhino still existed somewhere in the vast area to our north, between Marsabit and Laisamis. It seemed that this animal was the sole survivor of what had once been a large population of black rhino and had only survived because he was very wary and always on the move. In January 1993, on receipt of very recent information on his whereabouts, we and the Capture Unit decided to try to capture him. We succeeded but because of the presence of Somali shifta in the area we had to move him south immediately, giving him no time for recovery. We found we had ourselves a small but very powerfully built rhino with no ears, probably caused by a near miss with spotted hyena when he was a baby.

From the start it was obvious that Kenu, as we named him, was a very dangerous animal and hated humans, for which he could not be blamed. But he was also a rogue animal towards his own species being directly or indirectly responsible for the deaths of both Samia and Shaba, both of whom were his own mates. (When we scoured the area above the cliff to try to understand why Samia and Samuel had fallen to their deaths, we found

Kenu's tracks mixed with theirs.) But what does it do to an intelligent animal to possibly witness the deaths of all the members of his social group and to grow up in solitude and under constant persecution? There is ample evidence of what it does to chimps. I tried not to blame Kenu too harshly for Samia's death. But when he subsequently killed Shaba in an outright fight, the KWS decided to move him and shortly after that he too died falling off a cliff.

The end of 1991 saw the death of the old black female, Rongai. She was one of our founder rhinos and as she had spent much time near my house, I knew her well and had spent many happy hours watching her and learning from her. A cliff was her undoing, too; she overbalanced and fell, and died in the river below.

Rongai's sub-adult daughter Julali promptly joined up with Juno and her daughter Jupiter, and Samia was sometimes seen with them too. Julali had her first calf in June 1997 but most tragically died three and a half weeks later, when an elephant-damaged tree fell on her, killing her instantly. Her calf, a male whom we have named Laringoi, is being hand-raised by Jane Craig and so far is doing well. Having had colostrum and milk from his mother, his digestion was (unlike Samia's) in good order, and his mother had already started teaching him how to browse, so we are hopeful that he will survive and flourish.

In 1993, I and my two trackers had a somewhat hilarious encounter with Juno which is indicative, I believe, that rhinos do have a sense of humour. We were watching Kenu attempting to mate Juniper and so was Juno. Mama was obviously not in agreement with these goings-on as every time Kenu managed to mount Juniper, Juno promptly knocked him off her daughter's back. However Kenu persevered and Juniper was obviously willing, so eventually Juno gave up interfering and wandered off out of sight. My trackers and I continued to follow Kenu and Juniper to observe their mating and we quite forgot about Juno who managed, on large silent feet, to get right behind us and then let out a huge snort which effectively scattered us like so many startled rabbits and informed us in no uncertain way as to her views on Peeping Toms. In January 1996 Juniper calved, but probably as a result of a subsequent mating with Amuri.

In 1992 Juno produced a very small and possibly premature male

Anna feeding Samia

calf, who sadly died after five days from an infected umbilical cord. Juniper, who had left her mother on the birth of this calf, promptly returned to her and remained with her until Juno died in December 1994. It appeared that she died trying to give birth to her next calf, seemingly because of old age.

Solia, Samia's mother, and Stumpy both had female calves in 1991 and again in 1995, all four fathered by Kelele, Rongai's son. In 1996, Solia's second calf, Zaria, herself fathered by Godot, had a male calf by Kelele. This youngster is doing very well.

In 1992, Shaba gave birth to a male calf, Shimba, who sadly died in the flash floods of 1997 when, it appeared, he lost his footing and drowned. Shaba herself was killed in a fight with Kenu at the end of 1996 while she was carrying an almost full term calf.

Mwingo, who was brought to us in 1989 having been injured and blinded in Nakuru, at long last, in July 1997, had a baby, also fathered by Kelele. The gentle Mwingo was showing every sign of being a good and highly protective mother so we hoped that her calf would survive, but one night when it was just three weeks old it was killed by a large male leopard. Could Mwingo's bad sight been responsible? I do not know.

In 1994 two white rhinos, Sungari and Gororika, both produced female calves by Makora. Both then produced male calves in 1996, again by Makora. The third of our original white rhinos, Marembo, had a male calf in 1995.

A last message

Samia, during the eleven years of her life, had truly been both a rhino of two worlds, and possibly also the best ambassador her species has ever had. Her death left a gap in my life that will never be filled, because between us there was a reaching out towards each other, between two wholly disparate species, towards a mutual understanding. And the choice was hers. I never either controlled or tried to possess her, our friendship was her choice. Yet because of that she impressed all who saw her in the flesh or in the film the Bellamys made of her, with her gentleness and her outstanding intelligence. At Lewa, all of us are determined that the splendour which these great beasts bring to our lives shall not pass away. We realize that if the bell tolls for the rhino, all five species thereof, it tolls also for us and our children and we have vowed not to let it happen.

Appendix
Medical Data and Formulae

STANDARD CAPTURE DRUGS

M99 and Fentanyl Citrate (F.C.) are mixed together in the dart. Azaperone is injected deep intra-muscular before the antidote M50/50 is given - the effect lasts 8 to 10 hours. M50/50 neutralises the M99 and F.C. and leaves the Azaperone. Five out of 900 captured rhinos died from this treatment, and of these five, four probably had cancer of the liver. Thus it is likely that the liver did not have time to remove the M99 by the time the effect of the M50/50 was over, so that the M99 took over again and the animal collapsed and died (R. Henwood). If this happens, there is little that can be done, except to try to revive the animal with small doses of Nalorphine hydrobromide.

	M99	Fentanyl Citrate	Azaperone	M50/50
Adults	1 to 1.5 mg	30 mg	200 mg	6 mg
Sub-Adults	0.5 mg	20 mg	100 mg	4 mg
Juveniles	0.25 mg	10 mg	50 mg	2 mg

After injecting Azaperone, an injection of long-lasting antibiotic such as Penimycin (dosage: adult 40 ml, sub-adult 20 ml, juvenile 10 ml) is injected deep i.m. Antibiotics containing cortisone are never used as they will usually cause any pregnant female to abort. Streptopen is used to treat the eyes and dart wounds. Eyes have to be treated as soon as the animal is on the ground and covered with a sack, as Azaperone dries out the eyes and the animal can be blinded.

When Godot was captured (3 April 1988) and moved from the sanctuary another drug was used, and this proved satisfactory. He was darted with 0.82 cc Carfentany and then given 1.5 cc Azaperone. When his breathing was down to 3 breaths per minute, he was given another 0.2 cc M50/50 + 1 cc Azaperone + 50 cc Combiotic (Dr Dieter Rottcher).

DRUGS GIVEN TO AMBONI AT THE TIME OF CAPTURE

The drugs were given for an unknown ailment, the symptoms of which were weakness, bloody urine, dim eyes and a swollen head:

8/7/86 He was captured with 0.80 cc Immobilon + 2.5 cc Azaperone. He was found to have a temperature of 36°C and was immediately treated with 50 cc Longlasting Terramyacin + 6 cc Multivite + 10 cc Deltacortril + 8 cc Ferrofax + 1.5 packets of Berenil (2.5 g each).

20/7/86 Since it was likely that he had worms, he was treated with four 6.75 g sachets of Strongid P., each containing 5.18 g Pyrantel embonate.

20/7/86 He was further treated with 30 cc Catasol + 30 cc Bykhepar + Longlasting Terramyacin (50 cc). A severe helminth infection was diagnosed from a dung sample.

22/7/86 Further treatment for worms: 16 cc Imovec (not effective).

29/8/86 23 cc Imovec (not effective).

12/9/86 6 packets of Equizole (thiabendazole), 30 g in each. This was effective, and the egg count, which had been 4/6000 eggs per gram strongyle worms, fell below 1000.

DRUGS GIVEN TO MORANI FOR WOUND INCURRED FROM FIGHTING

27/8/86 40 cc Strypen; wound sprayed with Terramycin spray.

28/8/86 40 cc Strypen.

DRUGS GIVEN TO SAMIA FOR DIARRHOEA

Lectade, rice water, kaolin + Sulphaguanidine tablets (1.5 per feed).

DRUGS GIVEN TO SAMIA FOR PROTECTION AGAINST TETANUS

3 injections of Tetanol 2.5 cc each. The initial two were given one month apart when Samia was 2 1/2 years old, and the booster a year later.

DRUGS GIVEN TO SAMIA TO TRANQUILLIZE HER FOR THE JOURNEY TO NAIROBI

2/8/85 0.5 cc Azaperone (not effective).

17/8/85 0.7 Rompon intravenous (effective).

DIET FORMULA FOR SAMIA FROM BIRTH TO WEANING

10 measures Lactogen + 1 tbs Nestrum + 1 tsp Energex - increased pro rata.